Watercolor

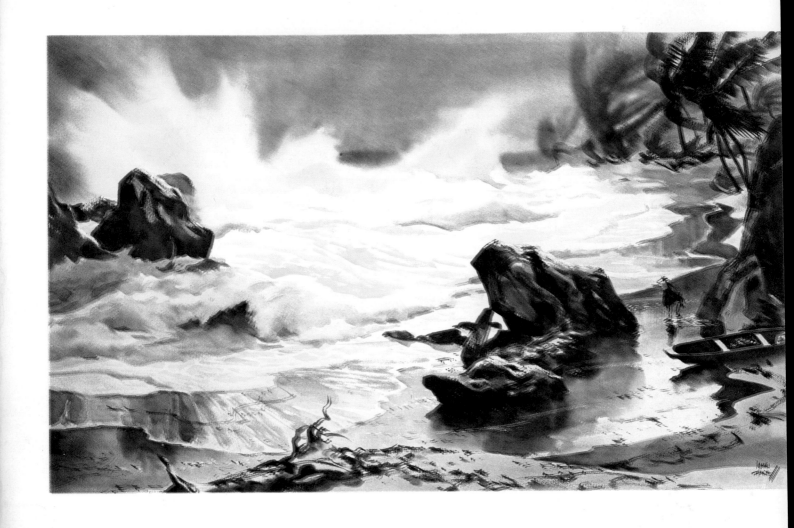

BREWING STORM, JAMAICA, W.I., *23″ x 38″.*
Collection, Mr. R. P. Risenburgh, Florida.

Watercolor

BY JOHN PIKE N.A., A.W.S.

NEW, ENLARGED EDITION

Watson-Guptill Publications / New York
Pitman Publishing / London

For Zellah — who knows

Library of Congress Cataloging in Publication Data

Pike, John, 1911–
   Watercolor.

   1. Water-color painting—Technique. I. Title.
ND2420.P54 1973   751.4'22   73-5552
ISBN 0-8230-5651-1

First Edition, 1966
   First Printing, 1966
   Second Printing, 1966
   Third Printing, 1968
   Fourth Printing, 1969
Second Edition, 1973
   First Printing, 1973

Contents

Preface

A cinema star, musical celebrity, golf or chess champion, or comparable personality may (and frequently does) arrive at the pinnacle of fame while still in his teens. I suppose the qualities needed for such success are what might be called natural or God-given, latent in certain individuals, awaiting only to be called forth.

A God-given interest is also required for the development of an artist of importance. But a vast amount of study, practice, unbelievably hard work, and experience are also required; for this reason, a painter or sculptor seldom makes his mark until middle age—and sometimes a great deal later. Many artists have done their best work after seventy. I think I know most of the outstanding artists of this country, and I couldn't name more than half a dozen who achieved recognition early. Those who "arrive" before thirty are astonishingly few in number.

It was during the thirties that I first heard of and began to see watercolors by John Pike. He was then about twenty-five and was being acclaimed by the art press as a painter-prodigy or "boy wonder." I had to wait a number of years—until early in World War II—before meeting him personally.

Half-a-dozen couples had assembled at a New York Club on 57th Street to do him honor. He had been a regular illustrator for *Colliers* and his representative, John Locke, had asked if I could fill in for Pike while he was away in service. That would have been quite an assignment for anyone, but, in any case, pressure of other work prevented my even attempting the job. Happily, however, the matter did serve to bring us together: the Pikes, the Lockes, Eileen and me.

Preparing to leave for Egypt, handsome John, in his army captain's uniform, really did cut quite a figure. It was then that I learned that he had many strings to his bow in addition to the one labeled *art*; for example, he was as smooth a dancer and musician as he was a painter. Since then, John and I have been close friends, so that I have had occasion to see what makes a prodigy function.

Discounting a season's study with Charles Hawthorne and Richard Miller, in his sixteenth year, John has been a self-taught painter and, moreover, has earned his keep from the beginning. Working at glassware etching, theatrical designing, advertising, commercial illustration, mural painting, and teaching —to say nothing of his wartime service in the air force and army—he has always held fast to the core of his ambitions and accomplishments: painting pictures to please himself. Yet he has always found time for other creative work: in Jamaica he designed and built a half-million dollar theatre for MGM; he bought and ran a night club there; and he helped manage an 1100 acre plantation and cattle ranch in North Carolina.

But remembering that prodigies do not always carry through—they may burn out before middle age—perhaps we should check John's prospects against the possibilities. The prospects look good. If anything, his force increases. He is now in his fifties—a grandfather—perhaps the most youthful appearing grandfather you ever saw, but a grandfather, nevertheless. He grows younger and more vigorous with age, and the promise apparent in his youth has expanded to place him among the best known watercolorists, illustrators, and teachers of the country.

In Woodstock, New York, he now runs the John Pike Watercolor School and sits on the city council; he conducts European teaching tours, does a considerable amount of commercial painting, and still contributes to most of the national competitive exhibitions.

In painting, John has always held to watercolor. A less resolute or more calculating soul would have selfishly chosen the oil medium rather than watercolor; rewards in the former had always been greater and more readily obtained because the public has erroneously considered oil more durable than watercolor. But dedication to an ideal does not admit of opportunism. John's dedication has brought results.

It was not until about fifty years ago that watercolor began to acquire the high standing in this country which the medium had enjoyed in Britain for a century and a quarter. True, Winslow Homer did wonders with watercolor, but he had few contemporary followers of ability. American Watercolor Society catalogs of about 1880 show that Homer watercolors could be bought for seventy-five dollars. During the first quarter of this century, a dozen or more great watercolorists demonstrated the wondrous possibilities of their medium—a self-sustaining, major medium—and since then its popularity and progress has snowballed so phenomenally that watercolor is now referred to as "the American medium." At open, national exhibitions of paintings in various mediums, one repeatedly hears the expression, "The watercolors were the best part of the show."

Thirty years ago, John Pike foresaw these possibilities and, in a magazine article at the time, expressed the hope that he might be able to participate in their achievement. The hope has been realized. In the development of watercolor to its present high level, John has more than done his share.

Frederic Whitaker, September, 1965

Introduction

This is a book on transparent watercolor. Great adventures and excitement lie ahead—as well as disappointments—but if you're game and willing to give it the old college try, it can be most rewarding.

Someone once said that watercolorists and pilots have much in common: "They're flying on their own and nothing can help them but their thorough knowledge of the mechanics of their craft."

It's those mechanics you're out to learn.

I've found watercolor an exciting and challenging way of painting. I hope you'll find it so.

Exciting because watercolor has an "action" all its own. It moves, it crawls, and it fights back.

Challenging to see how much of this diabolical behavior we can learn to guide and control through the hard, fun work of finding out what makes watercolor tick.

My purpose is to try to give you all I've gleaned over a lifetime of intimacy with my elusive love—watercolor—and show you its many tricks. In most media, various treatments are known as *techniques;* unhappily, in the *tricky* medium of watercolor, they're known as *tricks*. I hope I can help you learn the absolute fundamentals, the mechanics, the reasons why watercolor behaves as it does, and what we can do about controlling it.

The first part of your job will be to learn the scales before you go on to create the symphonies. But you must do it yourself! You can *read* forever about how to ride a bicycle, but you learn only by trying the machine itself. You have to get the feel of it.

What is watercolor? Watercolor is defined, roughly, by most of the leading watercolor groups and associations as "any pigment soluble in water, either opaque or transparent, and the painting executed with water." In brochures it's usually called an "aqueous base." What this really means is that watercolor is a type of paint made of pigment (powdered color or dye) and some form of glue (usually gum Arabic) to form a paste that can be thinned with water. The mixture is usually transparent when you add water, but can also be made opaque if you (or the manufacturer) add white paint or an opaque white filler. A watercolor must *look* like a watercolor: very few watercolor exhibitions will accept a watercolor painting that has been varnished or lacquered like an oil painting.

What is transparent watercolor? Transparent watercolor is unique among water based paints in that it *is* just what it says: *transparent*. Visualize transparent plastic sheets of several different colors; let's say we take our three primaries, red, yellow, and blue (remember the old color wheel we used to make in the 4th grade?). Lap one plastic sheet over the other. Yellow on top of blue will produce green. Red over yellow will produce orange, etc. In other words, there's a "compound" buildup as each color underneath affects the next *wash* or color you put on. You can see through all the layers of color. This happens in a hundred ways, depending on the sequence and character of the washes.

The white of your paper is your *only* white. So when you're painting, you must *plan* your project and remember to paint *around* those whites. Here's an example: when you're painting a portrait in oil or tempera, practically the last thing you'll do will be to put that little highlight on the end of the nose, because you're painting in an *opaque* medium. But, working in *transparent* watercolor, the *first* thing you must remember is to *leave* that little spot and keep it white throughout the painting session. This takes careful planning, but it's great sport when you pull it off! We'll go into these procedures later. In the meantime, remember: this book is about *transparent watercolor*.

What is OPAQUE *watercolor?* Opaque watercolor covers a large area. Gouache, casein, egg tempera, and the new acrylics are all water based media, all relatively opaque, although they *can* be handled in a tranparent way for special effects. But *all* of them are more opaque than transparent watercolor and are generally handled somewhat as you'd handle an oil painting. However, the exceptions to this are legion. Many fine artists work the middle road between opaque and transparent (with brilliant success) by adding a little opaque white to all their watercolor washes. I've worked in all of these media. However, the pure, transparent form of watercolor is my greatest love. Since this is a book on *transparent* watercolor, let's learn to fight this wildest of all painting media.

I believe firmly that you cannot properly express yourself without first having a thorough knowledge of the tools with which you're working. Whatever form, style, or "ism" you wish to embrace is your own free choice, of course, but it's logical that you'll be able to convey your thoughts far better if you're not being defeated by the medium. Occasionally a "happy accident" reaches the public eye, I think all too often. Painting is probably the only art form where this can happen. Music, sculpture, the dance, theatre, and literature all need basic knowledge and skill before a thought may be fully expressed. I think painting needs these too.

As you read this book, your first step will be to examine the "tools of the trade." These can cover a wide range and you can make your equipment as complicated as you wish. There's always an art dealer or manufacturer who's more than willing to sell you that "magic" brush or paper or pigment. Unhappily, there *is* no "magic"; there's only *you* and joyous, hard work. So keep it simple; you'll be happy you did when you go on your first field trip. However, I'll try to cover the whole area so that the decision will be yours.

Once you're past the "tools of the trade" and a series of preliminary exercises in their use, I'm going to give you a sequence of painting projects to help you "see" and interpret the wonderful beauty around you. You'll find that painting is an endless return to nature, where you'll perhaps rediscover things you'd long forgotten, but, even more important, where you'll find new thoughts, new shapes, new ideas.

Two definitions are basic to this book. The term *values* will be used a great deal. Value means simply the darkness or lightness of a color: a *value* (whatever the color) is a tone or shade between darkest dark (black) and lightest light (white). A *high* value is light in tone, like pale yellow or pale pink; a *low* value is dark in tone or shade, or low in *key*, like deep red or deep blue.

A *wash* is a passage of fluid color, usually applied rapidly over a large area. Learning to lay a wash with skill and confidence is basic to watercolor painting.

One day, as I was putting in a large, complicated sky wash, a non-painter friend called on the telephone. I shouted, "Hold it, I'm in the middle of a wash!" He waited while I finished. When I came back to the phone he said, "Brother, has your wife got you trained!"

Transparent watercolor is said to have limitations. Certainly there *is* the outer perimeter of what *has* been done. Your great challenge is to see what you can do about punching some holes in that perimeter and penetrating new territory.

Good luck! Have fun and help prove my belief that it can be done. I'm giving you all I know. I hope it will help you reach that new, great horizon.

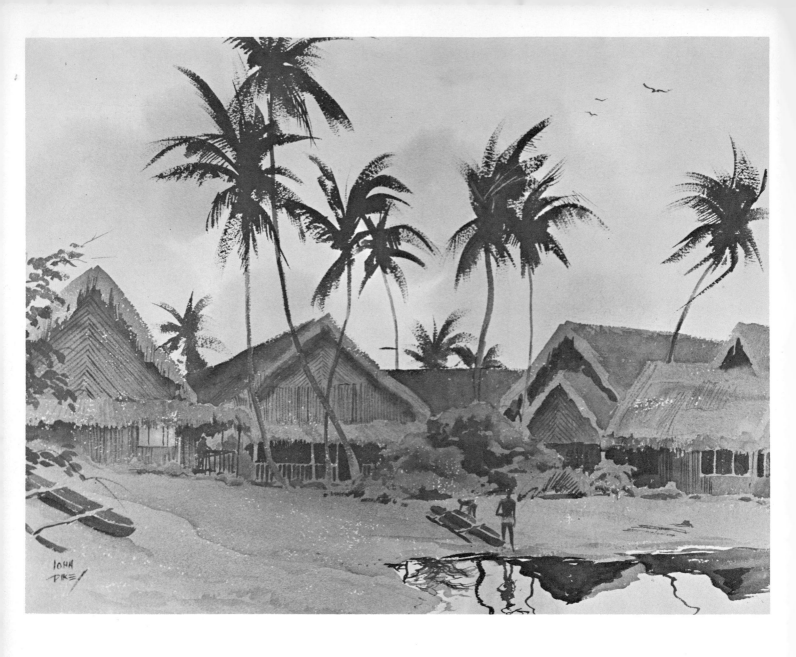

LAGOON AT DAWN, *22" x 30". Private collection.*

I was up early enough to paint this picture
because I had just flown in from New York
and had lost five hours on the way. We might
call it a very simple "two value" painting.
Care must be taken in planning the dark
silhouette against the light sky.

1 Brushes and other painting tools

Despite the enormous variety of brushes available in the stores, you need surprisingly few tools to paint with.

ROUND SABLE BRUSHES

First, let me say a word about sable. Sable, undoubtedly, makes the finest watercolor brush you can buy, but it's also the most expensive.

Sable has fine resiliency and yet has soft texture. It has the ability to snap back to its original shape even when very wet. The round brushes are numbered from #1 up through #12; #1 is the smallest and #12 is the largest. The round sables are for general painting. A fine brush if you can swing it financially.

FLAT SABLES

Flat, or *chisel* brushes have some advantages over the rounds. With the flat, you can lay in a large wash and immediately put in a fine line by turning the brush sideways, using the sharp corner or the full width of the brush. With

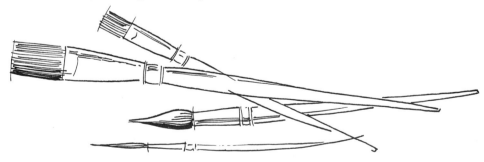

BRUSHES *Round brushes are available in sable or oxhair. The flats come in sable, oxhair, and hog bristles (mainly for corrections).*

the round, it's usually necessary to shake out the brush violently to regain the point. Also, the round will eventually lose its sharp point through wear.

I prefer the flats, with one or two exceptions, explained under "Recommended Brushes." Flat brushes come in *inch* measurements. Common ones are ¼″, ⅝″, 1″, 1½″, and 2″.

OXHAIR BRUSHES, ROUND AND FLAT

The oxhairs are my pets. I was a young student in the Depression years and the cost of a #8 or #10 sable was a month's room and board. So I found *oxhair*! In the years since that dreadful time, I've used an occasional sable, lent by a painter friend. But between you and me, the oxhair does the job every bit as well, and at one fifth the investment. (Art supply dealers aren't overly fond of me for saying this.)

As to their length of life, I have some oxhairs that I *still* use, although they were with me all through World War II, in the cold of the Arctic and in the heat and humidity of Egypt, India, and the Philippines. Sounds romantic, doesn't it? It wasn't, but the brushes stood up under all conditions, even if I didn't! Here's a photo of some of my old friends.

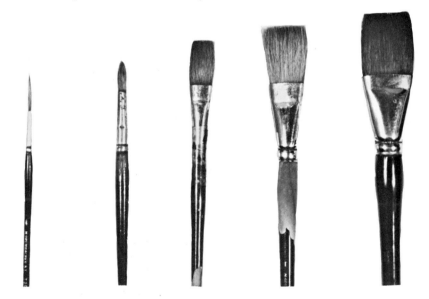

MY OWN BRUSHES *My big brushes are the flats, used for the large washes and bolder passages; my small rounds are for more intricate brushwork.*

To me, oxhair brushes have all the sparkle and bounce of sables, but you have to pick oxhairs more carefully. Be sure, in your buying, that you test each one for springiness and bounce-back qualities. All brushes come with starch in them to hold the hairs in place in the store. Ask for a pan of water to wash the brush out. If he's a good art supply dealer, he'll have a container of water right beside the brush storage drawers. See if the brush holds its shape when wet.

Oxhairs, if chosen carefully, can be excellent companions for many years.

14

BRISTLE BRUSHES

Bristle brushes are usually made of hog's hair, sometimes nylon. They're quite stiff and are generally used for oil painting, tempera, and the acrylics. In transparent watercolor, they're used to correct mistakes: to lighten small areas where the pigment is too dark; to soften an edge that has become hard when we wanted it soft or graded. This *can* happen; "goofs" in this medium are most common.

The bristle brush is a scrubber-outer. Dip your bristle brush into clear water and scrub *lightly*, so as not to harm the paper's surface. Have a rag or cleaning tissue handy to blot up water and pigment immediately. The sables and oxhairs will pick up *some* pigment, but not as cleanly as a bristle.

As in all cover-up tricks, don't depend on it too much. Try to do the job correctly the first time; but have a bristle scrubber-outer in your bag just in case. You can sometimes save an otherwise good painting. About a #5 "bright" is a good general purpose size.

LETTERING BRUSHES

Actually, all the flats were originally intended as lettering brushes, but were adopted many years ago by some of our finest watercolor painters and teachers. There are all sorts of lettering brushes on sale and the choice is a matter of personal preference, based on trial and error.

Be careful with your square ended brushes. Don't get mechanical with them so that you get squared effects (unless, of course, that's what you're after). Learn to twist the brush and turn it, drag it and squash it, to gain exactly what you want. Try a lot of practice exercises so you'll know exactly what the flat brush will do.

RECOMMENDED BRUSHES FOR THE BEGINNER

This basic list can be cut down to an absolute minimum. I've found that if I have a 1½″ flat, a 1″ flat, a ⅝″ flat, a #8 round, and a #4 rigger, my brush equipment is quite complete.

A rigger, by the way, is a long, slim brush. I choose the #4 as it's in between #2 and #6 and can do the work of both. It has hairs about 1″ long and has a slightly magic, ouija board quality. You put the rigger on the paper and the brush almost guides itself. It's delightful for little tree branches, tall grass, and a thousand other places—it's a fun brush!

I can't see that you're going to need much more than the brushes listed here. They should be most adequate. I have a couple of dozen brushes in my kit, but these five are really all I use. Perhaps you may want to add a #4 and #5 round, and possibly a #1 or #2 round for fine work, but you can get along very nicely with the first five.

CARE OF BRUSHES

After a day of painting, you pack up your gear to go home and, very often, the wet brushes become jumbled up in the tackle box, or whatever you use to carry your supplies in. Then, the next time you take them out, they've dried in twisted, agonized shapes. There *are* both a preventive and a cure for sick brushes.

The *preventive*: buy one Hong Kong split bamboo table mat; a yard of ¼″ garter elastic; a shoe string. Weave the elastic in and out through the

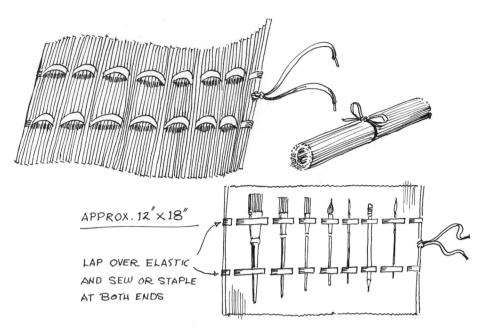

APPROX. 12" X 18"

LAP OVER ELASTIC
AND SEW OR STAPLE
AT BOTH ENDS

Brush Carrier   *I carry my brushes in a homemade
device which I concocted out of a Japanese bamboo
place mat, two strips of elastic, and a shoe lace.*

bamboo, leaving loops for the number of brushes you use, and sew firmly
at each end. Double knot the shoe string around the last two or three strips
of bamboo. Then slip your brushes under the elastic loops, roll up the mat,
and tie. This brush carrier takes up very little more room than the brushes
themselves, and they'll always remain straight.

The *cure*: when you find your pet brush all bent and twisted, wet it, rub
it on a cake of soap until the brisles are quite saturated. Then, with your
fingers, model the brush back to its proper shape and allow it to dry over
night. The next day, wash out the soap and you'll find the brush well again.

But try the preventive; it makes life easier.

Clean your brushes once in a while, particularly after you've been using
any of the Thalos (dye colors). At the art supply store, you can buy something called "brush cleaner." The bottle contains about 2½ ounces and will
do the job perhaps twice. At the supermarket, for the same amount of money,
you can buy a full quart of liquid kitchen detergent, which is every bit as
good and will last you for years.

Pour a little detergent into a cup—or into the corner of the sink—dip the
brush into it, work out the suds and dirt in the palm of your hand, then rinse
several times in warm water to be sure all the detergent is out. Then shape
the bristles and let the brush dry. I think you'll find this far better than the
old method of scrubbing holes in bars of soap.

STORING BRUSHES

My poor brushes somehow never get a chance to be stored. They seem to
be in use most of the days of the year. As I look at my side table, I see a

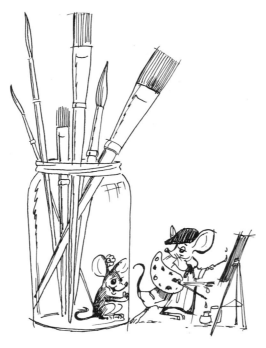

BRUSH STORAGE *If you use them frequently, as I do, the best place to store your brushes is in an empty coffee jar or Mason jar.*

cigar box with a lot of little upright cardboard partitions that once held some fancy cigars in glass tubes; I see a copper and silver Egyptian coffee pot that I bought in the old market place in Cairo years ago; and I see a Mason jar. I simply drop my brushes, *handle first*, into whichever one is closest. They all work.

However, if you *do* wish to store brushes not in use, particularly in the summer months, there are several methods. Remember, in a moth's evil mind, there's no greater delicacy than your favorite, most expensive brush. You can lay your brushes flat in plastic silverware trays, put in a moth ball or two (flakes are just as good), and seal with self-adhering plastic, or aluminum foil. Any jar with a screw or clamp down top—if the jar is tall enough—will do. So will the lacquered metal brush containers available in art supply stores. But always toss in a moth ball or two.

SPONGES AND THEIR FUNCTIONS

There are all kinds of sponges on the market: chemical or artificial sponges that come out of plastic factories across the land; and natural sponges that come from the East and the beautiful blue waters of the Caribbean.

But I must be unromantic and again go back to the kitchen for my source of supply. I find the artificial sponge more than adequate for my uses.

Its first purpose, to me, is to wash down a big piece of paper to remove the starch or sizing. (For explanation, see Chapter 3 on paper.)

Its second purpose is to pick up excess water, particularly where it's puddled along the rough deckled edge of your hand made paper. By removing this excess water, you avoid the chance of its working its way back into the painting, causing unattractive rings or *flowers*.

Third, the sponge is used to take out the big wash that you got too dark.

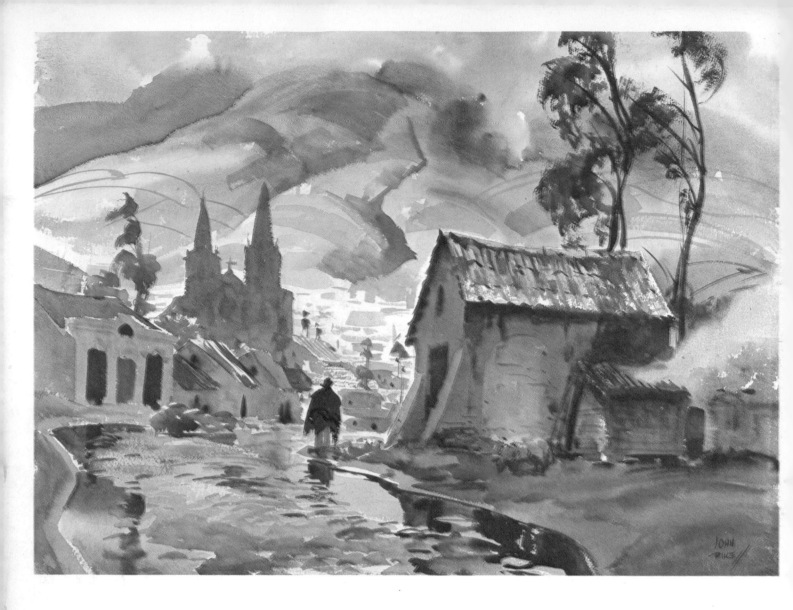

ECUADOR, 22" x 30". Collection, General Tire International.

Although this village is well over 9,000 feet high in the Andes, the surrounding mountains rise upward for many more thousands of feet. Their tops always seem to be shrouded in clouds.

To gain the clouds' softness, it was necessary to keep the whole upper area wet. After this was painted and allowed to dry, clear water was added to the underside, and the dark mountain tops were dropped in and allowed to flow upward, giving a soft edge.

The yellow-greens of the rolling cultivated fields were painted around the building at the right and around the church spires, leaving the distant town buildings white. Next came the silhouetting of the spires and the middle ground structures. I returned to the texturing of the distant fields with brush strokes following the contours of the mountains. The smoke at the right (from the cookhouse) was a blue-gray wash; the darks above and below it were dropped in while the wash was still wet, for a soft edge.

Next came the underpainting of the road, the grass to the right and left, and the pale blue underpainting of the tile roof, leaving the white paper for sparkles. Finally, I added the many small details: the tall eucalyptus trees, the textures on the tile roof and buildings, the figure, the sheep, doors, windows and the cobblestones of the road.

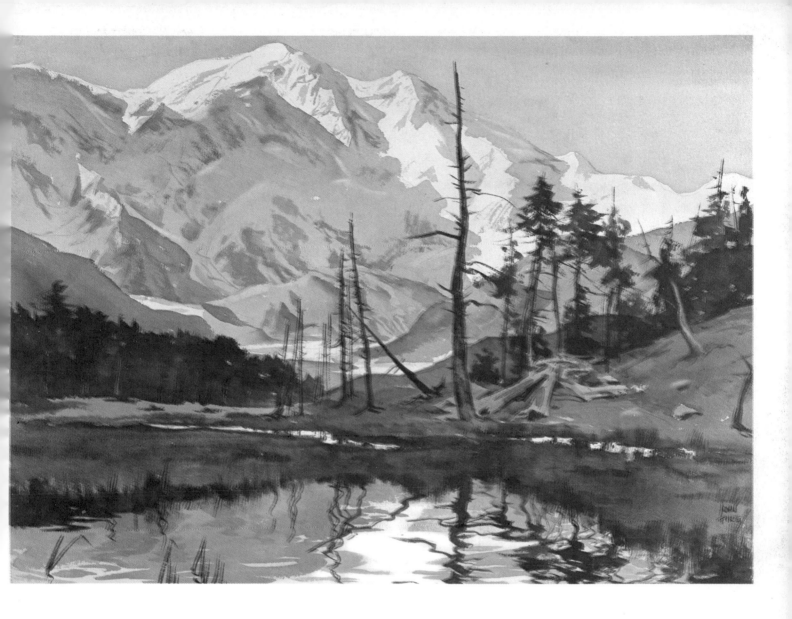

KARAKORAM MOUNTAINS, PAKISTAN, *22" x 30"*. *Collection, General Tire International.*

Here we have a rather subtle play of cool color against warm, making a good example of the rule: the colder the blue, the more it retreats into the distance. Although the blue shadows on the mountain are not *too* much deeper in value than the sky, they come forward because they are warmer, but still a blue.

The transition from distant mountain to foreground is achieved by the warm green on the rolling, middle distance hills. The very dark middle and foreground lead up to the viewer and, at the same time, push back the hills and mountain. The warm browns of the marsh grass also help to achieve a feeling of distance.

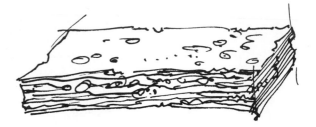

SPONGES *An artificial sponge —like the one in your kitchen —is enormously helpful.*

You may even want to wash off the entire painting. (At this point it might be best to turn the sheet over and start again.) The sponge can lift out large areas, as the bristle brush lifts out the small.

Keep two sponges in your kit: a clean one for sponging down the clean white paper at the start, and another for the bad judgments. A sponge is a very handy item to have, either on a field trip or working in your studio.

KNIVES AND RAZOR BLADES

The first function of a knife is to sharpen your pencil. It then comes into play on the painting itself in a very reserved manner.

After the painting is dry, little twigs, branches, and highlights may be lightly scratched in to give a sparkle and zing that can't be gained by any other method I know. (See the demonstration painting, "Fox in Snow," in Chapter 11.)

Again, let me caution you: this is only a bit of frosting on the cake and should be used sparingly.

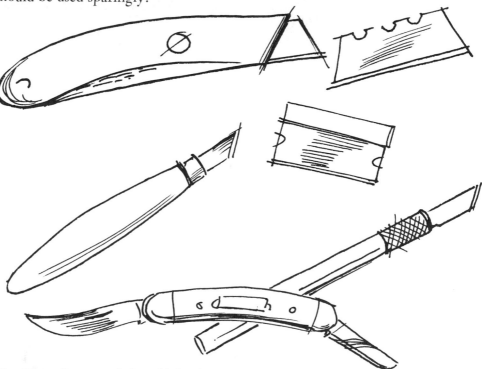

KNIVES AND BLADES *A sharp blade of some sort—a mat knife, razor blade, X-acto, or "utility knife"—comes in handy for all sorts of chores, and even for last minute touches on the painting itself.*

20

RAGS, BLOTTERS,
PAPER TOWELS,
CLEANSING TISSUES

The primary use of all these is *clean-up*. There are times when your palette is overloaded with dirty, pigment filled water, and you wish to work a light, clean wash. Clean off the palette; blot it all up! Sometimes a section of a wash is too dark; while it's wet, quickly pick it up with one of these clean-up agents.

Some brands of absorbent paper towels or tissues are more fibrous than others and will leave little particles on your painting; these particles will turn dark or mottled when you paint over them. Check any blotter, tissue, etc., to be sure it's lint-free.

Keep a few rags, paper towels, or tissues in your gear. You'll know what to do with them when the emergency comes.

One caution: don't get into the bad habit of holding a cloth or towel in your left hand, then dragging the brush (filled with water and pigment) over or through the absorbent rag or paper just before you make a stroke. You destroy the mixture you've just made up. If there's too much water in your brush, give it a good healthy shake and the devil take the wall-to-wall carpeting!

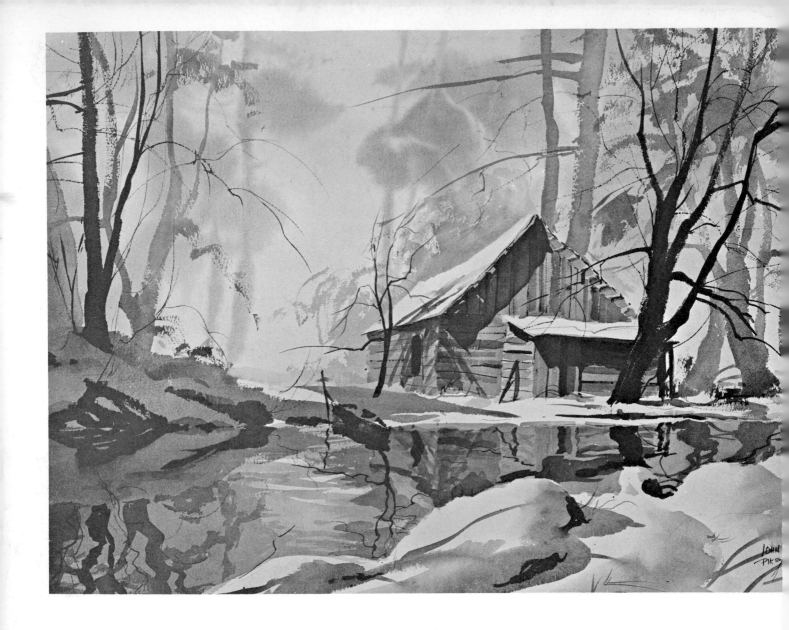

WINTER MIST, *22" x 30". Private collection. Photo, Russell.*

The entire background and the soft trees were put in at one time, leaving the white, snow-covered roof of the building. The middle distance trees are in a blue-gray to give them a sense of remoteness. When the lighter trees were dry, the dark trees were painted. Then the building was rendered, as well as the large mass of snow in shadow to the left. The round snow shapes in the foreground were modeled and allowed to dry. Finally, I did the reflections, always remembering what *causes* them.

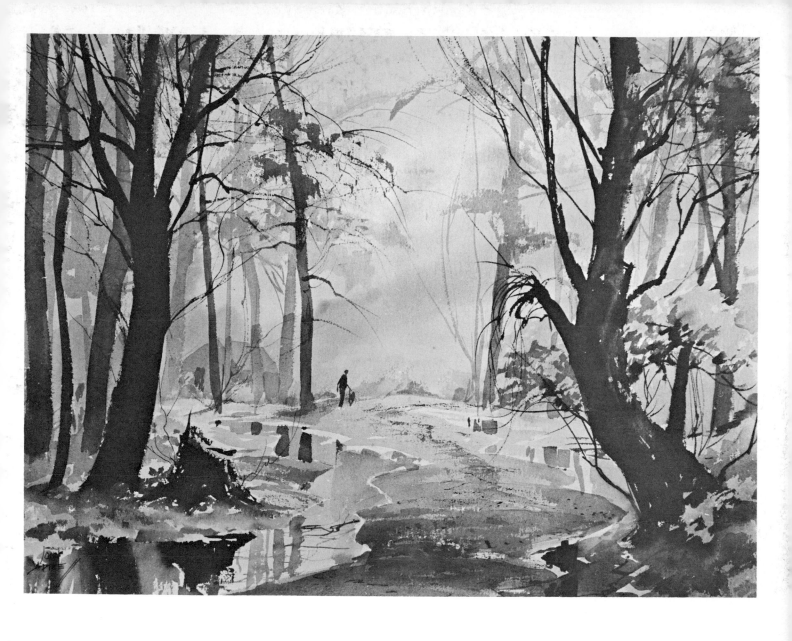

OCTOBER RAIN, *22" x 30". Private collection.*

This painting was a class demonstration to show our usual "three steps forward" treatment: (1) background, (2) middle ground, and (3) foreground. Note how the values correspond to these three planes.

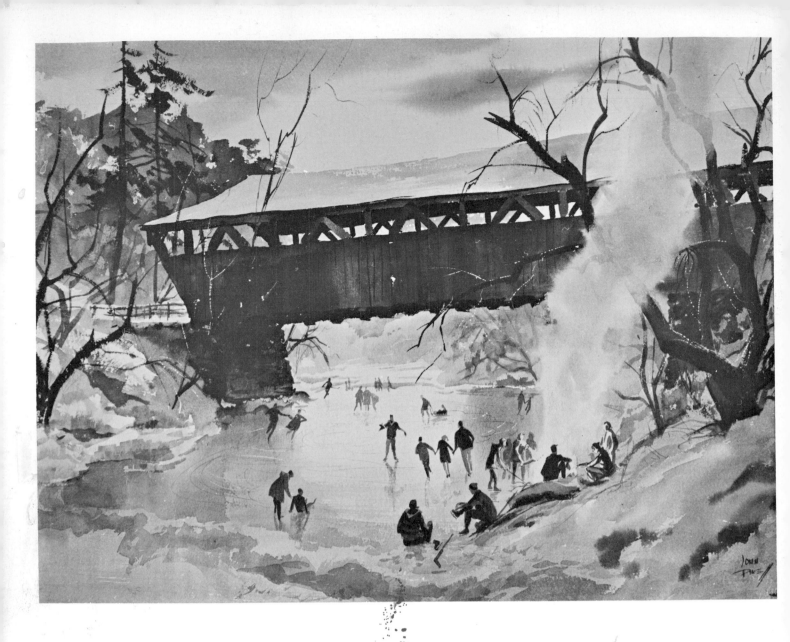

SKATING UNDER THE BRIDGE, *22" x 30". Private collection.*

In this picture, the center of interest was created by the intense back light. The sky and soft clouds were put in delicately, as well as the reflected light on the ice. A blue-gray wash was put over the snow in the foreground and up into the smoke to establish its pattern. The value of the snow on the roof of the covered bridge was studied carefully, to make the contrast between snow and sky *count*. To achieve the soft edge of the smoke, clear water was dropped in so that the dark of the bridge would run into it slightly. Where the willow trunks go behind the smoke, the pigment was thinned out, not scrubbed out. Finally came the dark mass of trees to the left behind the bridge, plus the figures and the little branches, to complete the painting.

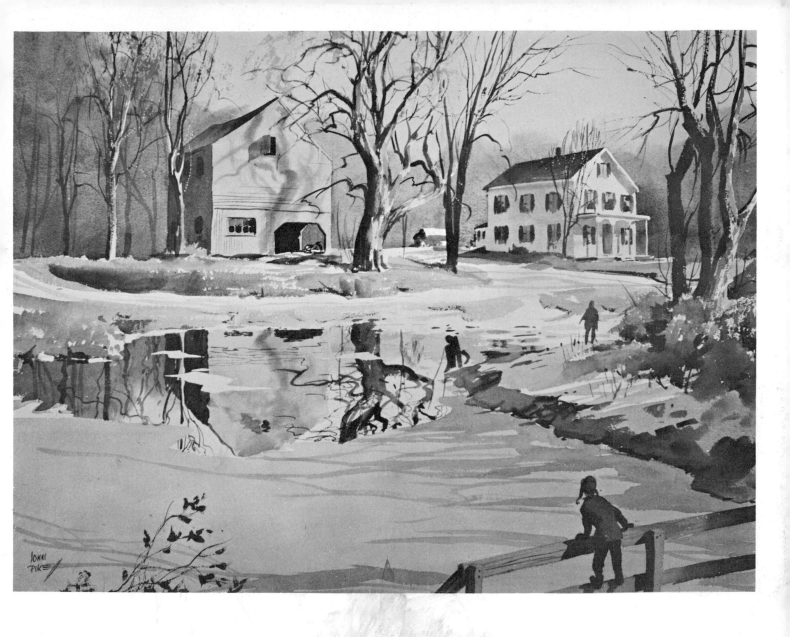

SPRING THAW, *22" x 30". Private collection.*

The entire area behind the building (with the soft trees) was washed in at one time, leaving a few of the tree trunks white. The snow and ice in the foreground were taken down in value to emphasize the sky reflection in the water. Then came the shadows on the snow, the building details, the rendering of the trees and figures.

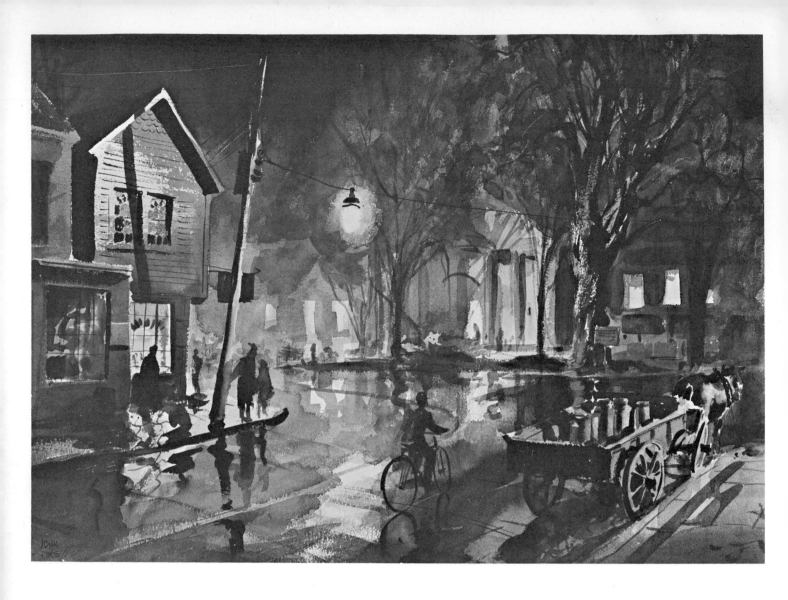

VILLAGE GREEN, WOODSTOCK, N.Y., *22" x 30",*
about 1946. Private collection. Photo, Juley.

Night pictures are much more complicated
than the comparatively simple sunlight
paintings. In the latter, you have the basic
light source, the sun; the object, which is a
building, a tree or a rock; and the cast shadow
of any of these. As simple as 1, 2, 3. In a night
painting, you have many light sources coming
from all directions. Added to that, you may
have wet pavement, which complicates things
no end. This is the time when you must
carefully consider all the influences of all these
lights, as well as the reflective surfaces.

2 Paper

Of all the tools you'll use in transparent watercolor, by far the most important one is your paper. Watercolor paper must be of good quality and have a permanent "whiteness."

HAND MADE VS. MACHINE MADE PAPERS

Good watercolor papers are 100% rag content. Bleached or unbleached fibres are made into a "soup," poured over a screen and, by the magic process of the individual paper maker, transformed into a sheet of paper with a surface that's a delight to paint upon.

Most machine made papers have a surface that seems too mechanical, often like a grid. I prefer good hand made paper for my particular work.

Some cheaper papers are made with a combination of wood pulp and rag, and so on down to the 100% wood pulp content of the construction papers that children use in early school. Papers containing wood pulp are absolutely no good for transparent watercolor. They take paint badly and will yellow —and finally crumble—with age.

CHARACTERISTICS OF WATERCOLOR PAPER

Investigate papers: work with different textures to see which one you like best, and to learn how these textures can contribute to your desired effect. Get the *feel* of various papers.

Most watercolor papers are manufactured with three different surfaces available: hot pressed (smooth), cold pressed (medium rough), and rough (very rough).

Different brands have varying degrees of absorbency, and this will naturally affect the drying time of your washes. As an extreme example, compare a wash on absorbent blotting paper and a wash on a completely non-absorbent piece of metal or plastic.

Learn to know what different papers' reactions are. Buy the three different textures as put out by several different manufacturers, and cut them into quarters, or smaller if you wish. Experiment until you find the one that's just right for you. It's a bit of an investment, but it may save you a lot of grief later.

SIZES AND WEIGHTS The standard size of hand made sheets is 22″ x 30″, although you'll find this varies as much as ¼″ in both dimensions. The large sheets may be cut in two, which gives you (in the heavy paper) four sturdy working surfaces, each 15″ x 22″. I don't mean to sound like a defeatist here, but let's face it, there just *might* be a time when you're not too happy with your painting; knowing that you've got that nice white side on the back of the painting—for a second try—can be rather comforting.

Generally, papers are listed in three weights or thicknesses: 72 pounds, 140 pounds, and 300 pounds. (This rating by pounds simply means the weight of a *ream*, or 500 sheets. I've been trying to find that out for years, and now I'm content to forget it!). As you might well imagine, the 300 pound sheet is about four times the price of the 72 pound, but it's worth it. I'll explain why in a moment.

The 72 pound and 140 pound stock—however fine the surface and quality—*must* be soaked and stretched smooth as a drum to avoid the wrinkles that hold water puddles, and that cause those unhappy rings and *flowers* to form just where we don't want them. Personally, I'm not a paper stretcher. I'm lazy and a bit of a spendthrift, so I use the 300 pound paper exclusively.

Actually, these aren't my real reasons for its use. I like the flexibility of a heavy sheet of paper that isn't pinned down to a board. I can bend and twist the sheet to better control the washes; to guide and direct them as I choose; and to get the painting to my fast drying agent with greater speed (see sketch of my gadget).

Many of the heavier papers have a slight starch or sizing on their surfaces. This causes thousands of fine little white spots that gray out your color when you lay a wash. This sizing may be removed by gently washing down the paper with a soft sponge, then allowing the sheet to dry before you start to paint. You'll find that the pigment *bites* much better and, in drying, the color stays much closer to what you put down.

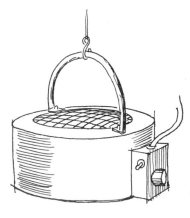

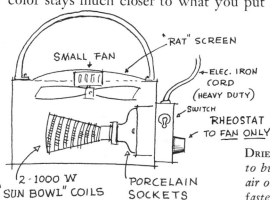

SMALL FAN

"RAT" SCREEN

ELEC. IRON CORD (HEAVY DUTY)

SWITCH

RHEOSTAT TO FAN ONLY

"2 - 1000 W "SUN BOWL" COILS

PORCELAIN SOCKETS

DRIER *This homemade gadget—very simple to build and terribly convenient—blows hot air on a wet watercolor, so washes will dry faster and I can get on with my work.*

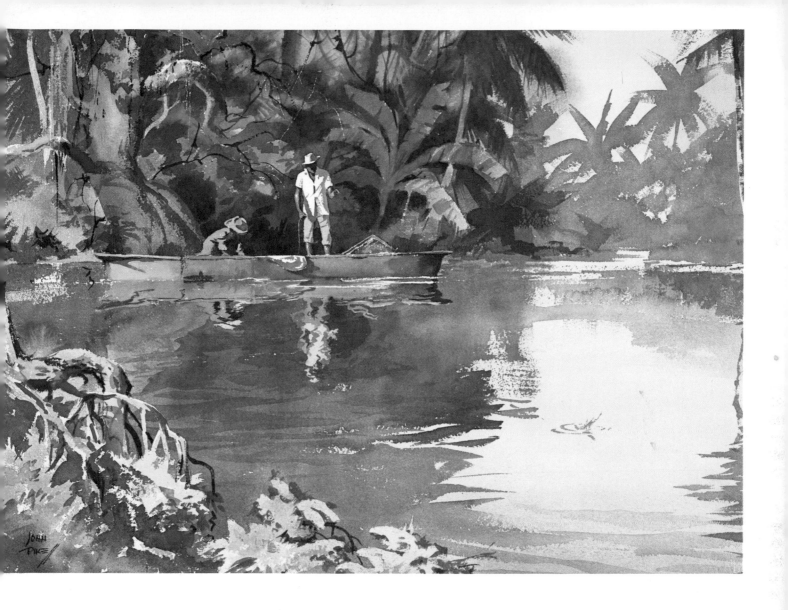

FISHERMEN, *22" x 30". Courtesy Osborne, Kemper, Thomas.*

This watercolor could have found its source material in any one of dozens of places in the lush tropical zones that circle the world: the coconut palms, the mangroves, the giant silk-cotton (kapok) tree festooned with "wis-wis" vines, and the still water of the inlet that might well hide a five foot barracuda relentlessly stalking the unwary.

1   Liquid frisket completely covered the figures and their reflection, as well as the boat and the mangroves in the left foreground.

2   I painted the light sky wash and the sky reflection in the water. These were faded off into the areas that would eventually be dark.

3   When the sky was dry, the distant palms were put in with fast, simple strokes. I also did the lighter greens of the dark tree areas, painting around the large kapok tree. All reflections were left until the shapes that caused them were established—a good point to remember.

4   Then came the deep darks and the texturing of the tree masses, both right and left. I added the light, warm underpainting of the big tree. When these were defined, I proceeded with the large reflections in the lagoon; this was done rapidly, but with careful planning, bearing in mind the reason for the shapes.

5   When all this was *thoroughly* dry, the masking agent was removed and the figures, the boat, and their reflections were rendered. The same applied to the mangrove and leaves in the foreground.

ROUGH PAPER

Rough paper is just what it says. Many watercolorists like its rugged texture. Its little mountains and valleys offer an opportunity to create rather sparkling effects; many times, the pigment hits only the tops of the mountains leaving the white in the valleys. This very interesting surface is conducive to many extreme styles and techniques.

COLD PRESSED PAPER

Cold pressed paper is much closer in texture to the rough than to the hot pressed. I personally prefer cold pressed for two reasons. First, it has enough *tooth* to allow me to gain a great variety of effects through proper brush manipulation. Second, I can lay down a wash much more rapidly than on the rough surface, where you have to fight your way down into those deep little valleys.

I say "personally" only because of the manner in which *I* enjoy working. In the development of your own particular style or technique—which I'm sure you'll do—you may very possibly prefer the rough or even the hot pressed.

To repeat myself, my sole purpose in doing this book is to try to show you—from the experience I've had—what happens when you go splashing around with water and pigment. From there on, it's up to *you*. Your life, your loves, your experiences, your ability to work and observe are the big contributing forces to *your* style. If you have a thorough command of the medium, you may interpret what you see in any manner *you* choose.

SMOOTH OR
HOT PRESSED PAPER

Smooth paper has quite a different reaction to pigment than the cold pressed and the rough. In its manufacture, the paper is squeezed in powerful presses at high temperatures, giving it a smooth, *hard* finish, much harder than the other two.

As a result of this hard surface, very little of your paint (with the exception of dye colors like Thalo blue) will sink *into* or be absorbed by the paper. Since the pigment sits pretty much on the surface, dried color picks up much more readily; when putting on a second wash over the first, be careful that the first doesn't lift up.

Experiment! It's a fine paper for gaining special effects. For example, it's fine for doing big sponged or painted decorative areas, then coming back in with brush or pen-and-ink line. Due to its hard surface, smooth paper can take almost anything: crayon, felt pen, tempera, transparent watercolor, chalks, acrylics—and lots of abuse.

COMMENTS ON
VARIOUS BRANDS

There are many fine papers, all worth trying.

I can't help but note here, with sadness, the demise of that grand old English paper, Whatman. It nobly served many generations all over the world, professionals and Sunday painters alike: the Homers, Sargents, Munnings, Flints—and Aunt Martha. Whatman will be missed.

Among the other big names in watercolor paper are: d'Arches (French, hand made); Crisbrook (British, hand made); Fabriano (Italian, mould made); Strathmore (American, machine made); Capri (Italian); R.W.S.

(Royal Watercolor Society, English, hand made).

There are others, no doubt, of equal quality, but I'm not as familiar with them.

As I've said, I prefer the texture and feel of the heavy, hand made paper. D'Arches is one of the few who still manufacture 300 pound stock, along with R.W.S., Capri, and perhaps a few others. I find it difficult to understand this because, to me, 300 pound is the ideal working weight for the watercolorist.

The toughness of a heavy paper, and the abuse it will take—aside from the ease in the painting—are all in its favor. I've served on an untold number of juries and I've seen how non-professional handlers can stack and unintentionally man-handle your matted watercolor masterpieces. "Oops! Hey, Charlie, where'd you put the Scotch tape?"

I put d'Arches first because I'm most familiar with it. I've learned to know its every little whimsy and how it will act under different conditions. Such as: How limp will it go on humid days? Can you pick up pigment from it, and just how much? Is it tough enough to withstand erasing, scraping, rubbing, and how far can you go with this? Is the quality uniform, sheet after sheet? This sort of intimate familiarity with your most important materials and tools can contribute greatly to the success of your painting.

But experiment around; try them all. Your personal approach to watercolor may require an entirely different paper from the one I happen to use. Find out what's best for *you*.

How to Stretch Paper	300 pound doesn't have to be stretched, which is one of my reasons for liking it. The 72 pound and 140 pound *must* be stretched for best results. Remember, a paper made by a reputable manufacturer, however light weight, is the same high quality as the heaviest; so, if it's properly stretched, you have an excellent working surface.

Here are three methods of stretching; I show them in order of preference. In all three methods, it's necessary to soak your paper in a bathtub or large sink until the sheet becomes soft and pliable. This won't hurt a good paper in any way.

Method One	This first one is very practical if you consistently work in one size. A recent student of mine had this device; I don't know if it was home made or store-bought. (Ask your art supply dealer.) Make your stretcher ¾″ smaller on all sides than the size of the paper you wish to paint on, because you'll need a fold-over at the edges.

Here are the supplies you'll need to build your own. *At the hardware store*, buy ½″ or ¾″ aluminum right angle extruded molding; eight 2¼″ light gauge bolts; eight wing nuts to fit the bolts. *At the lumber supplier*, get a piece of ⅛″ temper board (Masonite) cut to your desired size. *At the art store*, buy four canvas stretcher strips that, when assembled, will make up the size you want.

Assemble the stretcher strips. Nail the temper board to the strips with

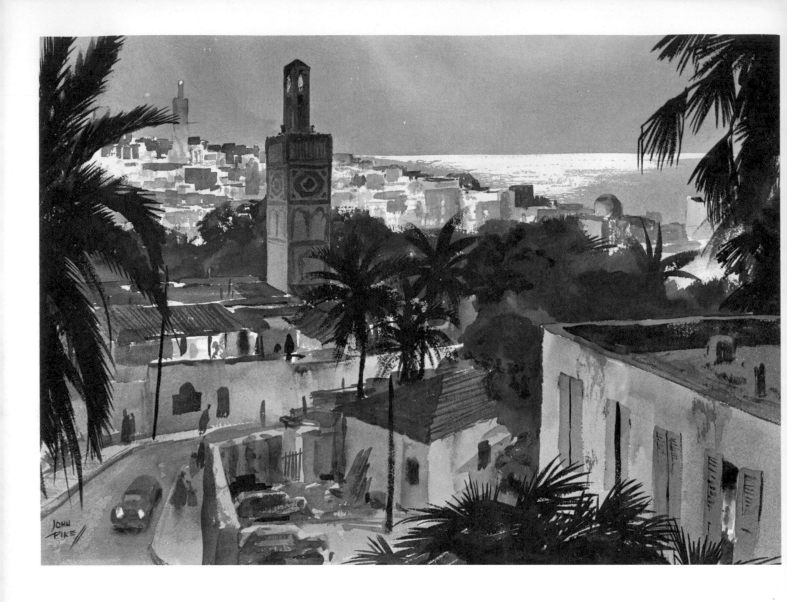

TANGIER, MOROCCO, *22" x 30". Collection, General Tire International.*

In most cities of great age in North Africa, the Middle East, and the Orient, you invariably have *two* cities, the *old* and the *new*. The new are usually as modern as tomorrow: beautiful parks, apartment houses, and shiny department stores. But it is the *old*, with its ancient architecture, the little hidden peddlers' stalls, the sounds and the colorful spots of sin, that hold magnetism for the painter. And rightly so, for time and "progress" are rapidly eliminating much of the beauty and charm of earlier architectural forms.

1   As unromantic as it may seem, a strip of masking tape made the horizon line where the moonlight falls on the distant sea. The sky was painted and the tape removed.

2   A masking agent was touched onto a few of the buildings to retain the lighted windows.

3   The warm, reflected light tones were spotted in on the distant city, as well as on the buildings in the foreground.

4   The brush was dragged over the water to give it sparkle. Then came the blues and brownish spotting of the dark sides of the buildings.

5   Next, I painted the large dark green mass of the middle ground trees and the blue-gray shadows of the foreground.

6   I added final little details and the very dark palm patterns.

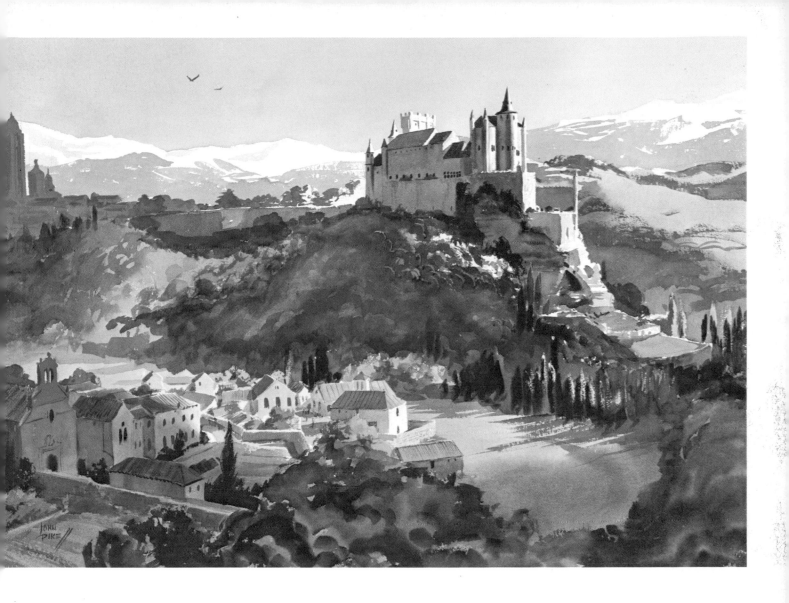

ALCAZAR AND CATHEDRAL, SEGOVIA, *22" x 30"*.
Collection, General Tire International.

It has been said that when you dream of
"castles in Spain," you see the Alcazar of
Segovia. Built high on a hill, with a shiplike
prow, the Alcazar sparkles against the
snow-capped Sierra de Guadarrama mountains
in the distance. In proper feudal fashion, the
charming shops and homes of the less
fortunate cluster at the castle's feet.
1   A masking agent was used only on a few
of the spires and light sides of the castle.
All the rest was painted directly.
2   In the usual light-to-dark procedure, the
color-graded sky was put in.

3   The masking agent was removed and all
the shadows were covered with a neutral
blue-gray wash. This established the over-all
value relationships.
4   The gray of the distant mountains was put
down, keeping in mind the light direction.
5   Then came the underpainting greens of the
middle ground hills and the foreground, plus
various warm tints on the castle and village
houses. All were allowed to dry.
6   I modeled the dark greens, as well as the
buildings.
7   I finished up with all the little details, such
as windows, roof tiles, little cypress trees.
And you have your castle in Spain.

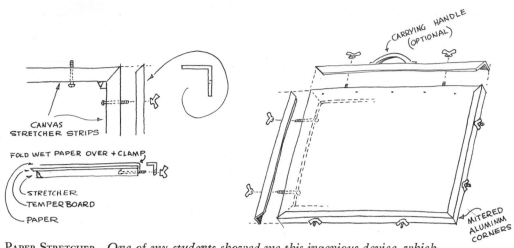

PAPER STRETCHER *One of my students showed me this ingenious device, which you can make with materials available in any hardware store and lumber yard.*

brads or screws. Saw the aluminum to the same length as the wooden stretcher strips; miter the corners with a hack saw (most of the aluminum in the "do-it-yourself" racks can be cut with an ordinary wood saw). Drill two holes in each length of aluminum, where the drawing indicates. Place each aluminum molding on the edge of the matching stretcher strip and mark the stretcher strip where the holes come. Drill the wooden stretcher strips at the marked spots and insert bolts from the *inside* out.

Now you're ready to place wet paper flat over the temper board; turn the edges of the paper downward. Slip all four aluminum moldings over the protruding bolts and tighten up the wing nuts. You'll need a small screw driver on the inside to keep the bolts from turning as you tighten the nuts. Allow the paper to dry and stretch; then go to work.

If you aren't overly happy with your own carpentry skills, show the diagram to your local handyman. It should take him about twenty minutes to build the unit. If no luck there, see your art supply dealer again and hope he can get one for you. If you fail on all counts, buy a sheet of 300 pound paper and skip the stretching!

METHOD TWO

The second system again goes to the ⅛″ temper board. Upson board, or what we used to call Beaverboard, will also do. This time it should be a good 1″ *larger* than your paper.

Spread your wet paper out on your board, push out all the air bubbles, sponge up excess water, then tape all around the edges with a *good* commercial (animal glue) brown tape. Masking tapes won't work. Let paper and tape dry and you're ready.

METHOD THREE

The third method involves the canvas stretcher strips again. Place your wet paper face down on a clean surface. Place and center the assembled stretcher strips on the sheet (no board this time). Fold the extending paper edges up the sides of the strips and onto the back of the strips. Thumbtack or staple the edges of the paper that fold over the stretcher strips. Some watercolorists tack or staple the sides or back of the stretcher strips; and some cautious souls tack or staple sides *and* back. Keep thumbtacks or staples close together.

MOUNTING PAPER

This is an old fashioned, tried and true method, but it cuts down the size of your painting surface by at least 2″ all around. When I feel like painting a full sheet watercolor, I want a *full* sheet. Like to try 300 pound?

Most paintings on light weight papers need mounting on cardboard to avoid wrinkling in their frames, caused by humidity and temperature changes.

Mounting board may be thick or thin, but be sure it is of good quality. Your art dealer friend will advise you. You'll need good wallpaper wheat paste (such as the trade name, Rex), plus a "strengthener" (such as Stay-rite). As they say, "the directions are on the box."

Mix your paste thoroughly to completely eliminate lumps; add the "strengthener" and stir. The mixture should have a heavy cream consistency.

Now, dampen the back of the watercolor paper with a moist sponge, and dampen the mounting board. With a large, soft brush paint the paste on *both* surfaces (paper and mount board) and remember, no lumps! Press the two surfaces together with the watercolor face up. With a clean piece of tracing paper held down with one hand to protect the surface of the watercolor, press out all the bubbles with the other hand, working out to the edge.

You can then cover the painting with a piece of clean wrapping paper (not newspaper) and iron with a medium hot, *dry* iron. After this, weight the mounted painting with a heavy wooden drawing board, loaded with books. Then allow to dry.

The ironing process isn't absolutely necessary, provided you have the watercolor absolutely flat on the mount board. Ironing just speeds up the drying a little. When dry, trim off the excess mounting board.

WATERCOLOR PADS AND BLOCKS

Most watercolor paper manufacturers put out *blocks* and *pads* of fine paper for your convenience when you're working in the field. These come in a variety of sizes, all the way from 6″ x 9″ up to 18″ x 24″. They're usually sold only in the lighter weights: 72 pound to 140 pound.

A *pad* is like a notebook; it may be hinged or attached either at the top or at the side. A pad may have a glued binding or a metal spiral binding, which is more convenient.

A *block* may or may not have a hard protective cover—like a pad—but it's bound on *all four* sides. There's one little open area on the edge (usually at the top) where you can slip in a table knife and cut all around the edge to loosen the entire sheet from the block. The table knife is better than a sharp one, as the blunt knife will not damage the sheet above or below.

There's one trouble when you work on a block: as soon as you start painting, the wet paper begins to wrinkle and heave up in the middle, due to the confinement of the edges. I've found that by freeing three of the four edges with the table knife, I can greatly reduce the buckling. You may get some curling at the loose corners, but it's better than having the Rockies in the middle of the sheet.

Pads and blocks offer a convenient way to carry small sketching or painting paper when you're working outdoors. I wouldn't be without them.

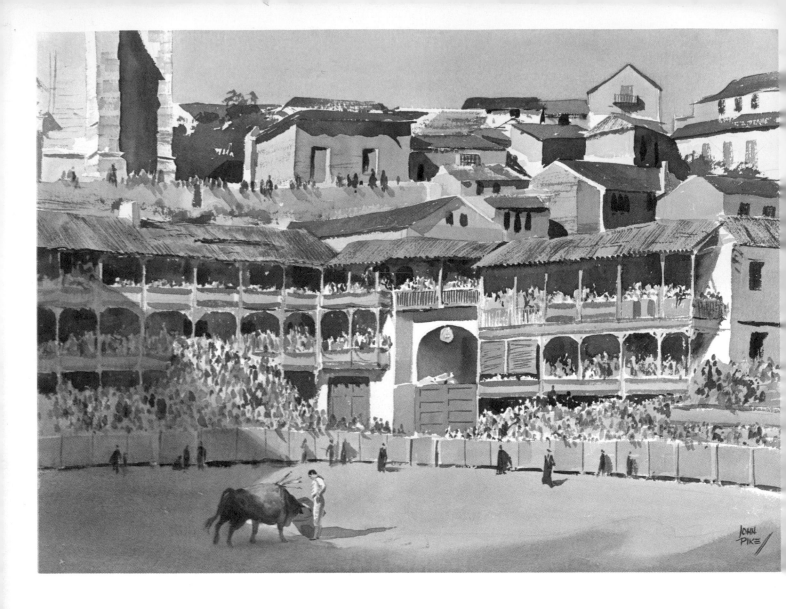

BULLFIGHT, SPAIN, *22″ x 30″. Collection, General Tire International.*

While this is primarily an architectural subject, it is also useful in showing the simple handling of larger masses of people. This *can* be made very complicated, or it can be kept completely simple by the impressionist approach shown here: just spots and patches of color.

The buildings, with their red roofs and stucco walls, create the atmosphere and indicate the locale. The packed in humanity, with all eyes staring at the center of the arena, focus attention on a great man and a brave bull, fighting here today. It is there, at the point of interest, that we put in our detail: there, where the matador and El Toro are performing their "ballet of death."

36

3 *Colors*

In talking about color, we always risk the pitfalls one finds in discussions of politics, religion, and Charles Darwin. Every painter has an opinion on the subject and usually a strong one!

It is American watercolorists who have given this exciting medium its present "gutsy," but subtle qualities, so that watercolor can take its place proudly with the "majors." In years past, it was known as the sketcher's medium. The dominant technique was the English tint-as-we-go method; works were usually given titles such as, "At Eventide, the Wild Woods Amongst." In the early days, watercolor was used mainly to record color notes for more ambitious works to be developed back at the studio in the only medium (at *that* time) worthy of the name—*oil*. Today, I hasten to add, there are many bold and brilliant English watercolorists.

TUBE COLORS

The introduction of moist watercolor—in tubes instead of little tins—was a great contribution to its development into a bold, large scale painting medium. With tube colors, one can quickly pick up enough pigment to hit that great dark at exactly the *time* it's needed. I don't happen to like scrubbing around in little pans; therefore, I suggest using tube colors.

CHARACTERISTICS OF WATERCOLOR PIGMENTS

In color, as in paper, get into the habit of using the very best you can buy. The *finest* are not that much more expensive than the so-called "student color," but the handling qualities, results, and permanency are far apart. Watercolor, unlike oil or any other opaque paint, isn't used in large bulk quantities. A little goes a long way, so you can well afford the *best*. Whoever the manufacturer may be, ask for his *top* grade of paint. Don't make that beautifully designed gown out of cheap burlap!

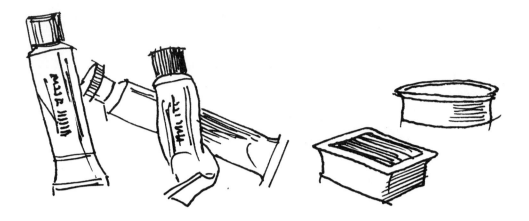

PAINTS *Moist watercolors in tubes are much easier to work with than hardened colors in metal or porcelain pans.*

Again, it's up to you; try them all, but I do think you'll appreciate the higher quality of the *vehicle* that makes the pigment adhere to your paper, in the better paints.

The actual *transparency* of transparent watercolor pigments runs the gamut from crystal clear—in some of the dye colors—down through the rather heavy semi-opaques, as in some of the cadmiums. It's your job to find out what the water-to-pigment ratio is, so that you won't make the error of using the heavier ones as opaque colors. Besides, they aren't quite opaque *enough* and look horrible if you try to use them in that manner.

You must also bear in mind that some colors are stronger than others in mixtures. The tiniest speck of Prussian Blue will do when you're mixing it with Cadmium Yellow to produce green; you'd need a lot more Ultramarine Blue in a similar mixture. Once again, you'll learn by trial and error.

Today, most good paints are produced under the highest standards. If the manufacturer says, either in his literature or on the tube, that his product is permanent, you can believe him. Some use the star system: *** absolute permanency, ** excellent permanency, * fair permanency. The chemistry and know-how of paint manufacture today is greatly advanced, compared to what it was only fifteen or twenty years ago.

The dye colors (of fairly recent development) have dreadful names like Chlorinated Phthalocyanine. M. Grumbacher, Inc., happily had the good taste to cut this monstrosity down to the simple trade name of Thalo. The English Winsor and Newton have skipped the chemical term entirely and simply call all colors with this base Winsor Blue, Winsor Green, etc. Other companies all have their own trade names for these colors. There are several Thalo colors available. I use only the *blue* and the *green*, which I'll explain later when I describe my palette setup. According to Ralph Mayer in *The Artist's Handbook*, these colors will, logically, become known simply as Thalo Blue, Thalo Green, etc.

PERMANENT COLORS There are fifty or so different colors available to the watercolorist and they vary considerably in permanency and opacity. Many are exotic, non-essential tints; others, I feel, are simply variations of a standard color. Below, I've listed some of the tried and true standards. All of these are permanent, but some are more opaque than others, as I'll indicate.

By *permanent,* I mean that the colors, under normal hanging conditions, will stay bright and clear long after our great grandchildren are gone. I've held original Winslow Homers in my hands; they were painted between 1865 and 1900, and they could have been done this morning! (I hope a little rubbed off on me.) And remember, today's paints are far better than those he used. *Any* pigment—oil, tempera, watercolor—all of them will fade if abused. Long periods of exposure to direct sunlight will naturally take their toll. But, if a painting is properly cared for, there's no time limit upon permanency. Here's a reasonably complete list of permanent colors for the watercolorist, with notes on relative transparency.

Alizarin Crimson: A rich red with a slight bluish cast; very transparent.

Alizarin Crimson Golden: A warmer red than Alizarin Crimson; very transparent.

Burnt Sienna: Golden brown; transparent.

Burnt Umber: Dark, rich brown; transparent.

Cadmium Red Light: A bright, orangy red; slightly opaque.

Cadmium Yellow Lemon: Very light yellow; slightly opaque.

Cadmium Yellow Deep: Yellow orange; slightly opaque.

Cerulean Blue: Light, rich, warm blue; slightly opaque.

Emerald Green: Light, cool green; slightly opaque.

Ultramarine Blue and French Ultramarine are much alike; the French is slightly warmer; both are transparent.

Gamboge Hue: A pale yellow; very transparent.

New Gamboge: A stronger pale yellow; very transparent.

Terre Verte: Warm earth green; transparent.

Hooker's Green Light and *Hooker's Green Deep:* warm, nature-type green; very transparent.

Lamp Black: A cool black; very transparent.

Ivory Black: A warm black; very transparent.

Payne's Gray: An elusive, bluish gray; very transparent.

Permanent Green: A strong, dark green; very transparent.

Prussian Blue: A slightly grainy, cold, metallic blue, very transparent.

Raw Sienna and *Raw Umber:* Both brown with yellow overtones; slightly opaque.

Sap Green: Pale yellow green, like Spring leaves; transparent.

Thalo Blue and *Thalo Green:* Both very powerful, cold, dark colors; very transparent. I like them as basic mixing colors.

Vermilion: A brilliant, Chinese type of bright red; slightly opaque.

Viridian (Vert Emeraude): Strong, dark, cold green; very transparent.

There are many other colors, but I feel they apply more to the other mediums than to transparent watercolor. In this list, you have more than enough suggested colors, certainly far more than I use; but again, I want the choice to be yours. Now, here are a few notes on certain colors.

PAYNE'S GRAY

Payne's Gray can be a fooler. It's one of the few colors that will dry about 50% lighter than what you put down; most other colors lighten only 5% to 10% when they dry. As an example, if you use Payne's Gray as a *dark*, you'll invariably find that it will dry too light; so you have to go back in again, and there you've taken the first step on the muddy road. Confine the use of Payne's Gray to light areas.

PRUSSIAN BLUE

Prussian Blue served its purpose well for many years, but I feel it's been replaced by a far superior color: Phthalocyanine Blue (Thalo, Winsor, and other trade names). The newer blue has greater brilliance; it's highly transparent; and it's smoother in handling. However, it's a dye, so don't get it on your white sweater.

NEW
GAMBOGE YELLOW
(WINSOR & NEWTON)

New Gamboge is a great improvement over regular Gamboge. The new color seems to have much greater strength and mixing power, along with great transparency. Although the Cadmium Yellows are beautiful colors, all Cadmiums have a tendency to be opaque. Since we're working in transparent watercolor, we should try to keep our colors as transparent as possible, which is why I like New Gamboge.

OPAQUE WHITE

It's a rather dirty word for the "purist," but opaque white should be discussed, if only briefly.

There are several approaches to its usage, as well as dodges for avoiding its use. In transparent watercolor, I use the dodges—rubber cement, masking tapes, liquid friskets, and other blocking out methods—not too often, but about as much as you see in the painting entitled "Suppertime." I use the dodges simply because I prefer the white of my paper to an opaque white on top of an otherwise transparent painting. Most times, I'd much rather see if I'm capable of painting *around* a white area.

The opaque color used on a transparent watercolor for little touch-ups seems out of balance in texture. Rather like the recipe for Moose and Rabbit Stew: "Take one moose, add one rabbit, etc."

Granted, in the days when I was doing magazine illustration in transparent watercolor, I became very handy with opaques so that they wouldn't show in the reproduction. But the opaques *did* show in the original, and weren't attractive.

The proper use of opaque white, as practiced by an old friend and fellow Academician, is to mix a little white with *all* your colors before each wash. This gives a beautiful, soft, semi-gouache quality. On this, the opaque highlights have a feeling of belonging.

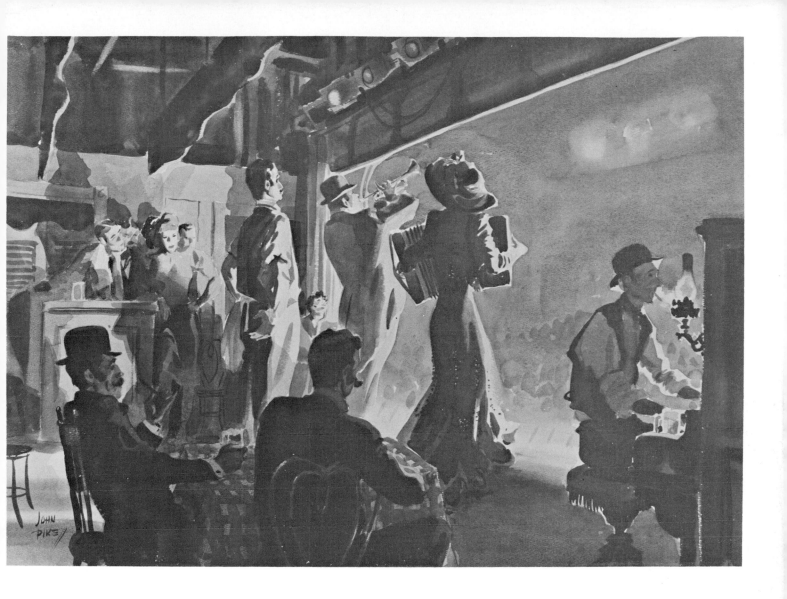

GOLD IN THE HILLS, 2ND ACT, *22" x 30", 1947.
Private collection. Photo, Juley.*

I did this semi-cartoon from a sketch done
backstage at one of the many shows we put on
for the benefit of the Woodstock Foundation.
Each year, we were able to give sizable grants
of money to worthy artists, writers, and
musicians to help them over a rough spot.

The man on the horn was the great Bill
Moore of the original California Ramblers
(around 1923); he played on through his
entire life and became more brilliant with each
year. The gal on the accordion was my dear
friend, Clementine Heinneman (Nessel). She
was soloist for many years with Ben Bernie
and helped Phil Spitalny organize his "all-girl

orchestra." (She refused to play in it as she
said she wanted MEN around.) A brilliant
musician! The man at the piano was famed
Broadway veteran actor, Harrison Dowd.

All are gone now, but I have delightful
memories of many years of wonderful times
we had together.

Note: I am the character in the bowler hat
at the left, disguised as Hawkshaw the
Detective.

This is a problem of value study to produce
a sense of the atmosphere and depth out in the
theater audience. Other than that, it is a simple
matter of strong light sources, objects, and
cast shadows. There was no masking agent
used in this watercolor. despite the crisp
patches of light.

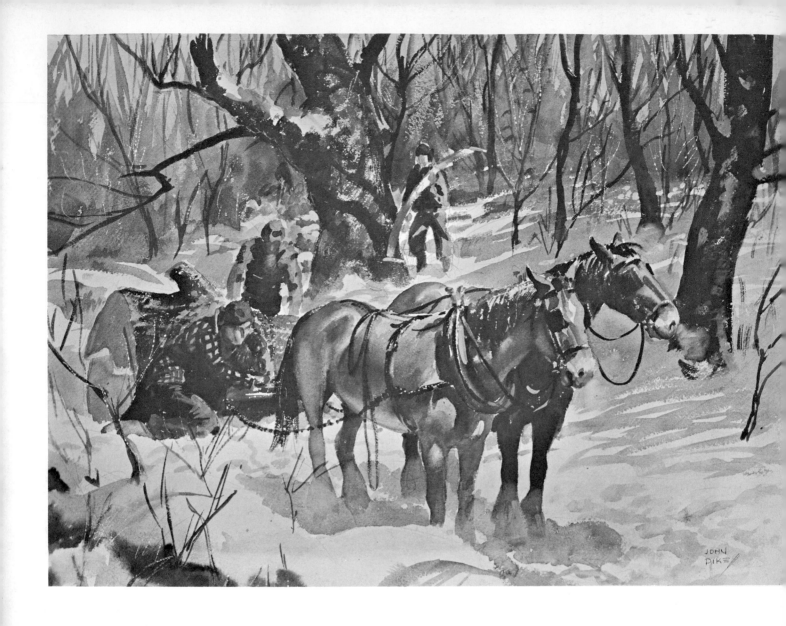

PATIENCE, OLD LYME, *22" x 30", 1938.*
Private collection.

After having lived for many years in the tropics,
I was completely intrigued with painting snow
at this time in my life. These old Clydesdales
have, no doubt, long since been replaced by
tractors. W. Frank Calderon, the great English
animal anatomist, has said that, in painting
horses, don't hesitate to let the contour of the
harness help in painting form and roundness.
I kept that thought in mind here.

CHOICE OF COLORS

Although I work in most mediums, I've simplified my transparent watercolor palette to the greatest possible extent. Many fine manufacturers are endlessly experimenting with beautiful, elusive colors. Now, in the opaques—temperas, oils, and the new acrylics—I find these colors fascinating and use them where applicable. But in transparent watercolor, I don't. I don't, because in the simple arrangement of the colors I use, I can gain everything I want very rapidly.

My simple palette was distilled over many years of illustration and painting. I found that I didn't need a Hooker's Green or a Sap Green; I could *make* it before I could get the cap off the tube. I didn't need an Ivory Black or Lamp Black; I could make it with great speed, plus others. In other words, I gradually cut back, almost to the primaries.

First, I'd like to show how you *might* select a minimum group of colors to work with. Then I'll go on to my palette: what colors I use; their arrangement for greatest convenience in working; and the reasons why I chose them.

In choosing your colors, the logical place to start is with the three primaries; red, yellow, and blue. At the risk of sounding obvious, it's from these three that all other colors are made. But there are all kinds of reds, yellows, and blues; so which ones for a starter? Here's how a palette might grow . . .

Red: Try Alizarin Crimson. *Yellow:* New Gamboge or Cadmium Yellow Light. *Blue:* Ultramarine.

We can go on. Since Ultramarine and one yellow may not make the variety of greens you'd like, you can add *Hooker's Green* to the list.

But you find you're still getting warm greens and you want a cold one. Add *Viridian.*

You mix Cadmium Yellow and Alizarin Crimson to capture the colors of Mr. Van Valkenburg's red barn. Too red. You add *Burnt Sienna.* Also *Cadmium Red Light.*

And so on until you have a palette that works for your specific needs.

Let me make clear that I'm not *recommending* this as the palette for *you.* I'm simply suggesting how your own personal palette might develop, based on your specific requirements. Every artist has his own preferences and builds his own personal array of colors. However, there *is* the danger that you can go on—and on, and on—adding color after color, hoping each one will add its own little touch of magic, until you've bought out the store and all its fifty or more colors! So let me suggest how to simplify the job. . . .

MY OWN PALETTE

Over many years, I've gradually eliminated color after color. At the start of this chapter, I said I'd cut back almost to the three primaries. What I actually have is a warm and cool version of each of the basic three.

For instance, I use *Ultramarine Blue* (a *warm* cool color) and *Thalo Blue* (cold). These two blues, in varying combinations, give me a full range through all of the Ceruleans, Cobalts, and Permanent Blues; so I don't need any of the last three.

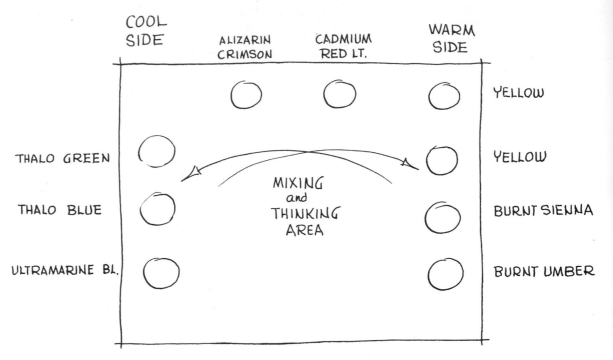

PALETTE LAYOUT *This is the way my colors are arranged on my palette: cools on one side, warms opposite, mixing and thinking area in the center. I use two squeezes of yellow (either Cadmium Yellow or New Gamboge) so at least one of them may stay clean.*

Here's my palette set-up.

Down the left side, I have my *cool* colors. Starting at the lower left is Ultramarine; above that Thalo Blue; then Thalo Green. Across the top are Alizarin Crimson; a *very* incidental accent color, Cadmium Red Light; plus two little mounds of the same yellow, Cadmium or New Gamboge (*one* of which I always think I *will* keep clean, and never do). Then, coming down the right—on the *warm* side—I have my Burnt Sienna and Burnt Umber. And these are all the colors I use in transparent watercolor.

This arrangement was arrived at for a reason. I happen to like the color located on my palette where I can get at it quickly. I also like a white palette space between my *cool* and *warm* colors as both my mixing and *thinking* ground. For instance, I want a warm, dark green. I dig into my Thalo Green as a starter; I move across to grab a little yellow and Burnt Sienna, then bring them back to the *white middle* to see what I have. It's too warm, so I touch the cool side again. Warm it up, cool it down, I keep reaching to one side or the other; it's all at my instant command. And every green, blue, red, or yellow in all the world can be found in this simple palette arrangement.

It comes out to seven colors, plus the Cadmium Red, which I don't usually count, as it's not for mixing. The most beautiful variety of grays can be made with Ultramarine, Burnt Sienna, and Burnt Umber. They have a luminosity that no tube gray can touch. And they can be greatly varied, all in one wash passage. Learn to think about color in that white space in the middle of your palette.

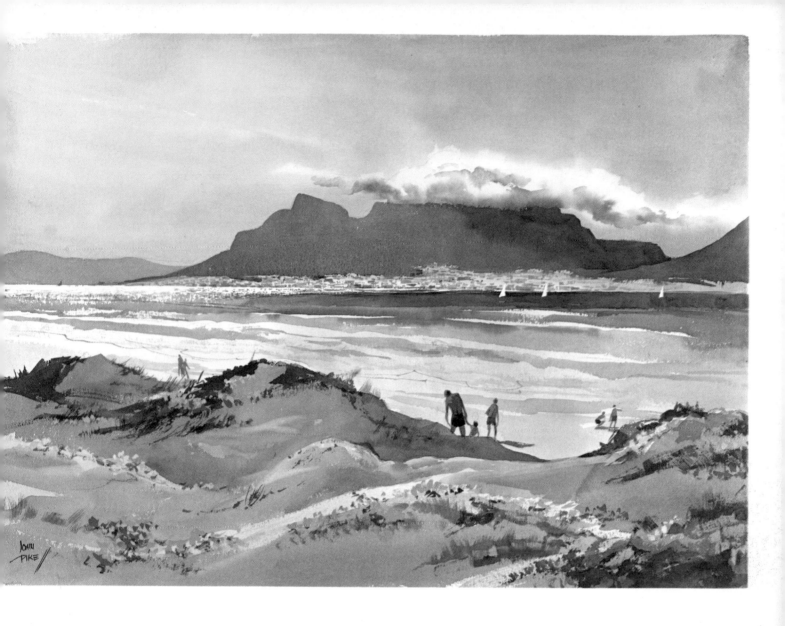

TABLE MOUNTAIN, SOUTH AFRICA, *22" x 30"*.
Collection, General Tire International.

This is Cape Town, seen from across the bay.
Devil's Peak is to the left, Lion's Head to the
right, and Table Mountain in the middle with
her tablecloth. The tablecloth is a mass of
cloud, formed by the cool air of the sea and
the warm air of the plateau behind.

After the drawing, plain water was put over
the entire cloud area; while still wet, the sky
wash was put in around the cloud, allowing
some color to flow into the cloud area and
down to the white, sparkling water, and to
the city itself. When this was dry, it was
necessary to add more clear water to the
white cloud area and put in its under-shadows.
This also allowed softness.

At this point, I was able to lay in the big,
flat silhouette of the mountains, darkening for
a shadow effect over Lion's Head. The warm
underpainting of the sand dunes came next.
Suggested details of the city, the sailboats, and
the water were our next move. Finally, I
added the modeling and texturing of the sand
dunes, as well as the figure. The only way I
could gain the hue of the flowers on the dunes
was by a touch of opaque color.

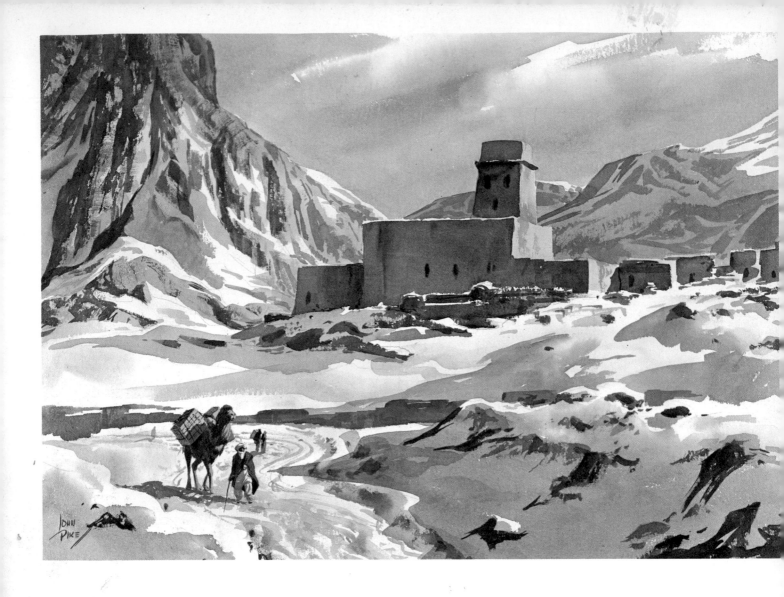

KHYBER PASS, 22" x 30". *Collection, General Tire International.*

The Khyber Pass is one of the more famous routes through the Hindu Kush, the untamed mountains that lie between the scenic lands of West Pakistan and Afghanistan. Many bloody battles have been fought in this area.
1   This watercolor was done without the use of any masking agent. Clear water was dropped into a few places in the sky to create the soft, trailing clouds. The cold blue of the sky was added at once—painting around the mountains and the old fort—and allowed to dry.
2   I painted all the warmer blues of the distant mountain, as well as the modeled shapes of the middle and foreground. In the right foreground, I added a little burnt sienna and yellow to gain reflected light on the bank.
3   Then came the warm underpainting on the cliffs at the left and the *entire* fort area, not just over the light sides.
4   When all the above washes were dry, I come back in with the texturing of the mountains, the dark sides of the fort, and the many small darks representing the rocks and boulders in the middle and foreground.
5   Finally, I added the old trader, with his loaded Bactrian camel, and the texturing of the road.

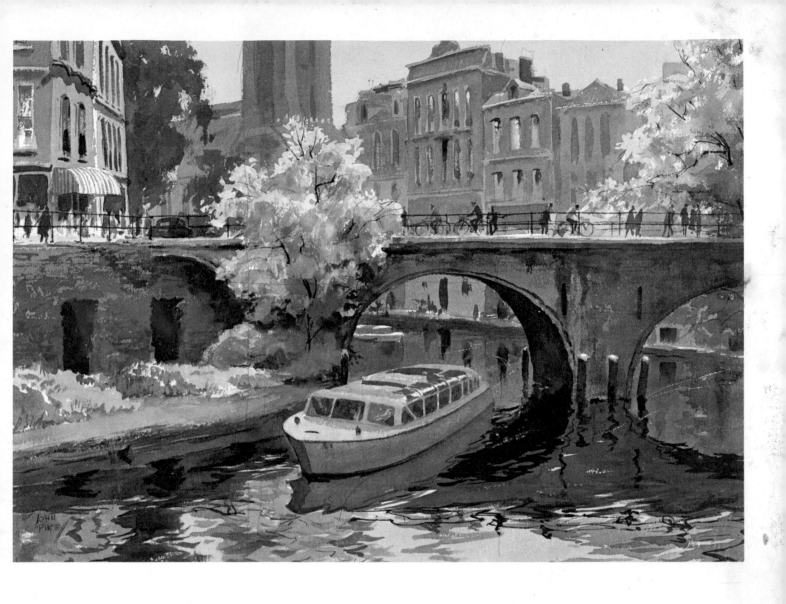

UTRECHT, HOLLAND, *22" x 30". Collection, General Tire International.*

This is a slightly hazy day and the sun is trying to burn through. In this watercolor, as in several others, blues have been employed to gain the feeling of distance, as in the buildings on the far side of the canal, beyond the bridge. The warm yellow-greens of the spring trees also aid in pushing the buildings back. Liquid masking agent was used to gain a lacy quality.

The warm grays of the old stone and the heavy dark arches give the bridge solidity and structure. The little figures give the bridge its relative size.

47

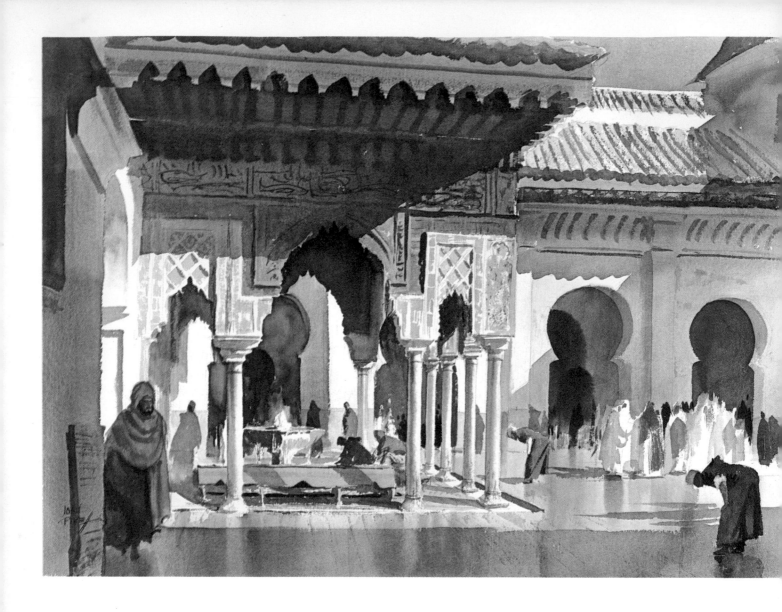

MOSQUE AT FES, MOROCCO, *22″ x 30″.*
Collection, General Tire International.

In an architectural subject such as this, great
care and attention must be paid to your
drawing and the patterning of the large
shadow masses. This mosque is a rambling
structure of incredible size. The painting
shows only a small portion of one courtyard.
The long foreground shadow, and the angular

shadow on the right rear wall, are devices
used to show that there's a great deal more
of the building "out that-a-way."

In drawing architectural subjects, think in
terms of the materials with which they are
built: the stone, tile, and wood that make up
the structure. It is a *building* and it must *stand*.
You can paint rapidly and broadly, but the
painting will be convincing only if your
drawing is correct.

4 Studio and outdoor equipment

This is a subject that's as loose as a broken paper sack of ping pong balls. It all comes down to what's best and most convenient for you.

DRAWING TABLES, WORK TABLES, TABORETS

An old fashioned drawing table or draftsman's table is fine, but not at all necessary. A light weight piece of Upson board or temper board (Masonite) which you lean against the kitchen table—or on your knees—is just as good.

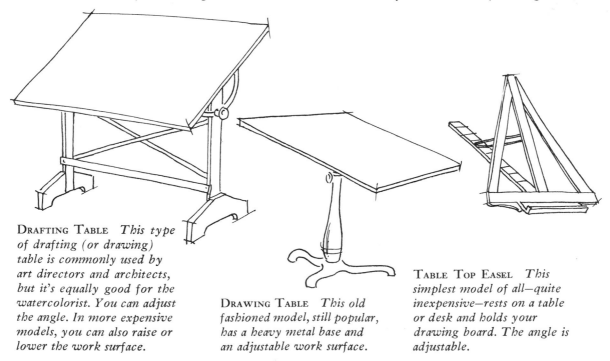

DRAFTING TABLE *This type of drafting (or drawing) table is commonly used by art directors and architects, but it's equally good for the watercolorist. You can adjust the angle. In more expensive models, you can also raise or lower the work surface.*

DRAWING TABLE *This old fashioned model, still popular, has a heavy metal base and an adjustable work surface.*

TABLE TOP EASEL *This simplest model of all—quite inexpensive—rests on a table or desk and holds your drawing board. The angle is adjustable.*

If you like to work standing up (as I do), lay the board flat on a table; any other small table will serve as a side table for your palette, water, paints, and brushes. Any of the new plastics (like a sheet of polyethylene) will protect the surface of the table. See your art dealer for suggestions. Find some place in an old dresser or on the top shelves of a closet to store your gear—remember the kids.

Work tables come in a couple of basic types: the cast iron base, single column, tilt-top, adjustable kind; and the all wood, tilt-top draftsman's type. Both are good and about the same price.

You can purchase taborets that have many convenient little drawers and special places to put ink bottles, etc. You can store everything but your large paper. Again, see your art dealer.

STOOLS, CHAIRS, ETC.

Use whatever is most comfortable for you. I have an old bucket seat from a 1948 Crosley station wagon, on a box base. Just fine.

NATURAL LIGHT

Improper lighting can really throw you off. Of course, the ideal is natural (or north) light from a window. This preference for north light probably sounds rather stuffy to your non-painter friends. So, for the record, allow me to explain.

A window facing due north will never, at any time of the year, receive the direct rays of the sun. It may seem strange, but that's the way artists like it, and for this reason: constant, sky-reflected light flows through the window; this light falls upon the object or person we're painting and *doesn't change all day*, except in intensity. The soft shadows all stay in the same place, as do the highlights. Therefore it's a *constant* source of light, to be enjoyed from dawn till dusk.

Photo, Roger Vandermark

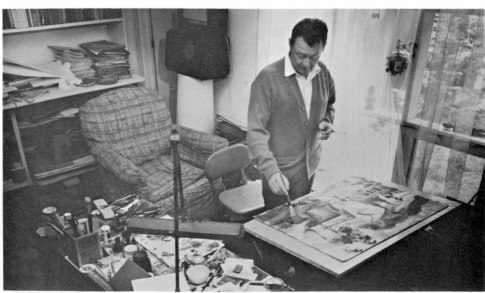

ARTIFICIAL LIGHT We're very fortunate to have our modern lighting advancements and discoveries.

However, the standard incandescent bulb puts out far too much *yellow* light; you can't really work under it with any semblance of color accuracy.

I have what I feel is a most satisfactory set-up. To my left is an 8′ square north window, right down to the floor. Above me, at a right angle to the window, I have a commercial fluorescent light fixture, 4′ long with two tubes of 40 watts each. One tube is *cool white*; the other, *warm white*. I turn the fixture on early in the morning so that, when the daylight fails, I don't even notice the difference.

The cool and the warm white arrangement seems the ideal combination for coming closest to natural light.

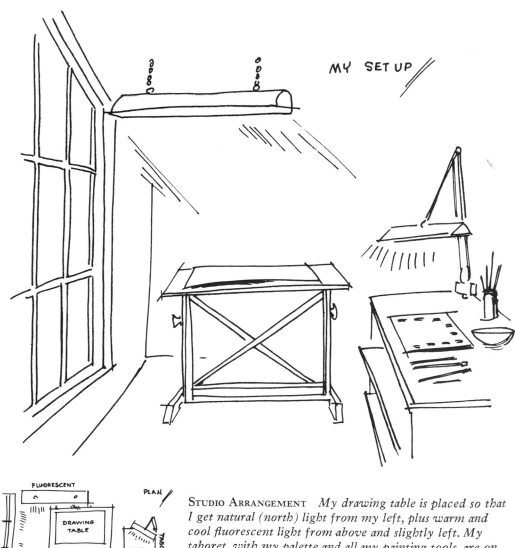

MY SET UP

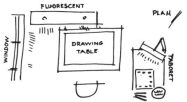

STUDIO ARRANGEMENT *My drawing table is placed so that I get natural (north) light from my left, plus warm and cool fluorescent light from above and slightly left. My taboret, with my palette and all my painting tools, are on the right, since I'm right handed. Obviously, you must switch things around if you're left handed.*

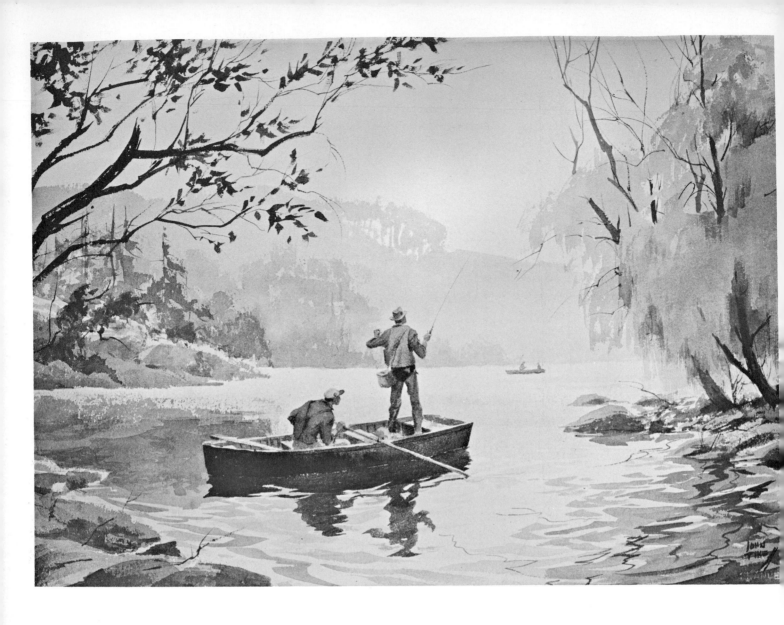

EARLY RISERS, *22" x 30". Private collection.*

Here we have the early, pearly morning effect. The sun will burn through later, but now the mist lies over the lake. The sky and basic water tint were put down over the entire watercolor. The distant trees and hills, since they have a hard edge, were put in after the first washes had dried. The entire background was subtle enough, and high enough in value, so that I was able to paint directly over them as I moved forward. The darkness of the boat, the framing branches and leaves in the upper left, the dark tree trunks of the willows, all tend to push back the distant hill and create the misty atmosphere.

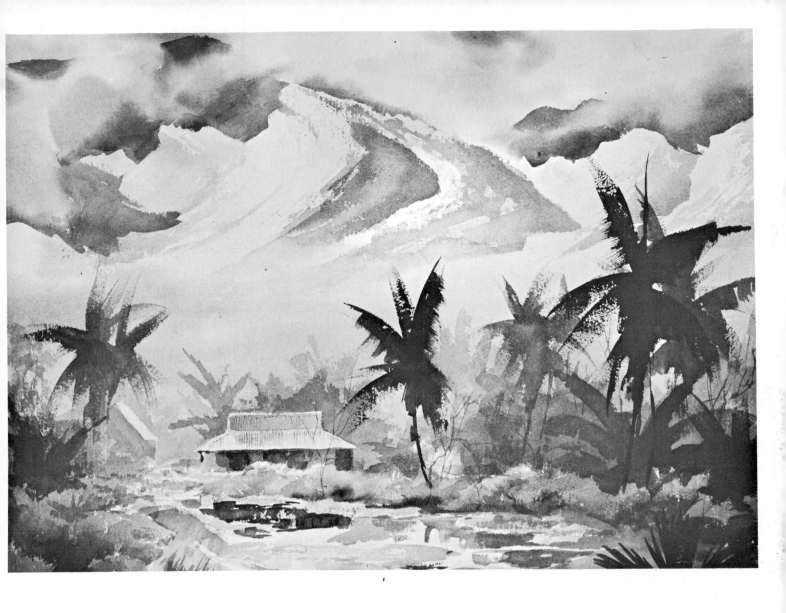

Hawaii Mist, *22" x 30". Private collection.*

In this watercolor, as in many others where
hard and soft are involved, we have procedures
which should become second nature to you.
Clear water is applied and then pigment is
dropped into it and allowed to take its own
action, as in the mountain and sky areas. The
illusion that objects come forward is created
by a theatrical series of planes, like flats on a
stage, one in front of the other. The values
correspond to the planes.

53

ARRANGEMENT OF
LIGHT SOURCES

If you're right handed, I suggest that your main light source be above and to the left, so that your brush hand won't cast a shadow over your work. Your palette and water jar will be on your right, so you may want an additional light there (see diagram). If you're left handed, you naturally reverse the layout.

STORAGE

Paper: The best way to store your paper and finished paintings is *flat* in large drawers, like blueprint files. This isn't always possible, as blueprint files are costly and hard to come by. However, any flat surface—such as a small table, or on the floor under your bed—will do. Be sure to wrap watercolor paper in plastic or wrapping paper.

Brushes, Tubes, etc.: Plastic silverware trays make fine catch-alls for these items. It's incredible how much junk you'll collect over the years: junk that has nothing to do with painting, but things that just might come in handy at some future time. Cigar boxes are good, too, for catching these things.

PALETTES, TRAYS
AND OTHER
MIXING SURFACES

Almost any *white*, non-absorbent surface will serve as a palette. I say *white* because it allows you to see better what you're mixing. I like plastic and enameled aluminum palettes best for their lightness, and also for their large mixing area.

The type with the thumb hole is fine for tempera, but pointless for transparent watercolor. The hole takes up working surface, and if you *hold* the palette (*à la* John Singer Sargent) you simply wind up with a wet thumb and Thalo Blue dripping off your elbow. But it does look arty.

I've developed my own palette, shown below, but a white enamel kitchen tray or butcher tray will also do the job.

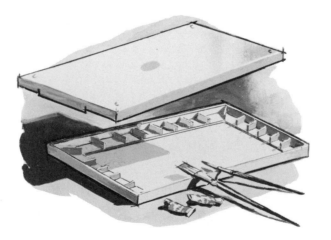

THE PIKE PALETTE *As far as I'm concerned, this is the ultimate in watercolor/acrylic palettes. It measures 15" x 10½" x ⅝", and it has a snap-on top which becomes a second working surface. (For information or order write: John Pike, Woodstock, New York 12498.)*

Here are some others. Try a square of white Formica, or som_ _ _ _ _ _ _ _ _ _ _ white plastic. You can use a sheet of clear glass, sitting on _ _ _ _ _ _ _ _ _ paper. A couple of flat dinner plates will work. Enam_ _ _ _ _ _ _ _ _ _ _ _ _ butcher trays are excellent at home, but they're heav_ _ _ _ _ _ _ _ _ _ _ _ down when you go into the field.

MISCELLANEOUS ITEMS

I think we've pretty well covered all of the bas_ _ _ _ _ _ _ _ _ _ _ _ _ _ few little items.

Pencils: For drawing on your water_ _ _ _ _ _ _ _ _ _ _ _ _ _ _ _ _ a #2 writing pencil or 2B drawi_ _ _ _ _ _ _ _ _ _ _ _ _ _ _ _ affect your color. They're also _ _ _ _ _ _ _ _ _ _

Erasers: I don't care for the old fas_ _ _ _ _ _ _ _ _ _ _ _ _ _ water-color; they leave little particles in the _ _ _ _ _ _ _ _ _ _ _ _ fect your washes. A kneaded rubber eraser is fin_ _ _ _ _ _ _ _ _ _ _ new vinyl plastics are fine for heavier jobs. Of course, _ _ _ _ _ _ _ _ _ dig in, you can use the round abrasive typewriter kind; bu_ _ _ _ _ _ _ _ _ er the erasure with a kneaded rubber eraser to pick up the gr_ _ _ _ _ _ _ you go back to painting.

As you develop your own personal approach to watercolor, you'll find many little things to add to your equipment.

Hardware stores and art supply stores, as long as I can remember, have seemed like roofed-over Heavens to me. (My wife says I'm a frustrated carpenter who has to paint pictures for a living.) I've purchased many wonderful things in both. But in the final analysis, it all comes down to a few tools and an endless love of what you're doing.

OUTDOOR PAINTING EQUIPMENT

This can, very quickly, be broken down into two categories of equipment.

If you're driving to the site and you'll paint by the side of the road, you can take the works: tables, easels, chairs, stools, etc. It's easy.

But if you're planning a cross-country hike to arrive at your subject mat-

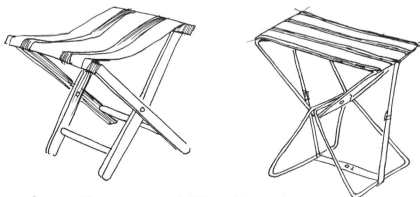

SKETCHING STOOLS *Here are two good, light weight stools for painting outdoors. The heavier one is made of wood, the lighter is metal. Both fold neatly and are easy to carry.*

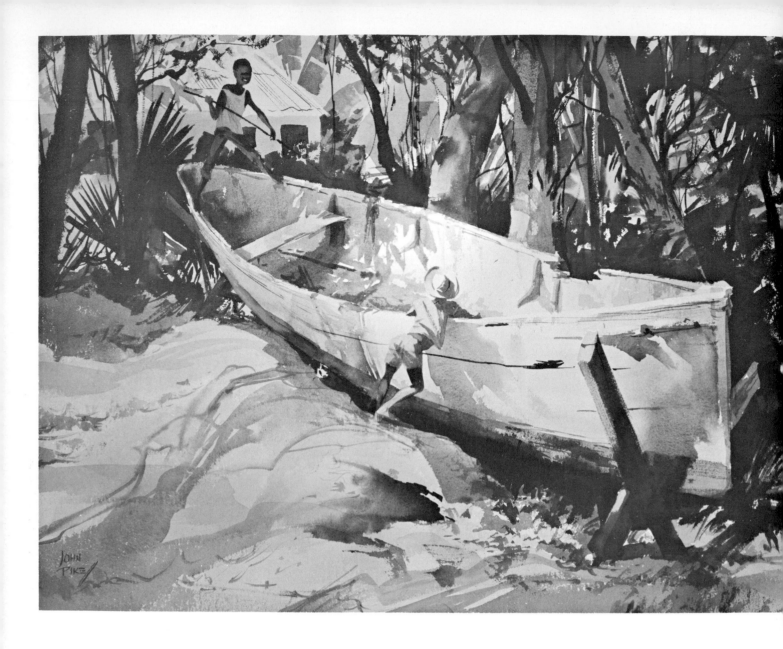

BEACHED SEA CAPTAINS, *22" x 30". Museum collection.*

This weather-beaten old Jamaica dugout was carved from the trunk of a giant silk cotton or kapok tree. These craft are very graceful and seaworthy, but fast disappearing from the islands. Care must be taken in drawing boats; the subtle curves must be accurately rendered. The dark foliage emphasizes the boat's high value, the brightness of the sunlight.

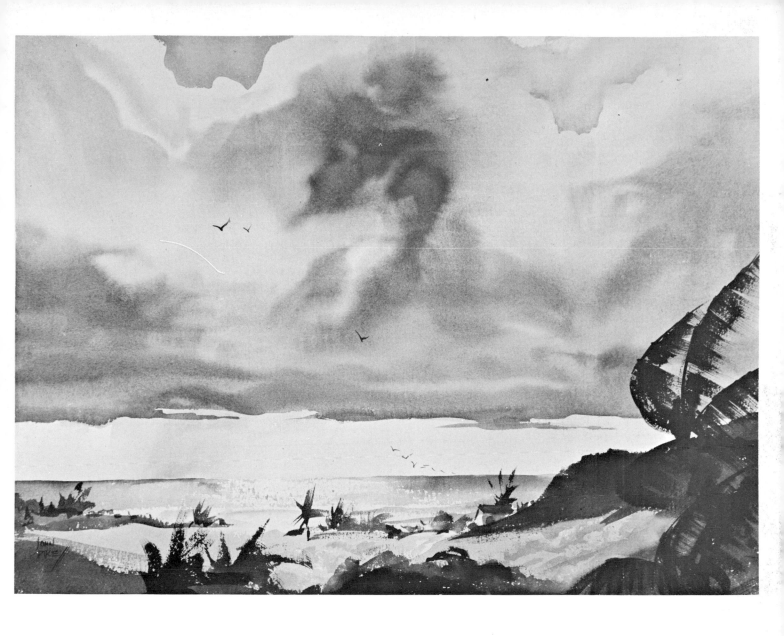

HAWAIIAN CLOUDS, *22" x 30". Class demonstration.*

The entire sky, with one or two exceptions, was washed in with a single pass. The hard, white edge of the clouds in the upper left was gained by leaving a small line on the paper dry, while all the rest of the area was flooded with clear water. The sparkle on the sea was achieved in the manner shown in the chapter on brush handling. The dark foreground tends to push the rest of the picture back.

ter, then you must gear up in an entirely different way. Say to yourself: "I'm a watercolorist; what do I need?" (*Actually* need.) The answer is (1) a light weight board; (2) paper; (3) paints; (4) water; (5) brushes, and nothing else (with the possible exception of a slight "spiritual lift" in a jug, for chill weather, but not enough to prevent you from finding your way back to the highway).

It all comes down to the question of *how much* you want to carry. You can sit on the ground; you can lean your board against a tree if you want an angle; and you can spread your paints, palette, and water on the earth beside you. Whatever you wish to lug around, beyond the bare essentials, is up to your own physical endurance. But remember, none of those extras has any magic. It's still *you!*

Your gear—with the exception of board and paper—can all be carried in a trout fisherman's aluminum tackle box. These usually have several compartmented trays that slide back as you open the cover. Mine has three: brushes on one tray; paints on the next; knives, erasers, etc., on the third.

Oh yes, I forgot one essential, terribly important: the insect repellent.

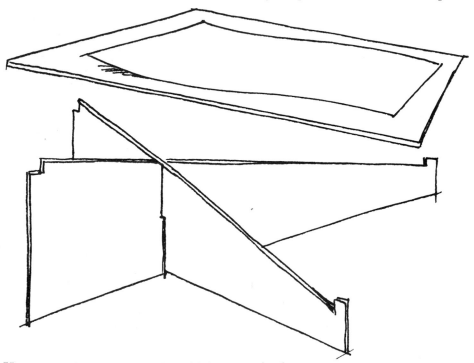

HOMEMADE OUTDOOR "EASEL"   *This is a very simple outdoor painting aid of my own design. You can make it out of one piece of cardboard, corrugated board, or even very light plywood. You can vary it to suit the particular size and angle you prefer. The plan shows only a suggested size. Whatever size and shape you make it, be sure both pieces are identical, except for the "egg crate" notches. This is a handy gadget, as you can take it apart and tape it to the back of your painting board for easy carrying.*

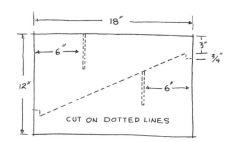

18″

6″

3″

¾″

12″

6″

CUT ON DOTTED LINES

58

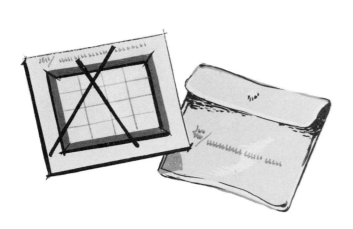

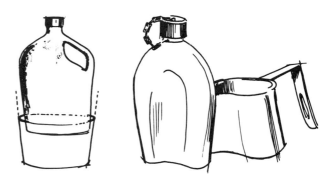

WATER CARRIERS AND RECEPTACLES *(Above Left) For outdoor painting, you can carry water in a plastic detergent bottle. Make a cup by chopping the lower half off a second bottle. They'll "nest" when you carry them. (Above Right) An old army canteen and cup make a fine water carrier and water receptacle when you're painting outdoors.*

PIKE'S "WONDERFUL PERSPECTIVE MACHINE" *Here's a handy device of my own design that you might want to include in your outdoor painting kit. Crisscross your canvas lightly with three vertical and three horizontal lines. Hold the "machine" at arm's length, then scan around and find a composition that you like. Move the thin steel strips around on the magnetic border to line up with the angles of the building, street, mountain, or whatever, then mark the same crossings on your canvas or paper. (Again, for information or order write: John Pike, Woodstock, New York 12498.)*

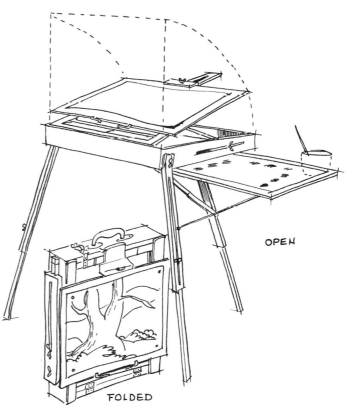

OPEN

FOLDED

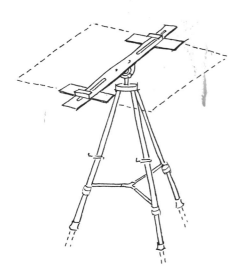

WATERCOLOR EASEL *This light weight, portable easel will hold a drawing board. The legs telescope for carrying and the whole thing folds something like a photographic tripod. If you're handy, you can probably make one out of an old photographic tripod and a few pieces of lumber.*

A PORTABLE STUDIO *To me, this outdoor (and indoor) portable compact easel is the finest on the market. It's sturdy and easy to set up. The white Formica palette tray saves carrying an extra folding table, if you like to work standing. You can carry all your gear in it, including a half dozen (or more) half sheets of watercolor paper. It's adjustable to sitting or standing positions and the rack goes from completely flat to vertical. Fine for oils too. It's manufactured by the Wilkins Simpson Studio, Box 72, Grossmont, California.*

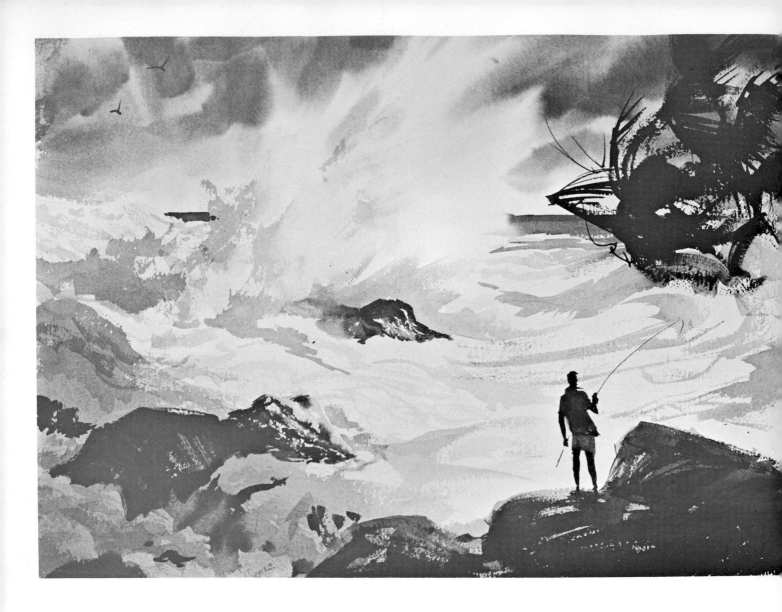

HAWAIIAN SURF, *22" x 30". Private collection.*

To gain the feeling of the great impact of the pounding tons of water, I wanted the top of the breaking wave to go almost into a mist; so my procedure was to wet the entire sky with clear water, then brush back into the top of the wave with the dark pigment of the sky, letting the fluid color take its own violent action. That, plus the patterning of the light and shadows on the swirling suds, is really the key to this painting. Where you're working in large areas of white—as in this picture, as well as in snow paintings—every brush stroke is obvious; so great care must be taken to put strokes in the right place the first time.

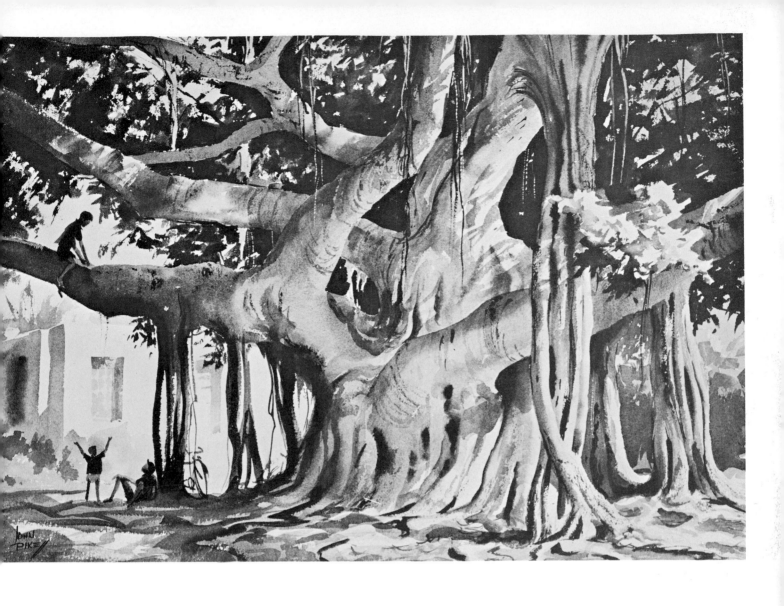

JUNGLE JIM, *22" x 30". Norton Collection.*

This giant banyan tree might well be in India
or Africa, while actually it is in West Palm
Beach, Florida. Nature did the patterning for
me. The illusion of the roundness of the huge
limbs, as well as the supporting branches, is
achieved by many reflected lights. It took
careful study, both of the "architecture" and
the values.

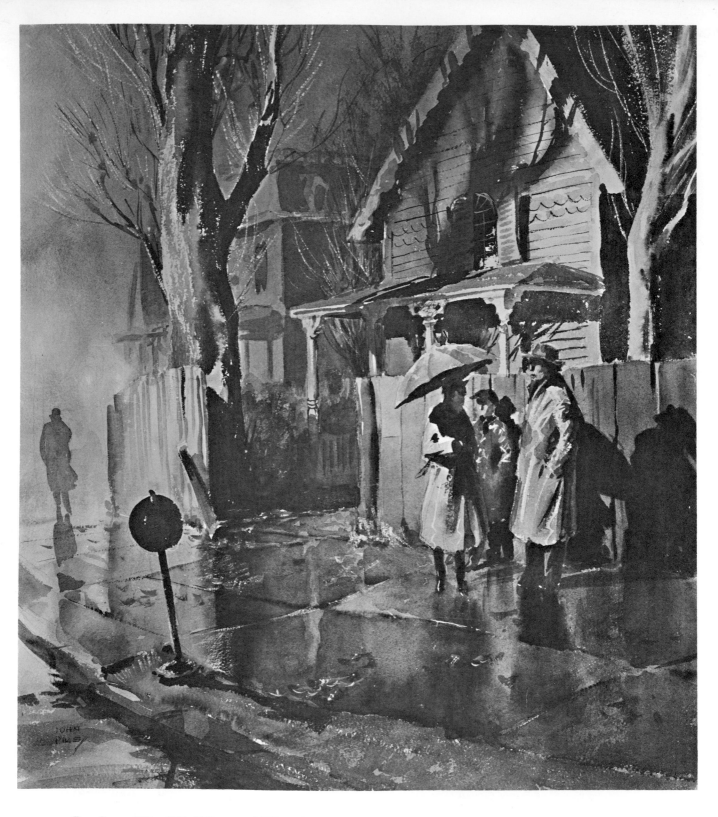

BUS STOP, *22" x 30". Winner, A.W.S. Award,*
1942. Private collection. Photo, Juley.

At this time, I had just been accepted for flight
training and was not thinking too much about
painting. I didn't really appreciate what a
great honor it was until after the war. This
watercolor is a matter of simple but careful
planning, with one big light source casting the
shadow of the tree on the house and behind
the figures, and a secondary light source to the
left, soft and fuzzy to create atmosphere.

5 *Washes and corrections*

In watercolor painting, the first thing you must learn is how to apply a large area of liquid color, called a *wash*. Actually, there are many kinds of washes, each serving a different purpose. Try them all and master them.

FLAT WASH
Applied on dry paper, this is a standard flat wash, all of the same value and color, not much variety in tone or texture. If the wash is to cover a large

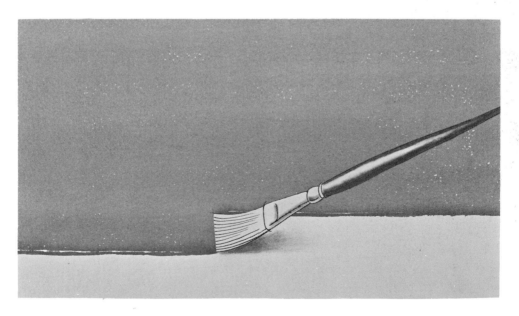

FLAT WASH   *This is your basic wash, more or less even in color and value, with relatively little texture.*

area, it might help you to mix up a batch in a teacup, testing the liquid color on another piece of paper before proceeding.

Now, tilt your board at an angle of about 10°. Start at the top of the sheet, with your brush fully loaded, and make your pass horizontally across the paper. The angle of the board will cause a little wall (sort of a long, narrow pool) of pigment and water to form on the downhill side of the brush stroke. Get another brush load and make the next pass just below the first, just slightly overlapping. (Don't waste any time, as a hard edge may form). The wall of water will flow into the second pass. This procedure is repeated, pass after pass, to the full extent of the wash.

In the illustration, the wall, or bead of water, is the dark line behind the brush and to your right, from the preceding pass; a new bead is forming to the left of the brush as it moves across the paper.

When you reach the bottom, or wherever you wish to go, be sure to pick up this excess—the last wall or bead—by shaking out your brush and touching it to the *top* of the water mound, *not* to the surface of the paper. Your brush will draw off the remaining liquid, almost like a sponge.

Do a lot of practice sheets. This exercise is vital.

GRADED WASH

Graded washes—which go dark to light, light to dark, etc.—are arrived at in various ways.

First, you can start off with your dark pigment and water on dry paper, and then add more and more clear water—pass after pass—as you come down

GRADED WASH   *This wash moves from dark to light, or vice versa, as you alter the ratio of pigment to water in your brush.*

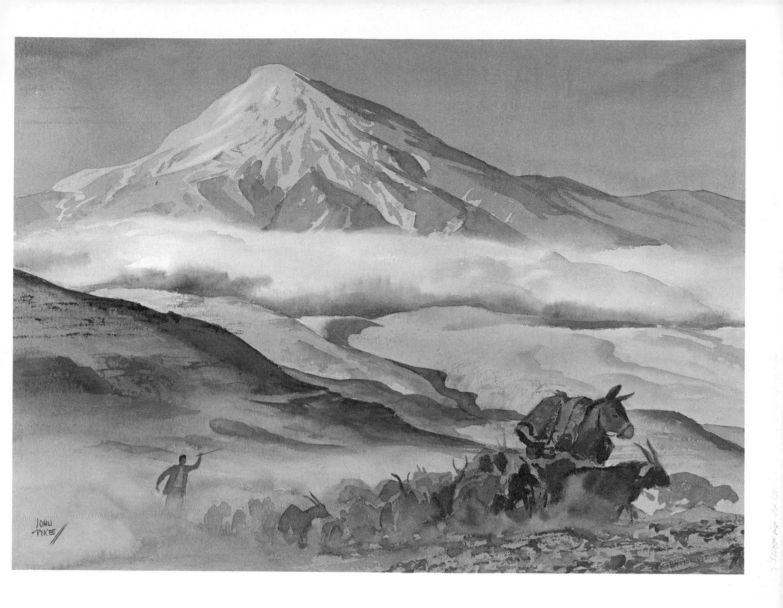

MOUNT DEMAVEND, IRAN, *22" x 30".*
Collection, General Tire International.

In this picture of Mt. Demavend in northern Iran, I wished to create the feeling of late afternoon, as well as the dry and arid quality of the land. Here, the endless search for pasturage goes on and on.

A pale, yellow-pink wash was put over all areas where the sun hit, including the sky. When this was dry, a medium cool blue was washed into the sky and a coolish green underpainting put over the rolling, middle ground hill. The low-lying cloud, just beyond these hills, was arrived at by a cool blue wash with a dark underside dropped in while still wet; the pigment was allowed to take its own action.

The modeling of the distant mountain was done in two moves: first, a middle value blue-gray; when dry, a slightly darker blue-gray for accent. Then came the contouring of the middle ground, remembering to soften the edges toward the light source; and last, the indication of the sheep and goats in the dust, and a hard texture of the barren earth in the right foreground.

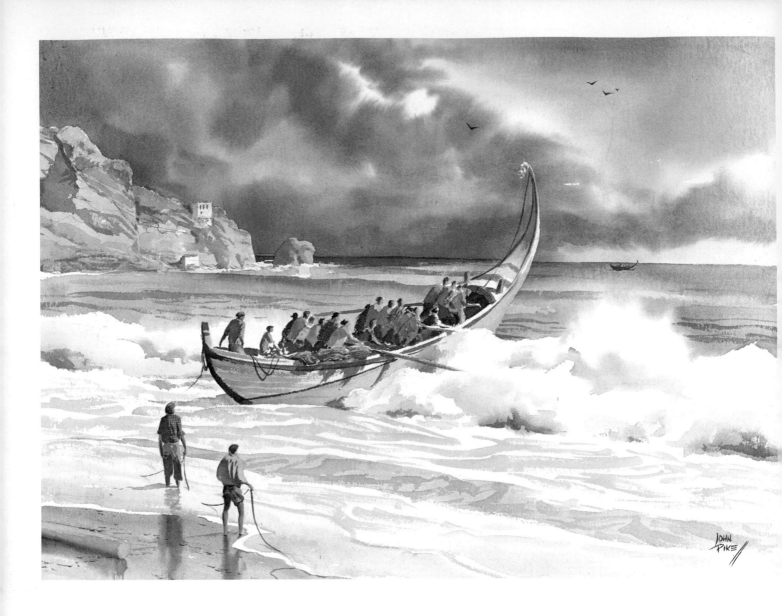

FISHING BOAT, PORTUGAL, *22" x 30"*.
Collection, General Tire International.

This is a rather good example of hard and soft treatment, along with a couple of "tricks." Masking tape was used on the horizon. The portion of the bow of the boat that protruded up into the dark sky was painted with liquid frisket. Then the sky was painted all in one pass.

To gain the soft top of the wave, clear water was used, and the distant sea was rapidly painted *down* to it, allowing the color to take its own action. Clean water was also used to model the tumbling surf. All the rest is straight painting; study the reflections on the wet sand.

These giant boats are interesting in design and have changed little since the time of the Phoenicians.

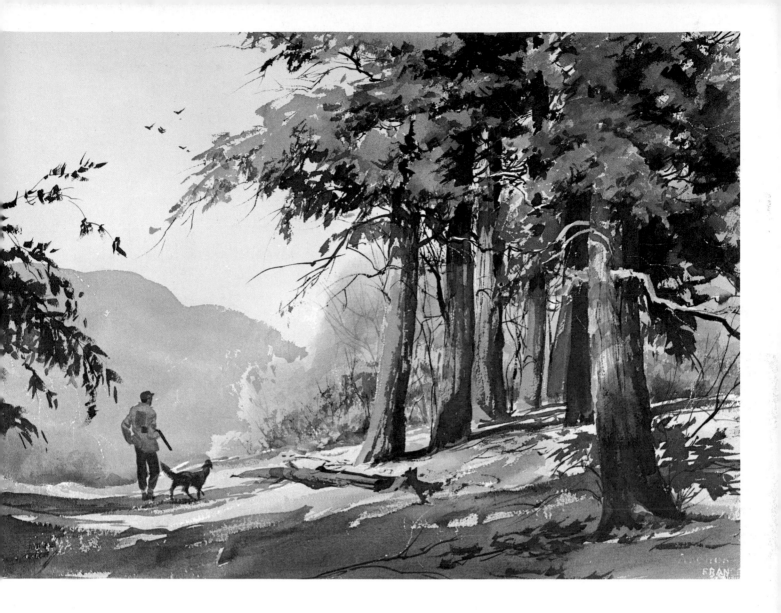

HUNTER'S HILL, 22" x 30". *Private collection.*
Courtesy Osborne, Kemper, Thomas.

The Irish setter in this picture was one of
the finest friends of my life. I had her for
fourteen years and used her so much in
illustrations that she practically became
a trademark. How she loved the big pine
woods!

This comes very close to being a two value
picture. The sky and the place where the
sunlight hits the bed of pine needles are the
highest value. All the rest, with all its little
detail, are the darkest.

The procedure is simple. The big sky wash
went completely over the area and all the way
down to the dip of the hillside at the left.
When this was dry, the cool sihouette of the
distant mountain was put in, drag-brushing
around the middle ground scrub foliage.
Next came the basic underpainting and
patterning of the leafy tree mass, as well as
the warm tones on the tree trunks. A light
wash was also put in, at this stage, over the
ground beneath the trees.

From here on, it's a matter of texturing,
putting in the large shadow area in the
foreground, the figures and all the tiny rigger
brush details. Good hunting.

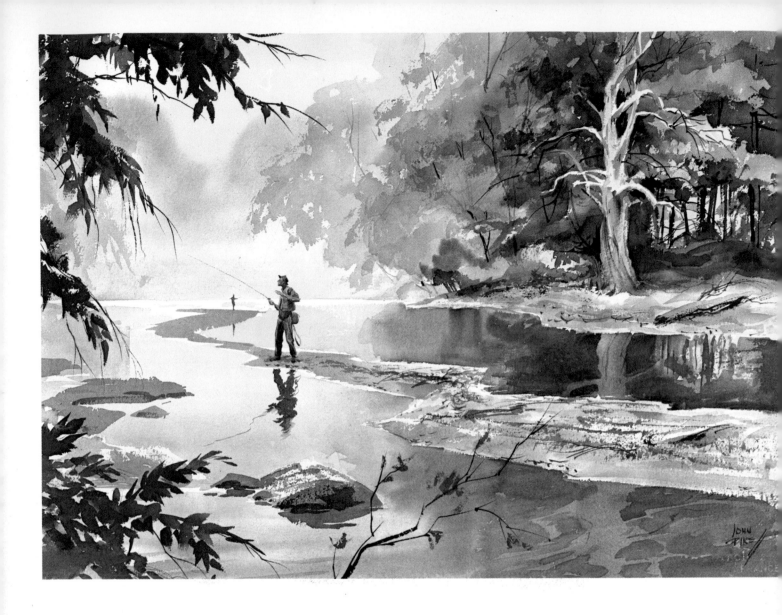

STILL STREAM, 22" x 30". *Private collection. Courtesy Osborne, Kemper, Thomas.*

The sky wash was laid in over the entire upper half of the painting, leaving only the whiteness of the dead tree on the right. At the same time, I ran in the basic wash on the water, leaving the white edge at the horizon. While the sky was still wet, darker cool pigment was dropped in to give the illusion of the distant, misty trees. When this was dry, the first of the hard-edge trees were scrubbed in, bringing the wash in all the way under the next step.

I could then go to the dark underpainting of the trees as they come forward on the distant bank, remembering to paint around the dead white tree. Next came the warm tints on the shore and on the sand bar. When the large clump of foliage on the right had been completely rendered, the dark reflections could then be put in. (Remember, never paint reflections until you've painted the objects that cause them.) The wind-up was the dark framing branches and leaves to the left; the silhouetted figures and rocks; and the texturing of the bank and sand bar.

the sheet. This increases the water-to-pigment ratio, so of course the color gets lighter. You handle the brush and the wall or bead of water just as you do when you lay a flat wash. The trick is to alter the quantity of water in each successive stroke.

Sometimes it's more convenient to work upside down, particularly where you have to paint around intricate shapes. Example: you have a group of buildings you wish to keep light. You want your sky to go from fairly light at the horizon (but darker than the buildings), graded up to the dark dome overhead. Turn your paper upside down, paint around the buildings until you're in the clear with the wash going all the way across the paper. Quickly add more and more pigment with each pass of the brush until you reach the top. Again, be sure to take up excess water with your brush, after your last pass.

WET-IN-WET

This is a typical wet-into-wet wash, which means that the color is brushed onto paper which is already wet. This is known as the soft or wet surface method. It may be done in several ways.

In this demonstration, I wetted the paper down lightly with a sponge, as I didn't have to paint around anything where I needed a *hard* edge. I put on my basic, fairly flat wash, then *immediately* came back in with my cloud-like dark pigment and let it run where it wanted to go.

There are a couple of points to remember here.

After you've put on your basic wash, if you wait too long before hitting

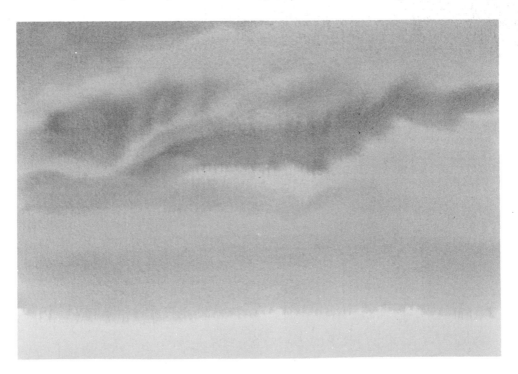

WET-IN-WET *Here your color is applied on paper which is already with clear water or an earlier wash, not yet dry.*

it with the dark, you're going to get hard, sharp edges to your darks.

When you have a large passage like this, study it carefully and plan exactly what you intend to do before you ever lay brush to paper; then, when you've decided, *bang* it in, cross your fingers, and hope your judgment was right! You can lessen the failures a great deal by doing many practice sheets; thus, you become completely familiar with just what happens under all kinds of conditions.

One tendency I've noticed is to get too much water and not enough pigment in the brush when you sail back into that first wash. The results can be disastrous.

Also, bear in mind that if you're working on a thoroughly wet paper—really soaking wet all through—all action is much slower. In this discussion, I'm talking only of a *surface* wet method in which the paper is wet only on top.

Another approach—when you wish to cut around objects and have sharp edges—is to lay your wash on completely dry paper and add your dark break-ins to the wet wash. But you must come back in with the darks with the greatest of speed, as your under wash dries even more rapidly than paper sponged with clear water.

Practice and find out. I can only warn you. You have to *feel* it. The real joy will come when it's all completely automatic. Well, I guess that's an overstatement; in this medium it never *will* be automatic, but that's what we're *working* for.

STREAKY WASH *As in the wet-in-wet technique, your color is applied on wet paper, but here the color is allowed to flow its own way, controlled by tilting.*

STREAKY WASH This is somewhat of a gimmick exercise, but there may be a time when you'll wish to use it. Furthermore, it *is* one more step in watercolor's *action* and it's important to learn the reasons why.

Flow clear water with a brush over your paper. While the paper is still very wet, drop in your dark pigment at the top, and pick up one corner of the sheet. Let the dark flow as far as you wish, then lay the paper back down to a flat position to stop the action. If it's streakier than you desire, change the angle and the streaks will blend together. Try it and have fun.

VERY DARK WASHES Dark washes are usually pretty difficult for the beginner. As I've suggested in my discussion of the flat wash, try mixing your color in a cup or glass until it's exactly the color, value, and fluidity you wish. Try it out and let it dry on scrap paper until it's just right.

One of the problems seems to be timidity about using sufficient pigment, and stirring up a large enough quantity. By using the cup method, you arrive at exactly what you want *before* ever putting brush to paper. With experience, you'll be able to mix right on the palette with great rapidity. This allows for greater variety in your color, too; but as a starter, try the glass or cup approach.

The procedure is identical to that used in laying a flat wash. Just be sure you have enough pigment in your brew. A thought to remember, just in case the wash isn't dark enough the first time, and you have to go back over it: the more pigment you have, the easier it *picks up* from your paper when you go back in. So get it right the first time around.

VERY DARK WASH *Most beginners find a dark wash toughest of all. The trick is to mix the wash in a cup beforehand.*

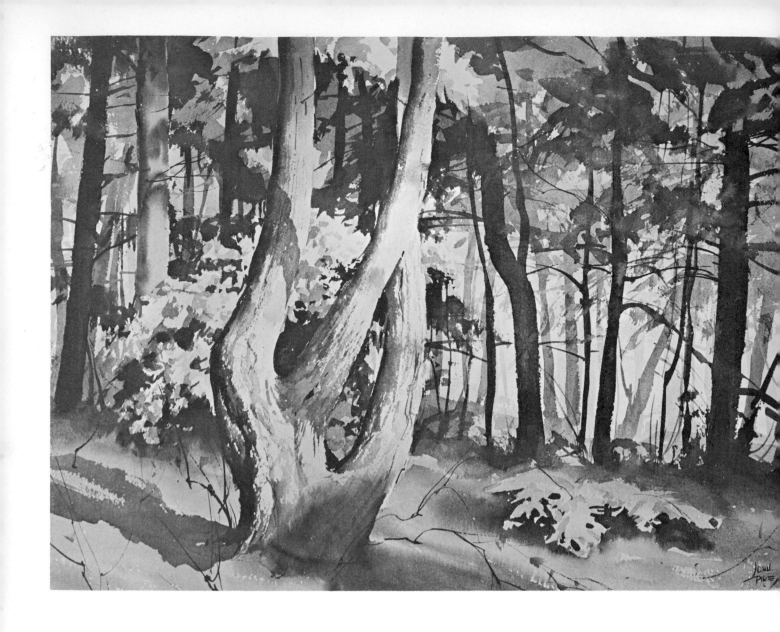

TRILOGY, *22" x 30". Private collection.*

The procedure followed in this watercolor
is exactly the same as in the step by step
demonstration painting of "The Fox in the
Snow." The problems of advancing and
receding planes are identical.

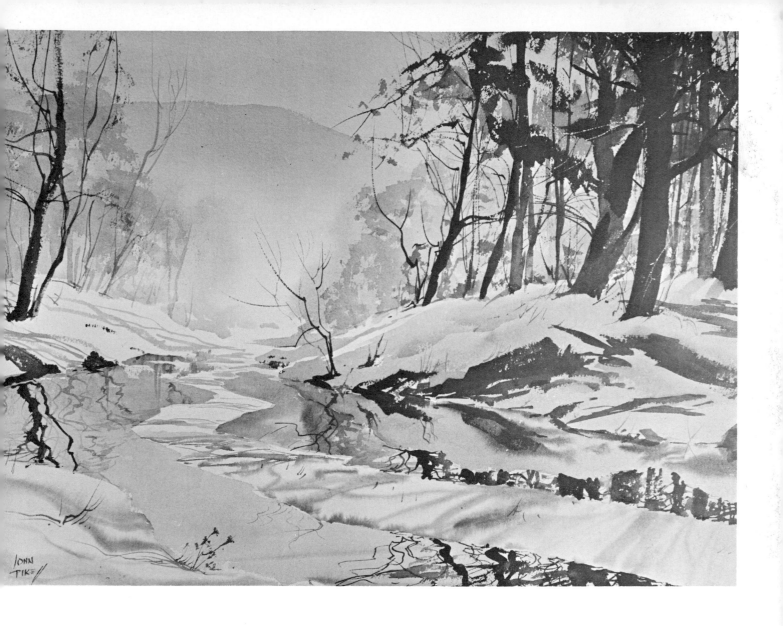

AUTUMN SNOW, *22" x 30". Private collection.*

The effort here was to gain considerable
subtlety in the whites. It is almost a two value
painting, with the pale blue-grays, the
mountain, and the sky being our lightest value,
while the extreme dark of the trees, foliage,
and reflections becomes the dark value.
Variation in color gained additional form
and shape.

73

A student once said that correcting a watercolor is like telling a lie; the more you try to fix it, the worse it gets!

Many years ago, just prior to World War II, I was doing a demonstration for the American Watercolor Society in New York City. I'd planned the painting very carefully and, as a result, I'd really completed the painting in about three quarters of my allotted time. However, I wanted to be sure the audience was getting its money's worth, so I was doodling a little here and a little there. At that point, a little old lady, who'd been sitting with her chin practically on the edge of my table, stood up, looked around at the sizable audience and said, "All right, where's the man with the hammer?"

A sense of knowing *when to stop, when to let the painting alone*, is difficult to develop, but it must be learned.

Ideally, we should put our colors down as we want them for the first time, but we all know that this doesn't always happen. So this discussion would be incomplete without some description of corrective measures.

The six panels shown here are all the same basic wash.

1. The wash is untouched, just as it dried.

2. The wash was scrubbed with a sponge, except for the square in the upper left hand corner, which I left untouched to show the contrast of the old and new tones. This scrubbing was done after the wash had *dried*.

3. The cloud-like areas were picked up with a cleansing tissue when the wash was *wet*.

4. The pigment was picked up from the *wet* wash with a soft brush, well shaken out. The result can be pretty much the same as the tissue exercise in number 3.

5. This was done with an oil or bristle brush (see the chapter on brushes) on a completely dry wash. Scrub a little with a wet bristle brush, then pick up water and pigment with a tissue. It's possible to harm the surface of your paper, so be careful. You may find that any wash over the scrubbed-out areas will turn dark. This is because the fibers of your paper have been roughened on this spot, causing greater absorption of the pigment. The same may happen after you try number 6.

6. This was done with an old fashioned typewriter eraser on a *dry* wash. These erasers are hard, tough, and gritty, so come back with your kneaded eraser to pick up the grit left after you erase.

If these exercises look a little like outer space, the reason is clear. They were done on the day our fantastic astronauts made the first rendezvous in space—and I'm a space buff.

Flat wash, uncorrected.

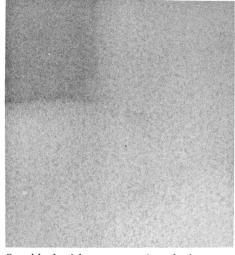

Scrubbed with a sponge after drying.

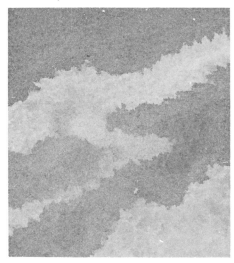

Picked up with a cleansing tissue while wet.

Picked up with a soft brush while wet.

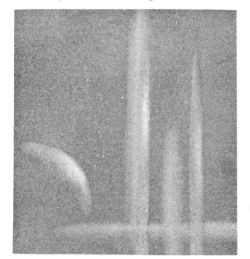

Scrubbed with a bristle brush after drying.

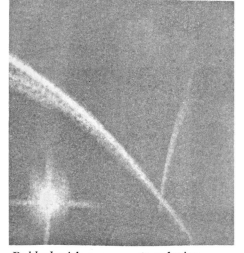

Rubbed with a eraser after drying.

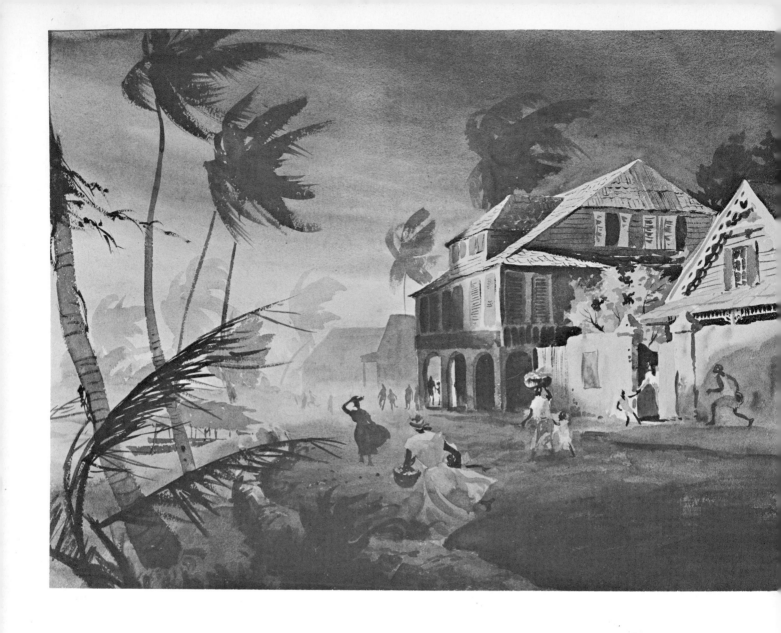

High Winds, Jamaica, *22″ x 30″. 1950.*
Private collection. Photo, Juley.

Here's the procedure: (1) careful drawing
and planning; (2) sky wash, allowed to dry;
(3) silhouette of distant palms and buildings,
bringing these washes down into the
foreground; (4) building details, as well as
dark foliage in the foreground; (5) and last,
the tall, middle ground coco palms.

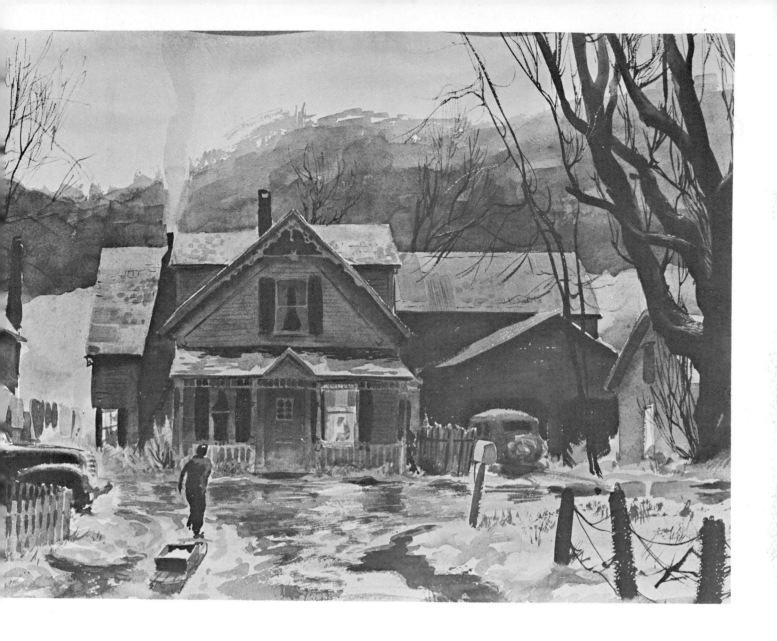

DUD SHULTIS' HOUSE, *22" x 30". Private collection.*

I see this charming little house every day when I drive into town for my mail; it's right at the end of my road. In this watercolor, I tried to create the slush and the puddles of early March. By the car designs, you can see that the painting was done several years ago.

The high, back lighting creates the interesting roof patterns and the dark vertical sides of the building. Procedure: (1) sky, down to the upper edges of the roof; (2) then the subdued light grays of the roof and the snow in the foreground; (3) the mountain behind. The darks of the building complete the big, over-all pattern. The rest is texturing and details.

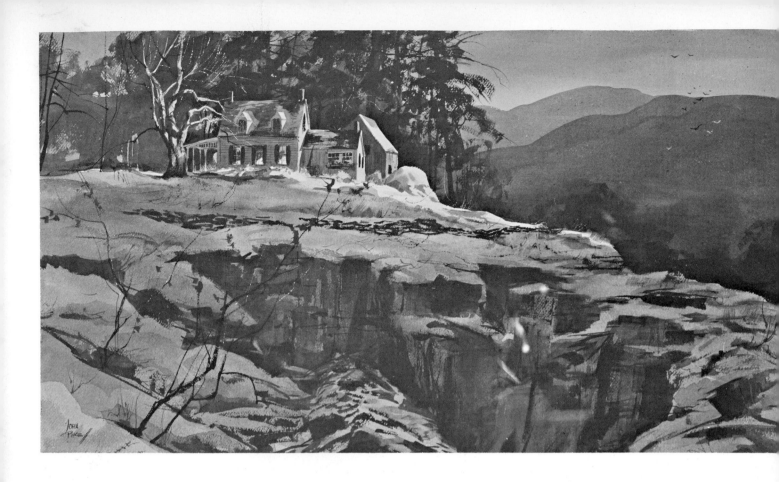

Bluestone, *20" x 38". Winner, Watercolor U.S.A. Award (A.W.S.), 1964. Permanent Collection, Frye Museum, Seattle, Washington. Photo, Juley.*

A great deal of the bluestone that helped build New York City came from the area of Woodstock in the 18th and 19th centuries. This painting shows one of the old, abandoned quarries.

A dramatic effect was accomplished by throwing the entire picture into shadow, with the exception of the spotlighted house and barn.

1 The sky wash was brought all the way down to the house and light edge of the cliff. I had previously masked out the tree to keep the fine branches white. I painted around the house and barn.

2 After the sky was dry, I put in the distant mountain, again bringing my wash all the way to house and cliff.

3 After drying, I painted the nearer mountain over the other. At the same time, I put in a blue-gray wash over the entire middle and foreground, of course leaving the white paper where you see the light hitting the buildings and ground.

4 The trees behind the house were painted in semi-dry brush, as well as the darks of the quarry walls.

5 I removed the masking agent on the tree in back of the house; then I rendered the details of the buildings and the snow covered haystack, and built up the texture of the stone and the snow. Incidental twigs and branches came last: a slight touch of the knife here and there for sparkle.

78

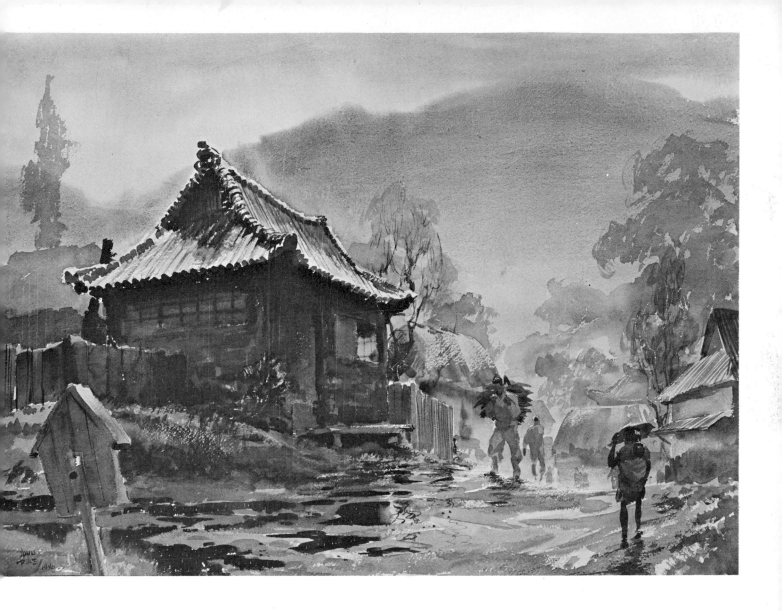

MR. KIM'S NEW ROOF, *22" x 30", Korea, 1946. Private collection. Photo, Juley.*

This painting was done from a sketch I'd made the previous year, when I was with the Corps of Engineers in Korea, on the outskirts of Yong Dong Po, south of Seoul. The Western equivalent of the Korean name, Kim, is Smith or Jones. There's a great deal of rain there in the autumn and early winter months, which is great for the rice crop, but doesn't do much for the lagging spirits of one hoping to get home for Christmas. (I made it!)

1   The sky and the mountain were all done in one wet wash. I was careful to paint around Mr. Kim's roof. The lower part, behind the figure carrying wood, was faded off or *lost*, by adding clear water as I went.

2   Then came the foreground, with its puddle arrangements—only the light earth part, not the dark reflections.

3   By this time, my mountain and sky had dried enough, so I could come in with the hard edged trees and distant buildings. Putting in your higher values, in this way, gives you the opportunity to study the picture as a whole and helps you decide *how dark* the rest of it must go.

4   I added the light, sparkling, wet roof, and the dark side walls. Then I did the quick little figures and the deep, muddy reflections. (In painting a reflection, always remember what causes it.)

At one of my exhibitions, a few years ago, a very sweet little old lady said to me: "You make better water on the street than anybody."

79

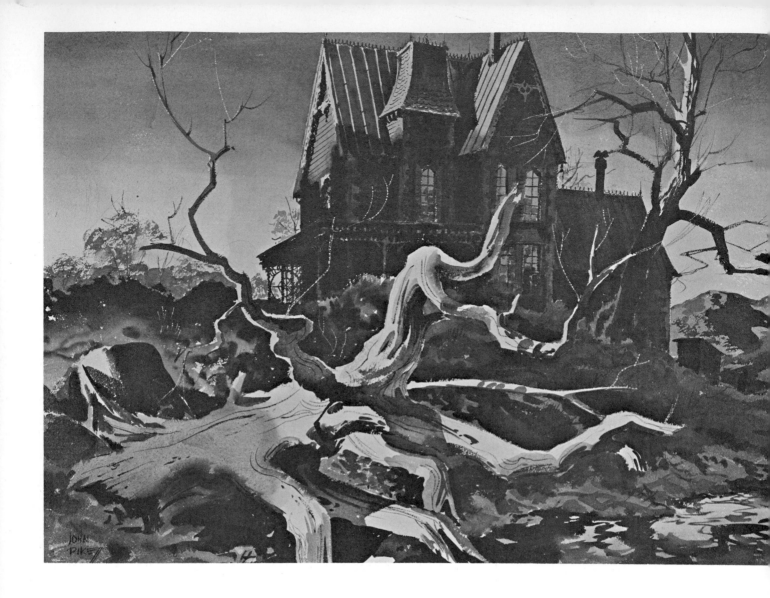

SEPTEMBER SONG, 22″ x 30″, about 1952.
*Presented by the artist to the New York
Hospital Fund. Photo, Juley.*

This is a "mood" painting: the old tree that
has been washed downstream in the flood
season; the old, decaying Victorian Hudson
River house; the long shadows of a late
September afternoon. (Now that I think of it,
perhaps it wasn't the best choice of a gift to
a hospital fund.)
1   Everything was "painted around," no
masking agents used. The sky is a graded
wash, leaving the building white.
2   A middle dark wash was put over the
middle ground; I painted around the contorted
tree in front.
3   The darks of the house, the distant trees and
mountain, the middle ground, all completely
silhouette the foreground tree, which is still
the white paper.
4   Last came the modeling and texturing of the
tree. A few dark accents were added here and
there, plus a little knife work for the twigs.

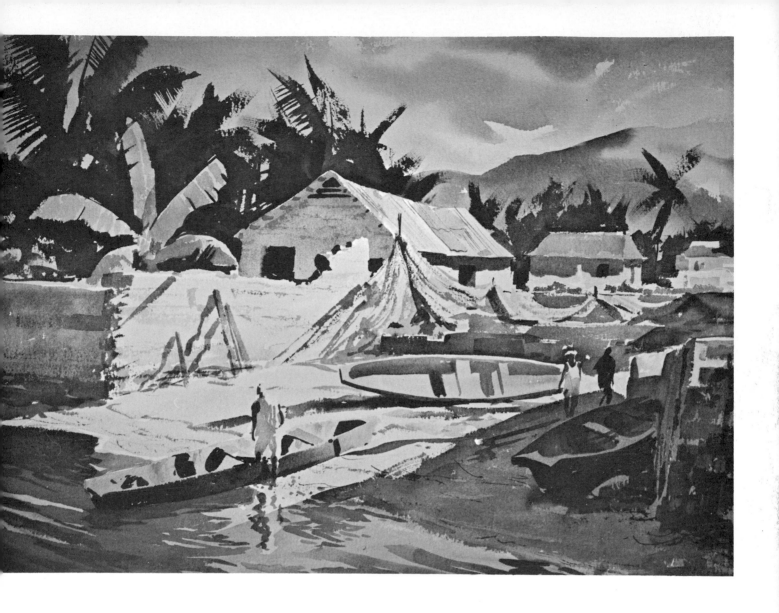

JAMAICAN FISHING COVE, *22" x 30". Private collection.*

Shown here are some cottonwood dugout canoes similar to the one in the painting, "Beached Sea Captains." The pattern here is simple; perhaps the only tricky part is in the combination of the cast shadow and reflections in the water. Study it and see the reasons why. The procedure is direct: (1) sky, (2) mountain, (3) buildings, (4) nets and finally, (5) the silhouetted darks of the coco palms.

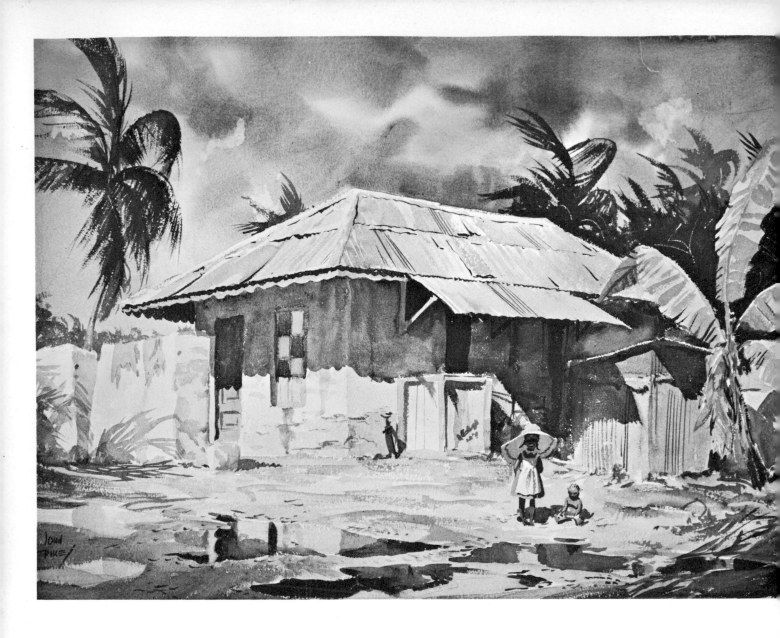

PANAMA HATTIE, 22" x 30". *Private collection.*

This painting was done on the spot near Balboa on the Pacific side of the Panama Canal Zone. It was an old shipyard where they were still building wooden ships, and these are two of the workers' children. The sun was very high, almost directly above and behind me, causing the long shadows from the broad overhang of the building. The procedure was direct. First came the cloudy sky, leaving the building in white silhouette, the palms to be painted in later. Next came the shadow pattern on the building and the warm underpainting on the ground. Finally, I added the light texturing of the tin roof, the ground, the little figures, the reflections, and the large darks of the palms.

6 *Tools and techniques*

In this final chapter on the "vocabulary" of watercolor, I've done a group of illustrations to show various ways of using your brushes; how to use masking agents; how to gain special effects; and how to use a knife.

BRUSH STROKES

This shows some of the differences between round and flat brushes. Notice how the flats lend themselves to the broad wash as well as to the thin line

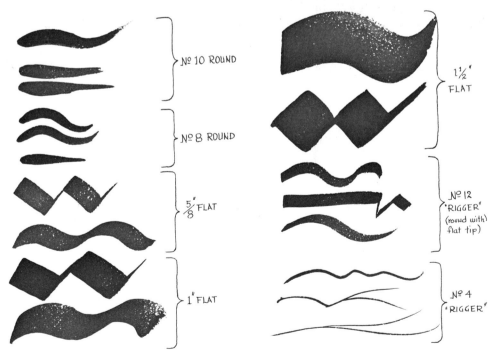

No 10 ROUND

No 8 ROUND

⅝" FLAT

1" FLAT

1½" FLAT

No 12 "RIGGER" (round with flat tip)

No 4 "RIGGER"

when used sideways; you can also use a sharp corner of the brush for small, delicate touches. I like the flats because there are many times when you can achieve a variety of textures without changing brushes; where time and speed are involved, this can be a great help. But as I said earlier in the text, don't let it get too mechanical looking. These strokes were *purposely* done mechanically to show the shape and flexibility of the different brushes.

TEXTURES AND BRUSH MANIPULATION

What appears here as *drybrush* isn't drybrush at all, but the effect gained by the *positioning* of the brush in relationship to the paper, taking advantage of the paper's roughness, its little *hills and valleys*.

All these examples can be done with a flat brush of any size; the reaction is about the same. Load the brush as you would for any normal wash.

1. To gain a sharp left hand edge and a furry right side, place the brush as shown. Depress the brush's upper corner, bringing the flat of the underside into contact with the top of the hills. The lower and front edge of the brush, being in a more vertical position, pushes the pigment down into the valleys as well, making a solid tone.

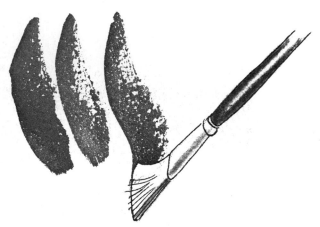

2. This is the same as number 1, but this time not pressing down as hard. All these textures, gained through brush handling, must be practiced to gain the proper feel of the brush for *you*.

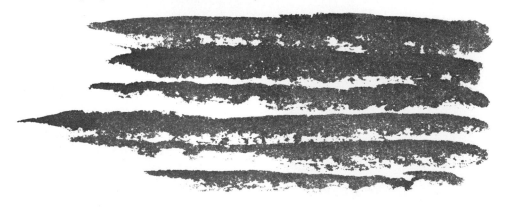

84

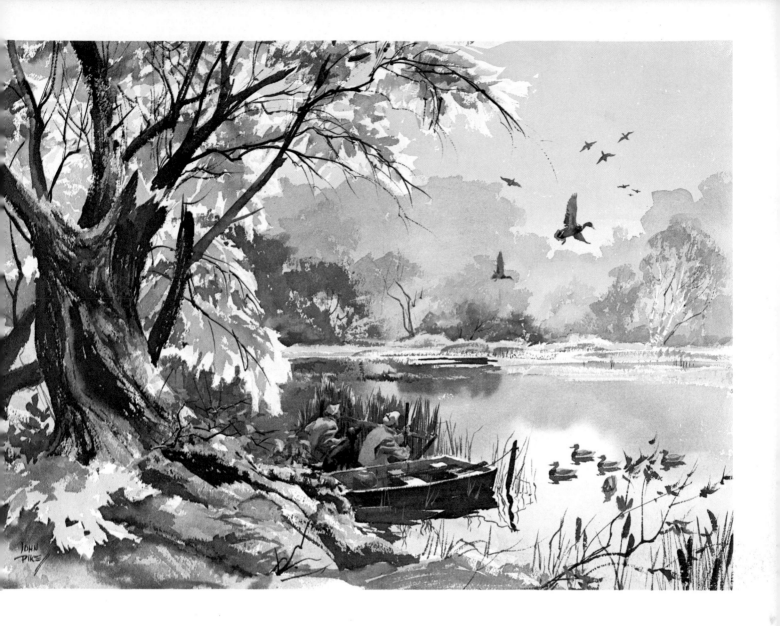

MORNING ARRIVAL, 22" x 30". *Private collection. Courtesy Osborne, Kemper, Thomas.*

In "Morning Arrival," I cheated a bit by using a small amount of opaque in the figures and the mallards. The compositional planning is very simple, but it had to be carefully thought out in advance.

I painted the sky and water in one pass, being careful to paint around the highlighted edges of the leaves in the tree at the left, as well as around the sparkle on the water near the distant shore. When this was dry, the simple silhouette of the far distant trees was put in, as well as some simple undertones on the tree trunks and the foreground. Next came the pale yellow underwash on the near leaves. The rest was all a matter of texturing and the detail of the birds and figures.

There are many paintings reproduced in this book that followed identical procedures.

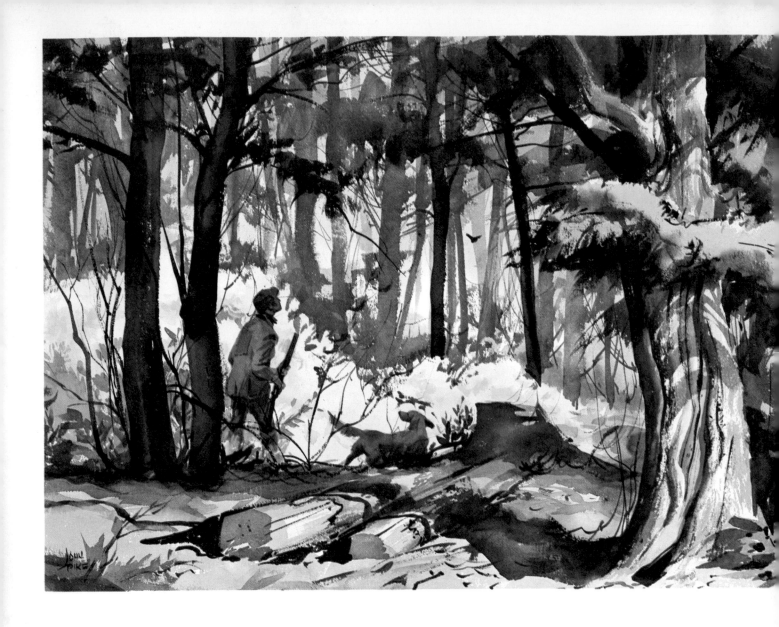

SPORTING PARTNERS, *22" x 30". Private collection. Courtesy Osborne, Kemper, Thomas.*

In this watercolor, as in the demonstration painting entitled "The Fox in the Snow," we have a very similar condition and a similar procedure: sky coming through distant trees, darker middle ground trees, and a light tree in the foreground. Study that demonstration and it will give you the key to this painting too.

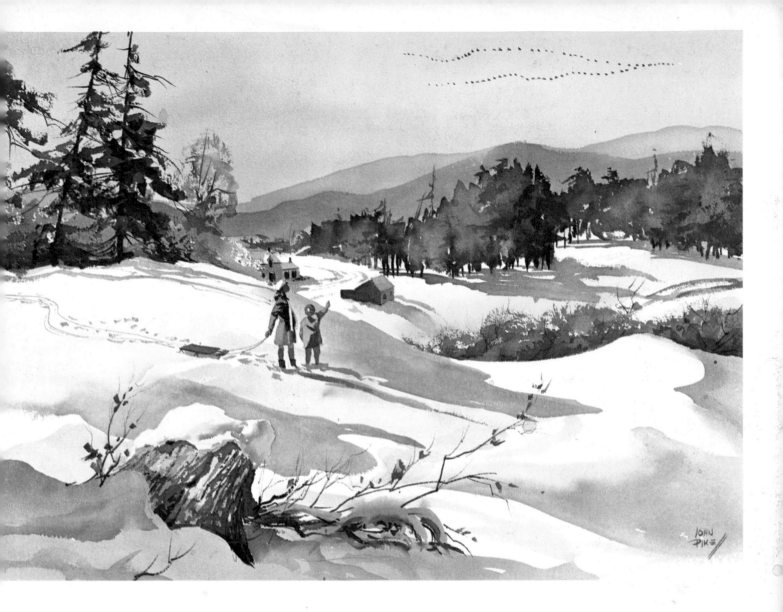

WINTER FORMATION, *22" x 30". Private collection. Courtesy Osborne, Kemper, Thomas.*

The tendency in painting snow scenes is to make the shadows too blue. I'm afraid I'm guilty of just that in this watercolor. However, the painting does show the simple modeling and shadow formation quite clearly.

The cool, blue-green sky was washed in and lost among the middle ground trees. When the sky was dry, the distant mountain was put in and allowed to dry, also losing itself in the dark middle ground trees. In this painting, as in "The Fox in the Snow,"

a clear water wash was put over the entire white area; while it was still wet, I dropped in small spots of the three primaries, red, yellow, and blue, then softly blended the whole together to gain a subtle spectral quality. This kills the deadness of pure white paper.

All the darks, including the figures, were left until last. The soft upper edges of the snow shadows were created by applying clear water in just that area, and the shadows were painted upward to the water. The crispness of the trees was produced by the drag-brush method described in the chapter on brush handling.

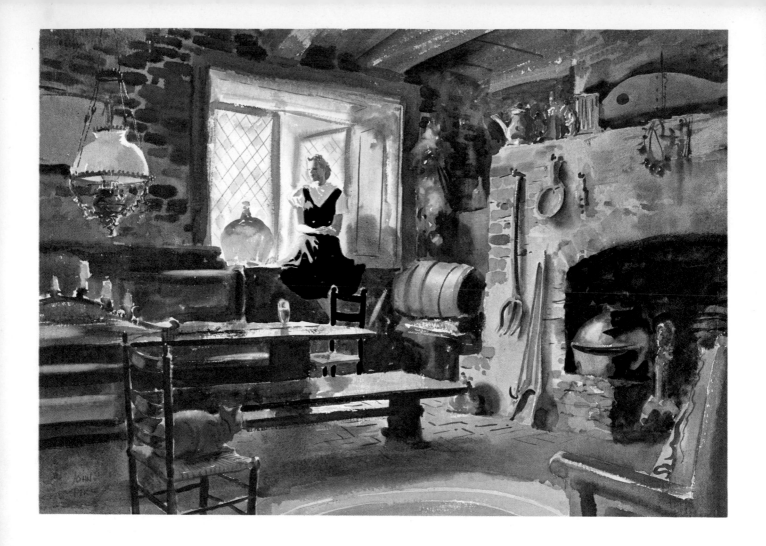

FRITZI AND FRED, *22" x 30". Courtesy, Donald Art Company.*

Aside from the fact that this is one of the few interior paintings in this book, I'm very sentimental about this old kitchen. It belonged to dear old friends of mine, and many wonderful evenings were spent here in front of the fire.

Interiors are usually affected by one or two strong light sources. In this painting, the entire light source is the window. This makes the window the point of interest. All areas are taken down in value from that point. The walls to the right and left of the window naturally receive the smallest amount of light. The fireplace, barrel, table top, and bench—being directly in front of the window—receive the greatest amount of light.

There were no masking agents used; everything was painted around. As I remember, a blue-gray wash was used over the entire back wall and ceiling, silhouetting the objects catching the light. From there, it was a matter of suggesting all the many details. Fritzi, sitting in the window, was painted very simply and directly, as was Fred, sitting on the chair. The glass of beer on the table was mine.

3. and 4. Turn the brush on edge, with the handle almost parallel to the paper, and drag sideways over the tops of the hills. This can be done in a light and airy manner, or heavy and scraggly. Again, practice.

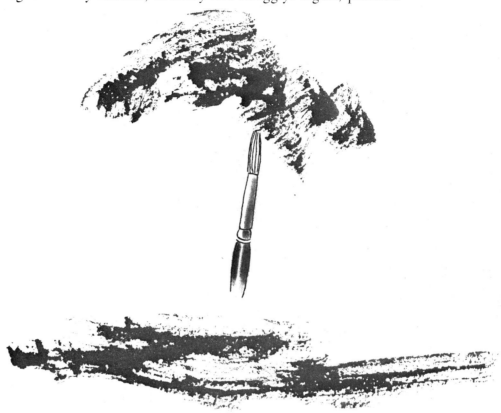

5. This is logical if you think of the reasons. The brush, held vertically at the left, naturally goes down into the valleys, so we have a solid wash. As the brush swings down and becomes more parallel with the paper, the flat of the brush hits only the tops of the hills, giving us the speckled effect. So: UP, solid; DOWN, speckled with whites—and on as we wish. This one exercise will apply in countless ways through all of your watercolor painting.

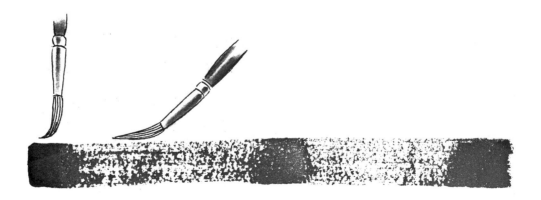

A flat brush was used in all these strokes with the exception of number 1, which was done with a rigger.

1. Riggers are fun brushes that seem to have an action all their own. The long, thin hairs follow your guiding hand in graceful arcs and curves. The rigger is most handy in hundreds of ways, any place a fine, free line is needed.

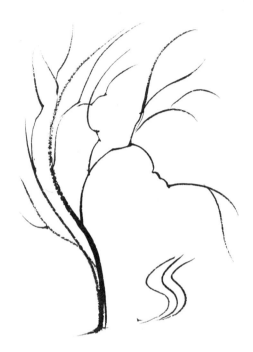

2, 3, and 4 are simply ways of handling the flat brush, taking advantage of its square chisel edge.

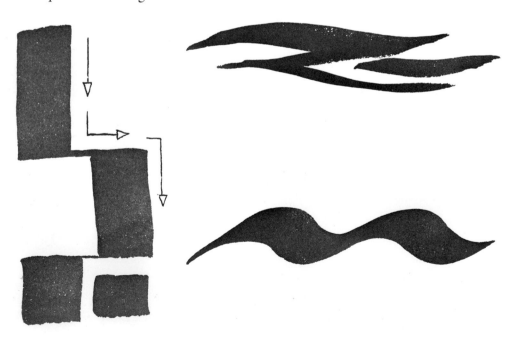

5. This is rather tricky, but you may find some use for it. It's semi-drybrush. Pick up your pigment in a half-wet brush and lay the brush flat on your palette; then bring the handle up to a vertical position. Leaving the brush hairs squashed flat, squiggle the brush sideways until the hairs separate, as shown in the drawing. Interesting effects may be gained when the hairs are separated in this way. Try it.

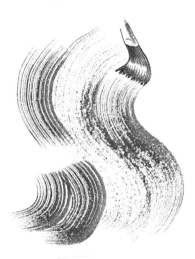

6. Here's how to soften an edge. The sphere was wet with clear water, then the pigment was dropped in all around the edge and allowed to take its own action toward the highlight. Naturally you have to guide the color a bit. The cylinder was accomplished by a direct stroke of pigment, then immediately softened on the right side with clear water. Again, watch it until the pigment has settled. These two methods will be used endlessly and in many ways through all your watercolor painting.

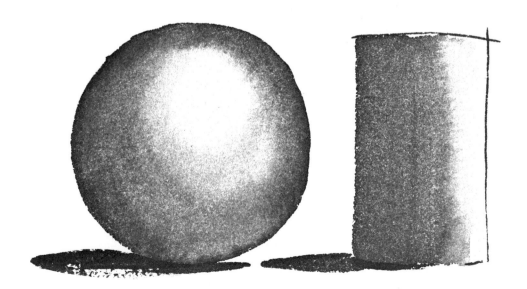

Here are some special effects you can do with things like a sharp blade, rubber cement, masking tape, salt, and wax crayon.

1. Using a knife or razor blade is about the only way I know to gain the sparkle of branches and other crisp little forms against a dark background. Don't overdo it. (The lights on the tree trunk were left.)

2. This is just a blob of rubber cement which I put on the paper and allowed to dry before the dark wash was applied. If you want it dead white, be sure it's thick enough. After the wash is dry, rub the cement off with your finger or a pick-up (a chunk of dried rubber cement).

3. Masking tape was pressed down firmly over the penciled outline and cut with a sharp knife to the desired shape; then the excess tape was peeled up. You can see through the *thinner* varieties of masking tape just enough to follow a pencil line underneath. Don't cut too deeply. Lay on the wash and, when dry, lift up the tape.

4. I stuck a straight piece of tape at the horizon line. I painted in the sky and the mountains, then peeled up the tape and painted the water.

5. If you like tricky effects in washes, you can have a lot of fun experimenting with ways to produce these effects. This illustration was made with table salt, sprinkled on a wet wash, allowed to dry, then brushed off. But there are all sorts of things—bread crumbs, coffee, cement, etc. Try anything that's absorbent.

6. This effect was gained by using a wax crayon, applied on the white paper before the wash. White candle wax does as well. Needless to say, a wash of color is repelled by the wax, leaving the paper white wherever the crayon or candle was used.

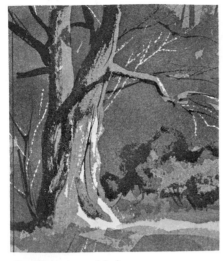

Knife or razor blade

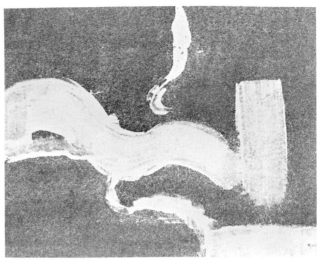

Rubber cement

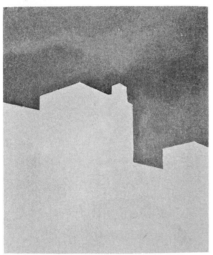

Masking tape

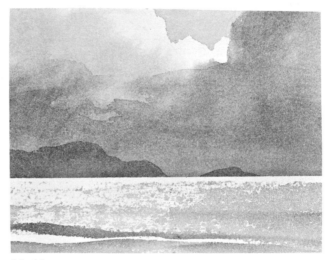

Masking tape

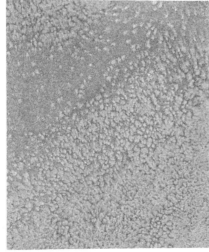

Salt

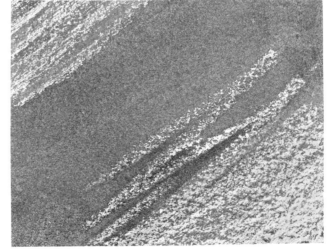

Wax crayon

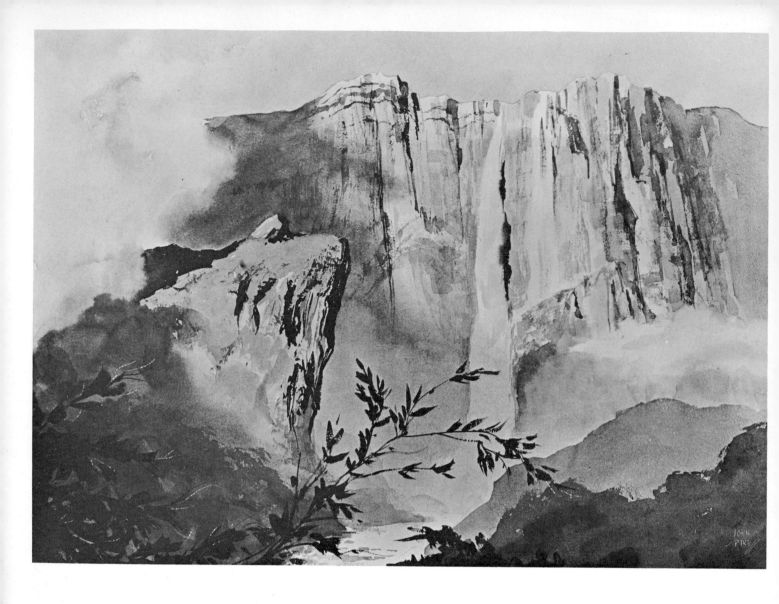

ANGEL FALLS, *22" x 30". Collection, General Tire International.*

This 3700 foot waterfall is in Venezuela. Notice how the towering rocky form looms up in the sunlight and then drops away into the mist below. These misty passages—like the one on the left hand side—must be handled with great care, combining subtly graded washes and wet-in-wet technique. The foreground shapes are kept in shadow to accent the sunlight on the center of interest.

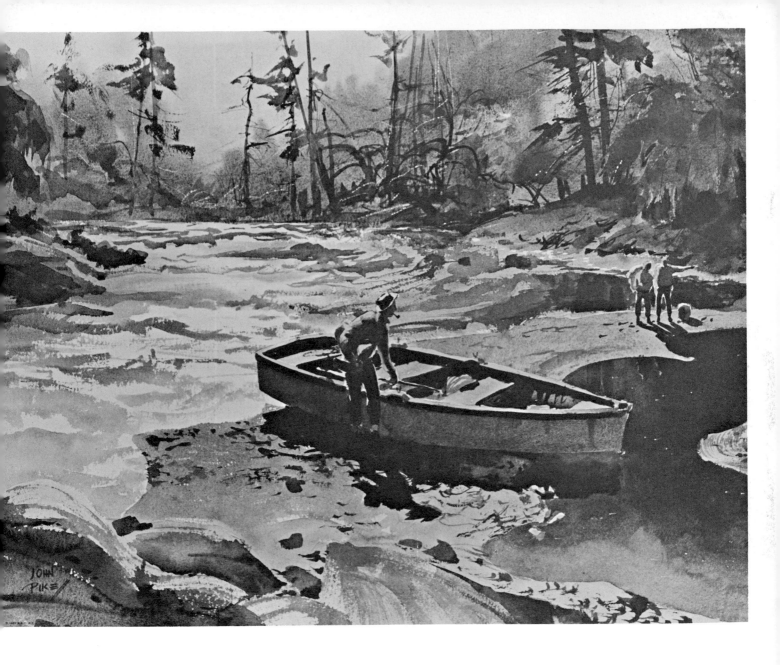

CAMPERS, *22" x 30". Courtesy Donald Art Company.*

The interplay of soft, blurry forms and crisp detail in the far trees—always a problem in painting woods—was accomplished by combining wet-in-wet with crisp brushwork on dry paper. First came the out-of-focus shapes, painted on wet paper. When this was dry, I went back in with the tree trunks and leaves. Analyze the direction of the light and you'll see that the picture is back lit. The near side of the boat is in shadow and the figures are in silhouette, edged with light.

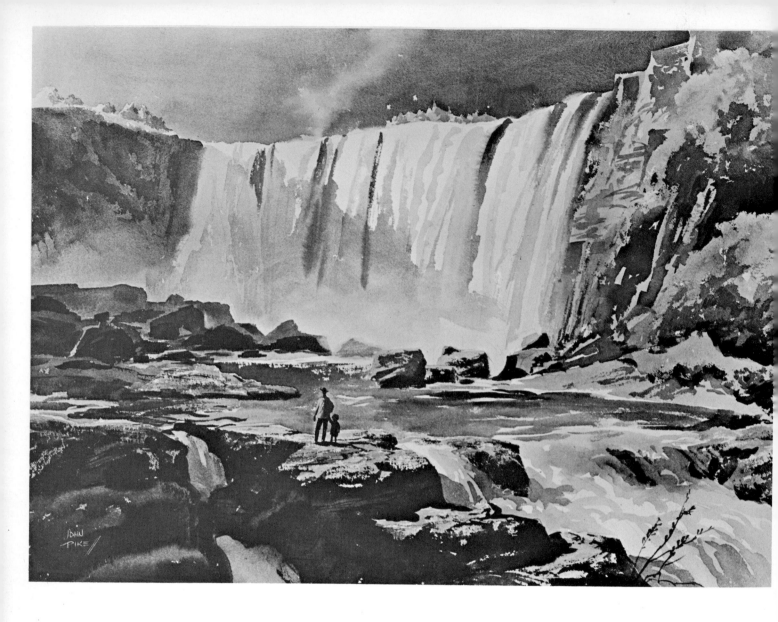

SALTO DEL LAJA, CHILE, 22" x 30". Collection, General Tire International.

The big, slanting shadow across the falls tells us the direction of the light. The strong contrast of light and shadow in the foreground rocks—the shadows are very dark and wet—accentuates the brilliance of the sunshine. The intense light on the water is accented by the dark cloud that appears just over the edge of the falls. The tiny figures are important; because they are so small, they show the viewer how large and majestic the falls really are. Without these figures, the falls might be *any* size, because the viewer would have no sense of scale. Put your finger over the figures and you'll see what I mean.

7 *Planning a watercolor*

The approach to painting in transparent watercolor is different from the approach in any other medium. The painting must be thought out in advance; it must be visualized in its completed form.

Granted, there are many fine watercolorists who rely on the *chance* method, sailing into the painting and hoping; without doubt, many delightful effects are sometimes the unexpected result. My old teacher, Charles Hawthorne, used to refer to these effects as the "divine accidents" of watercolor; the painter goes to work, thinking, "Let's see what kind of hell the old girl is going to give me today!"

But from a technical standpoint, I feel one should be master of his craft, rather than having the craft be master of him. This takes hard work and endless doing.

Once, in my summer class, I was stressing the importance of familiarizing yourself with the medium, of working with the medium again and again. A student told the story of a man lost in New York City, who approached a beatnik on 57th Street and asked, "How do I get to Carnegie Hall?" The beatnik answered, "Practice, Daddy-O, practice!"

And that is practically the whole story of a watercolorist's life. Work with it, play with it, practice until you *know* all its nasty little habits by heart. It's only *then* that you'll know how to make the divine accidents happen where *you* want them to.

THE TOUGHEST MEDIUM

I think this quote from John Carlson's book, *Carlson's Guide to Landscape Painting*, expresses the unique quality of watercolor in relation to other mediums. At the beginning of Chapter 2, "The Mechanics of Painting," he wrote:

"Do *not* for at least the first year of your study, attempt to work in watercolor [note that Carlson is speaking to the absolute beginner], but rather get your experience or knowledge in oil colors. Oil painting allows of much abuse in its handling. We can 'paint in' and 'scrape out' any number of times. We can lay one color over another, or keep correcting our color masses until the desired relations and transitions are obtained. We can construct and reconstruct, almost at our leisure, the portions of our canvas needing such corrections, all with very little difficulty.

"With watercolor, the case is rather the reverse. The speed of drying of the medium requires a masterly knowledge in its uses: a knowledge of all relations, transitions, juxtapositions and constructions involved in landscape painting. The transparency of the watercolor allows of no radical changes of color or composition in the picture.

"The clarity of the color depends (in watercolor) entirely upon the directness of its application or 'washing in' and . . . it is impossible for a student to be direct in a medium he does not thoroughly understand. . . . Once these principles of landscape are mastered, through much experimenting (in the more malleable medium of oil) the several other mediums such as watercolor . . . will be found easier to handle. This advice is in contradiction to the popular belief that an amateur should never essay oil painting, a fallacious theory that accounts for the many frail examples of art in our watercolor exhibitions. In such examples, solidity, form and color transitions, the very rock foundation of painting, have usually been sacrificed to the maintenance of a few 'clever washes' which, except for their daring, have no significance whatever. Watercolor is a master's medium."

John Carlson wrote these words in the middle 1920s. They are very sound and discerning. But I can't help wishing he were here today to see how far the "clever washes" have been taken by innumerable sparkling young watercolorists, who have contributed so much to making it the "American medium," and who also believe in "solidity, form and color."

SKETCHING
IN THE FIELD

In finding material and planning pictures, sketching in the field is most rewarding in many ways. Sketching on the spot trains you in observation, helps you get the feel of the great, wonderful world around you. Nature is the great source of truths; you must return to it endlessly for inspiration and guidance.

By this, I don't mean we must paint all things as they appear to the eye. The happy thing about painting—in contrast with photography—is that we can change, rearrange, eliminate, and add to our subject as we choose. Our own aesthetic tastes can hold full command.

Every little leaf and fern, every turned-over stone, offers magnificent design ideas. Study them. Use them. Become conversant with the *hidden world*, hidden only because we may fail to *look*. It's there to *see*. Learn to see it! All great landscape painting is based on the intimate study of nature, which is a far richer source of material than the wildest imagination!

Many years ago, I discovered the tremendous value of the preliminary black and white sketch. I used typewriter paper or a standard 9″ x 12″ bond paper pad. In making your sketch, you can use any drawing tool that will allow you to get down broad values: black Conté; chalks in a range of grays; charcoal (a bit messy); graphite sticks or 4B and 6B pencils—all good.

Let's say you're tramping across the countryside and you turn the magic corner. There it is! Patches of late sun fall in just the right places; the scene has everything! But then, by the time you've unwound your gear, gotten set up and ready to paint, your sun has changed. That first impact and impression are gone. Whip out your sketch book, quickly outline the light and dark areas that made the subject attract you, and then you have it. You've nailed it down.

I very often use a Polaroid camera with black and white film to catch those moments.

Even when I have plenty of time, I still go ahead and do my sketch, as it allows me three things, three bits of insurance against ruining a very expensive piece of paper. (There's a lot of Scotch as well as Indian in the Pike family.)

(1) I can explore my compositional possibilities. On the sketch, I can scrub around, change, manipulate the layout to suit me. You can't do this on watercolor paper as it will ruin the painting surface.

(2) I can firmly establish the light and dark areas. It's vital to stick to this; if you start chasing the sun around, trying this way and that way, you'll wind up with mud. You'll never arrive at the light effect that delighted you when you first spotted the subject.

(3) Most important of all, you've established your *values*: how much lighter, how much darker, is *this* area in relation to *that*. More about values in a moment.

In other words, your sketch session is your creative thinking time. The sketch helps you visualize the completed painting; it's your *blueprint*. Then, when you go to work on that big blank sheet of watercolor paper, you've nothing to worry about but the watercolor itself! (And Heaven knows, that's enough!)

VALUES

Probably the single most important thing to the painter or designer, regardless of his medium, is the ability to see and understand *values*.

In a painting, the proper relationship of the values to each other is what creates depth: the values push the distance away out back, pull the middle ground and foreground up to where you want them. Remember, you're working on a flat surface that has only two dimensions: height and breadth. So it's your values that will give you the illusion of going *in*, that give you the visual feeling of a third dimension.

A good way to learn to *see* values is to make a graded chart, or buy one with eight or ten tones (see illustration). There's a black at one end of the chart and the grays get progressively lighter until they reach white. This may seem mechanical, but it does fix an image in your mind. Some instructors

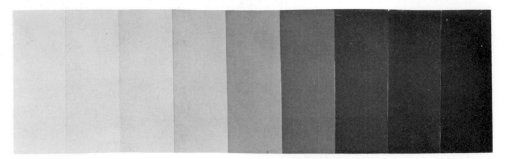

suggest numbering or lettering the different values: 1 to 10, or A through J, etc. I don't think this is necessary; but if it makes it clearer to you, be my guest.

ANALYZING VALUES IN YOUR SUBJECT

Now to analyze the subject you wish to paint.

First, pick out a value which you feel is exactly half way between the *darkest* thing you see and the *lightest*. This is your starting point, the place you hang your hat. Now pick the *lightest* area before you. With the gray values (on the chart) in your mind, are you *sure* these two are in proper relationship to each other? If so, pick the third, or *darkest* one. If these are all sitting in their correct places, you have it made! All the others, in between, are merely contributing minor factors to the three big, strong values.

This business of seeing values may seem a little complex in the beginning, but after you've played the game for a time, it will come to you so automatically you'll completely forget that old graded chart. Make it a game; endlessly look, observe, not just when you're going out to do that Sunday masterpiece, but all the time! Ask yourself: "Where's my hat-hanger, that middle value; where are my lightest and my darkest values?" If you do it enough each day, when Sunday comes, you'll *know!*

LEARN TO SEE VALUES

What constitutes a value? Is it only the dark side of a barn, or the light side? A large, flat blue sky? No, it *is* more complex than that, but perhaps I can simplify it a bit for you.

Look at the reproduction of "Fox in Snow" on page 132. Then half close your eyes; you'll find that all of the background—with all of its little trees, twigs, and "woods trash"—becomes *one large dark mass*. That's what I mean by a value.

For another explanatory example, look closely at a tweed jacket or tweed overcoat. Dozens of different colored threads make up its design. Now step back ten feet and you'll find they've all blended into a solid tone (unless your eyesight is better than mine). Each little thread (or twig) contributes to make one great over-all value.

One fine student suggested that if you're confused by all the little details, the best way to see masses is to look into the ground glass of a reflex camera, then throw it slightly out of focus. It's a good trick and it works!

But a much simpler method is half closing your eyes and looking through

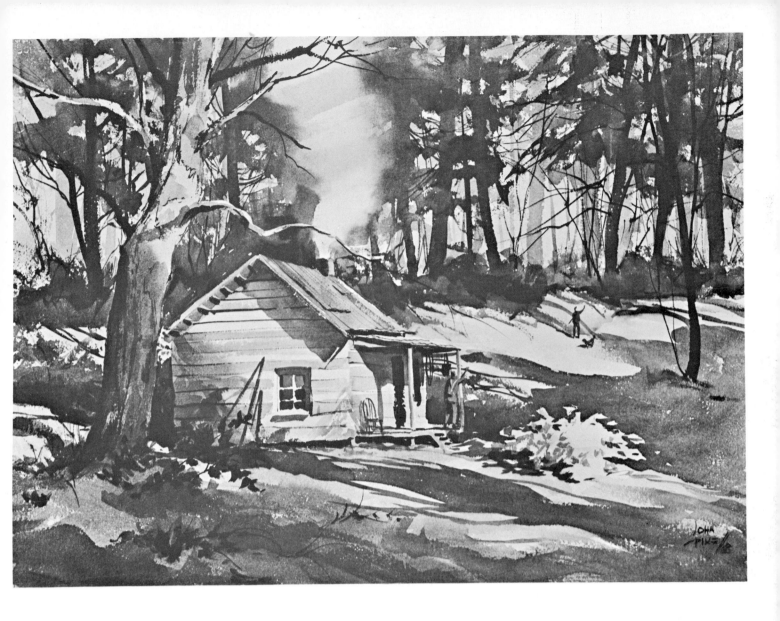

HUNTER'S SHACK IN NORTH WOODS, *22″ x 30″*.
Collection, General Tire International.

The composition is established by the long
sweeping brushstrokes that form the shadows,
which lead the eye to the focal point of the
painting. These long shadows also show the
direction of the light and even the time of day.
Study the trees in the background and you'll
see how they're divided into dark strokes and
light strokes, which correspond to two planes—
nearer trees and far trees. Notice the soft
edge of the trees where the light breaks
through above the shack.

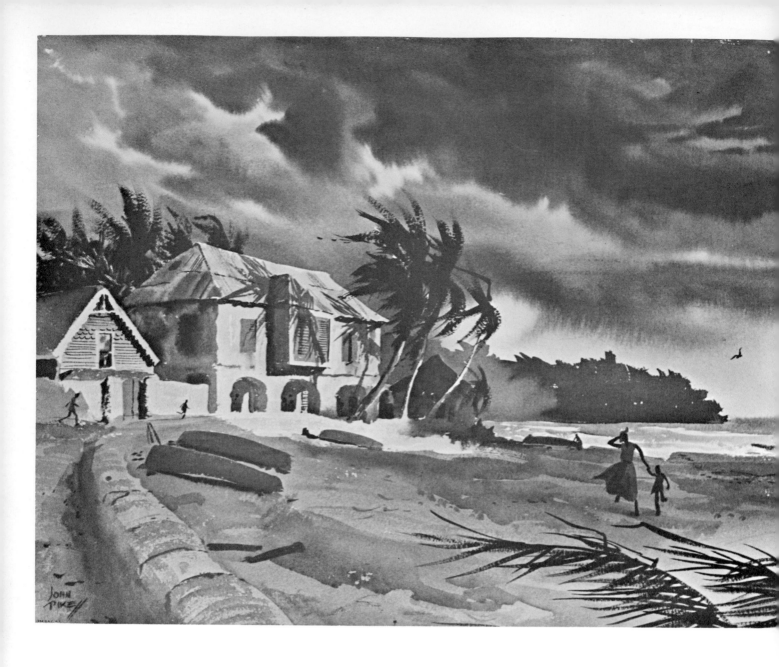

AHEAD OF THE WIND, *22" x 30". Courtesy, Donald Art Company.*

The drama of an approaching storm is heightened by the flash of sunlight on the houses, beach, and water. The dark storm clouds were painted wet-in-wet and allowed to form a variety of soft edges; this wash was carefully controlled to let patches of light break through the dark masses here and there. In contrast with the patches of light in the middle ground, the foreground is thrown into shadow by a cool, over-all wash. Notice the roughly textured drybrush in the trees.

your lashes. This may give you gals "laugh lines" (I like that term better than "crow's feet"), but, in spite of the hazards, this habit will also make you a better painter.

Back to the chart.

In a picture that's conceived with strong sunlight and shadow patterns, the values will pretty well cover the entire range, from *black* to *white*. On the other hand, a gray day might conceivably cover only the lower middle half of the value range.

Remember to pick subjects that will give you large, simple patterns. Once these patterns are established, you may play around with all the little details as you wish. But if the values are properly seen and conceived, the picture will hold together. Again, let me say, it's the *large value-related areas* that do it.

Play my little *seeing game*. Do it as you ride in the car, walking, or even at a cocktail party. You may see some things that aren't too attractive; but, in general, Mother Nature has wrapped a mighty beautiful mantle around us.

THE DEMONSTRATION PAINTINGS

In the next eight chapters, I'll reconstruct the stages I went through in painting eight pictures. Like the demonstrations I do in my school, these demonstration sequences are meant to show you how the painting principles I've described (in preceding chapters) work in practice. The demonstrations are graded in order of difficulty: the easiest comes first, the toughest last. If you were a student in my school, I'd assign these to you—or something like them—as projects. But since you may be several thousand miles away, I suggest that you assign them to *yourself*. I don't recommend that you *copy* my demonstration paintings, but find yourself similar subjects—eight or more—and try them in the same order.

I'm sure you realize that the black-and-white demonstration stages are *not* the actual step by step development of the full color painting you see reproduced. Except for the still lifes, I took finished paintings and back-tracked to show you the procedures I used in arriving at the finished job, and to explain why I thought it the best approach. The black-and-whites were painted approximately half the size of the originals to show brushwork and texture better. They're in black and white (blues and umbers for nicer blacks and grays) to clearly show the tremendous necessity for understanding values.

HOW THE DEMONSTRATIONS WERE MADE

How were the watercolor black-and-whites done? First, the outlines of my layout were made, just as I did when I painted the actual picture. The layout was then photographed. Next, I put on the first wash and photographed it. And so on, up to the finished watercolor, photographing each new stage as I went on adding washes, strokes, and details.

So help me, I never thought I'd be a photographer; but I hope these photos will convey to you some of the painting methods I've found easiest. A watercolor—with its freedom of movement, rapid brushwork, elusive washes, and one's own inability to do the same thing twice (you wouldn't be in this cult if you could)—is almost impossible to copy. But these scale reconstructions do seem the most practical way of showing you my procedures. Short of flying you to Woodstock, New York, it's the closest I can come (within the limits of a book) to letting you look over my shoulder as I paint.

A NOTE ABOUT THE SKETCHES

The chalk or Conté preliminary sketches (my *thinking* sketches) are also shown.

In the photos of the sketches, you'll notice a grid of three horizontal and three vertical lines. This is an old method by which you can gain the same *proportions* in your large painting as you have in your small sketch. Simply draw the same grid on your watercolor paper (lightly) as you have on your sketch. This speeds up the transfer of your drawing and saves a lot of erasing on that beautiful, expensive piece of watercolor paper, with its easily damaged surface.

This is sometimes called a *mural scale-up*.

If you don't want to damage your pencil sketch by drawing lines on it, you can lay out a grid on clear plastic with India ink or a China marking pencil. You can lay this plastic sheet over any sketch and use the grid over and over.

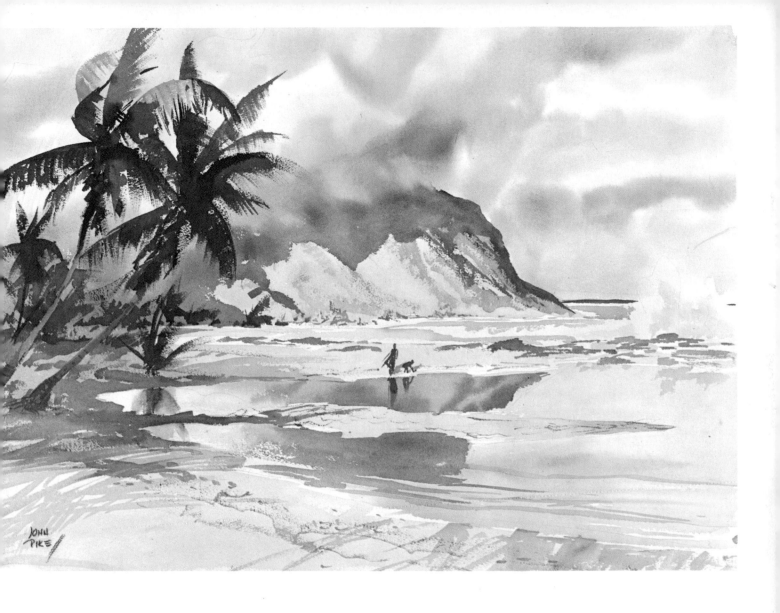

HAWAII, SHELL HUNTERS, *22" x 30".*
Collection, General Tire International.

The procedure in the upper section of this painting is almost identical to that in the demonstration series entitled "Chimborazo Volcano."

The breaking wave, beyond the second strip of reef, was produced by the use of clear water at the time the sky was laid in. The light warm tones of the beaches were put down and, when dry, textured with drybrush and small dabs for bits of seaweed and footprints. Then came the reflections of the promontory, plus the shadows on the sand.

Finally, I did the silhouetting of the lacy palm trees and the old gimmick of the central figure in a bright red mou-mou. I say "gimmick" as this is an old trick; wherever you have a predominance of one color someplace, put in a touch of its complementary color—in this case, green to red.

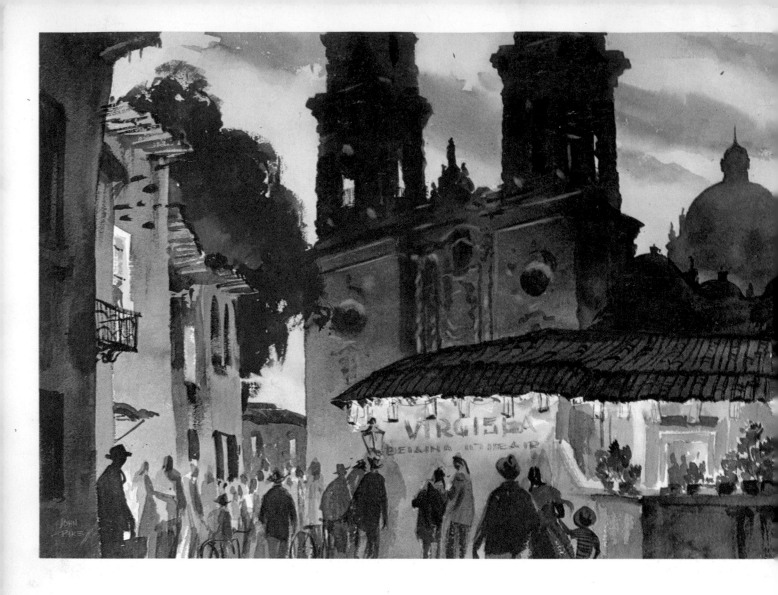

TAXCO, MEXICO, 22" x 30". Collection, General Tire International.

My purpose in silhouetting the cathedral against the early night sky was to create an atmosphere of mystery and age. This device also serves to direct the viewer's interest to the activity in the street below.

The sky colors were kept very cool to accent the warmth of the lights in the windows and shops.

Note the upward reflected lights on the carvings of the cathedral. After the large, dark graded wash was dry, these lights were lifted out with a bristle brush and a tissue.

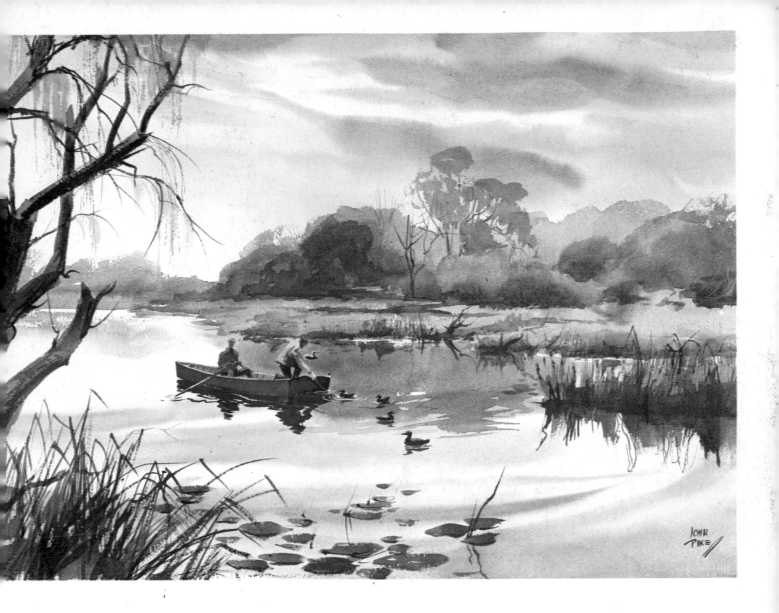

DECOYED AT DAWN, *22" x 30". Private collection. Courtesy Osborne, Kemper, Thomas.*

The cold, dank smell of the marsh lands at this hour can be a delight. Setting out the decoys in anticipation is part of the fun.

Again I started with a large sky wash, bringing it all the way down to the horizon and to the darks of the trees. While this wash was still wet, I flowed in the warm early morning clouds. The water, with its soft ripples, was put in at the same time.

From there, when this was dry, I worked forward in the various stages, softening and modeling as I went. The silhouetted tree, the rushes, and the lily pads frame the composition to bring the focus of attention upon the boat and figures.

107

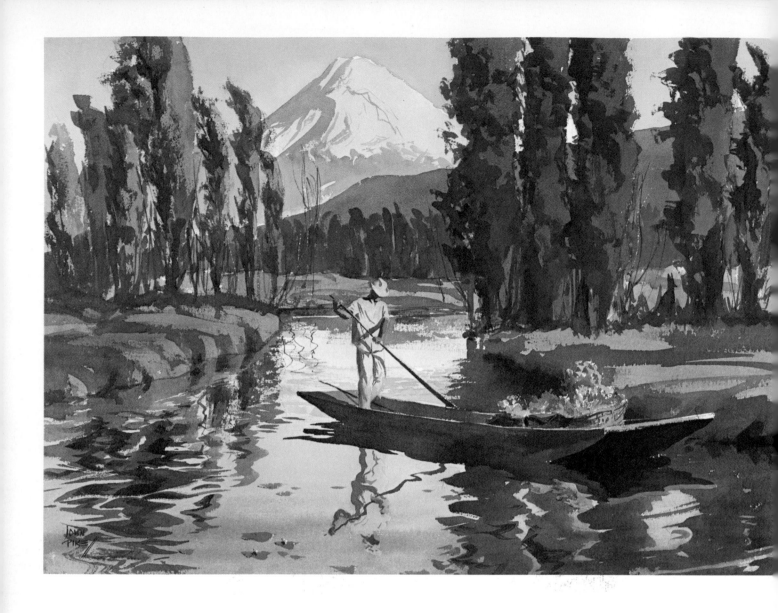

XOCHIMILCO, *22" x 30". Collection, General Tire International.*

The beautiful mountain, Popocatepetl, rises in the distance above Xochimilco's gardens. The steps are rather clear when you remember the stage set procedure in the demonstration chapters. First comes the backdrop: the sky and the snow-covered mountain. The next "cut-out" would be the distant blue hills, coming forward to the middle ground poplar-like trees, and on to the detail of the flowers, figure, and reflections.

One note on the sky wash: I painted *around* the middle ground trees for, even though they're dark, I wanted to keep them warm in color, and not have them affected by the blue-green wash of the sky.

8 *Geometric still life: demonstration*

This is a simple, but most instructive exercise, as it forces you to see the true values, so important in landscape painting. At this point, work only in grays. Combinations of Burnt Umber and Ultramarine make fine grays.

Wrap several cardboard boxes of different shapes and sizes in white paper —or paint them white—and set them up near a window or near any single light source. Make a pyramid of the shapes and then turn each so you have several different tones on their various planes.

After doing your drawing, lay in a dark wash behind the boxes, leaving them as a white silhouette. When this wash is dry, study the different values very carefully and lay them in as you see them. Remember to work from light to dark, and have patience to let each wash dry to avoid "bleeding." A hair dryer will speed your drying times. Repeat this exercise with several different arrangements of boxes, seen from various angles.

In my summer school, I ask all my students to do this project on their first afternoon. From the results, I learn three things: (1) how well they draw; (2) how well they can lay down a dark wash; and most important, (3) how well they see values.

This is a good exercise, not as easy as it looks.

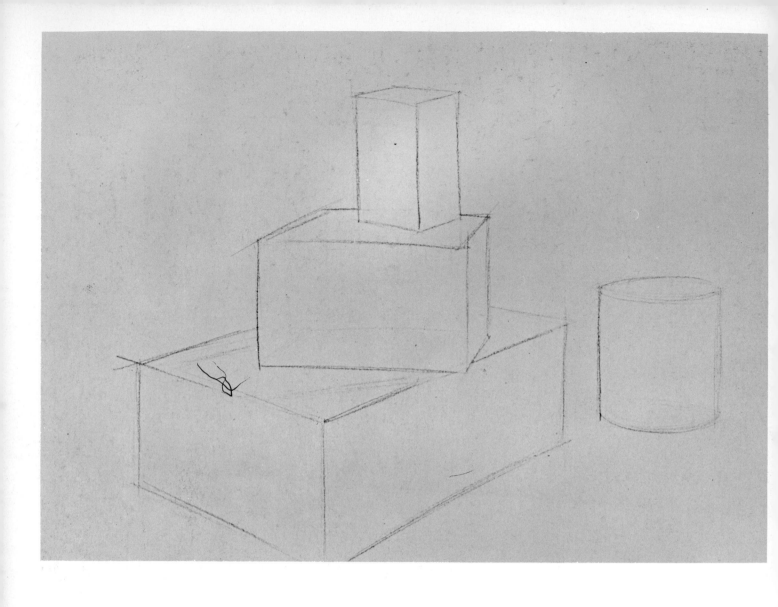

STAGE 1   This is the rough pencil outline. Note how no two planes face the light source at the same angle.

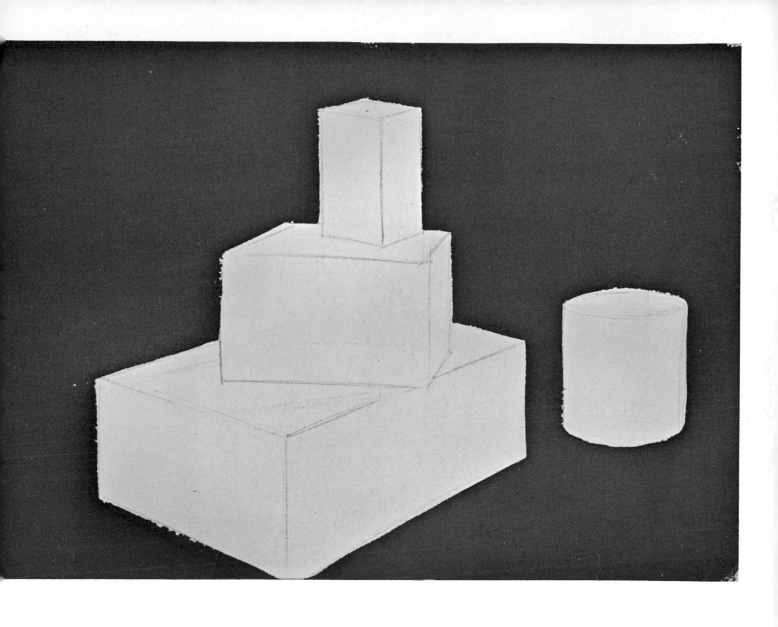

STAGE 2   I lay a dark wash all around the outer edges of the boxes and allow to dry before going on to the next stage. By silhouetting the forms in this way, you can see the subtleties of the values much more readily.

111

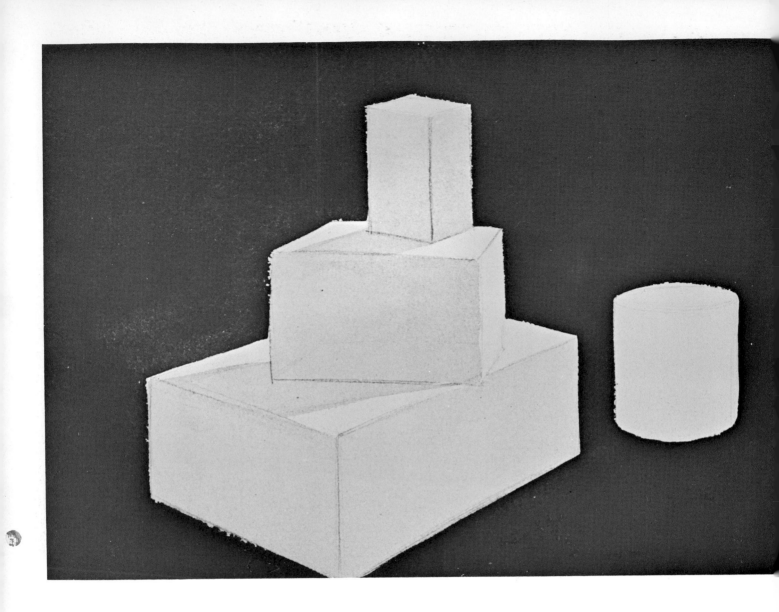

STAGE 3   Keeping in mind the idea of working from light to dark, I pick the value of the lightest plane just a bit down the tonal scale from the white of the paper. I paint this over everything other than the white paper areas I wish to leave. As you can see, the painting is already taking on form and depth.

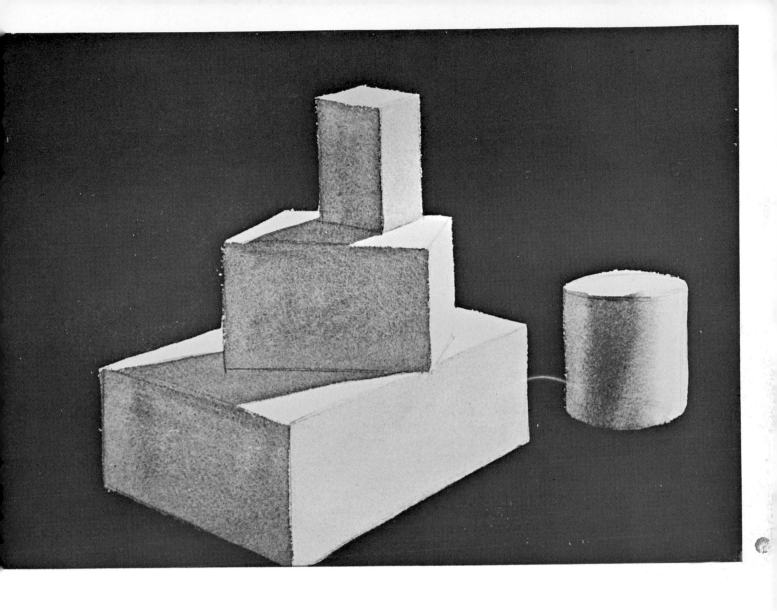

STAGE 4   Now what's the next value down
the scale? I decide and put it down.

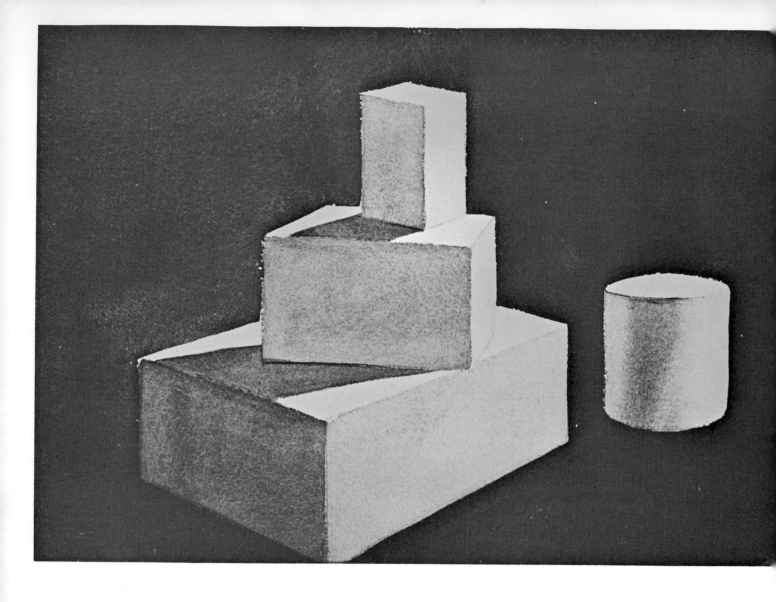

STAGE 5   Here, all I've added is the darkening of the direct cast shadows on the horizontal planes, cast from the top and middle boxes. Remember, a direct shadow on a *horizontal* plane is subject to few influences; a *vertical* plane in shadow is influenced by the direct light surrounding its base, and is therefore lighter.

9 Still life with regular and irregular shapes: demonstration

This isn't an overly inspired still life, but I'm using it here as the next logical step up from our white boxes. This arrangement of regular and irregular shapes also gives you further opportunity to dig into your value thinking.

Still life painting is one of the finest of all practice areas for the landscape painter. It teaches him to *see* under the most favorable conditions. Some students may find still life dull, but the thoughtful student won't overlook its possibilities.

In a still life, we have a *captive* subject. It doesn't move, and isn't affected by the weather, like a landscape. You can control the light and the arrangement of the forms; the subject just sits there, unchanging, so you may study its values and qualities at your leisure. Analyze every little subtlety, every change of value and color; think out the best procedure to arrive at your desired result.

(Side note. A student friend of mine worked way into the wee small hours on a fruit still life. I came to school the following morning to find a half finished painting. His set-up had disappeared. I asked him what had happened. "At 2 A.M. I got hungry and *ate* it!")

In my value thinking, the sharp highlights on the glass bottle and on the pottery bean pot present a problem. These highlights are so very much higher or brighter on the value scale than anything else in the picture. This means just one thing. Everything else in the picture *must come down* in tone or value to make these brilliant spots count. So I put a graying (or subduing) wash over everything except the highlights.

From here, I painted in the normal manner. But it's like painting on a gray background; all future color is influenced by the subdued wash underneath, leaving the sparkle of the highlights untouched.

A good trick, to add a bit of zest to those white highlight areas (particularly if you're using artificial light), is to put a tiny rim of yellow around the outer edge of the space, leaving the center white.

Your still life doesn't have to be an "arty" one. Everybody's kitchen has all kinds of objects that will serve for practice studies. (See rough sketches for ideas.)

When you go into the great outdoors, try to break the landscape down and analyze it, just as you've done with the still life. All the same rules are there, although they're more difficult to recognize and apply out there under the sky.

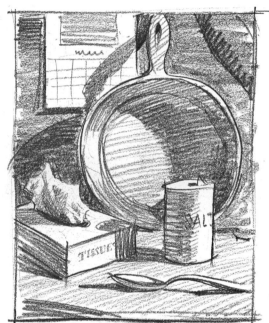

Pencil roughs of still life

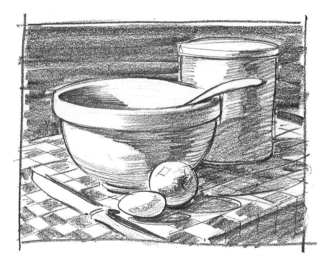

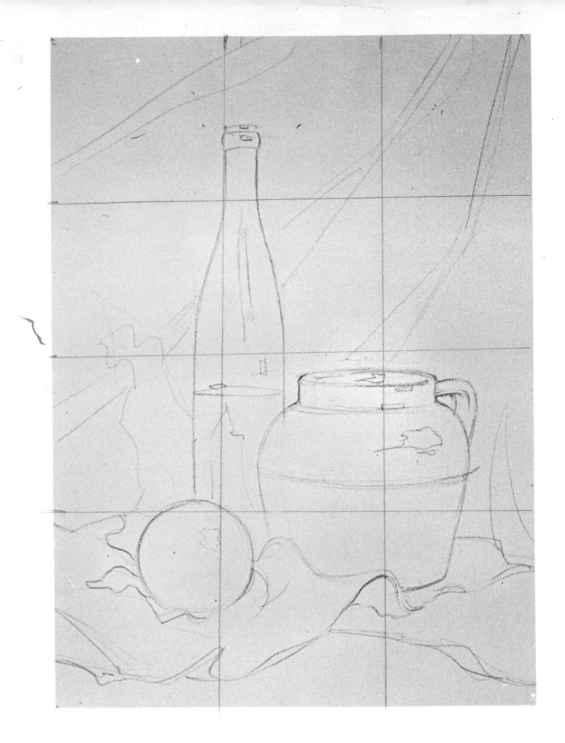

STAGE 1   When you've arranged various objects, when your lighting is to your liking, when you feel you're gaining the most in contrast (all the way from the sparkle of your highlights, through the middle values, to the darks of the cast shadows) then pencil in the composition. In all these step-by-step paintings, I've gone much darker than I usually do, to make the values more legible in the reproduction. Note that I've sketched around the highlights as well as the cast shadows.

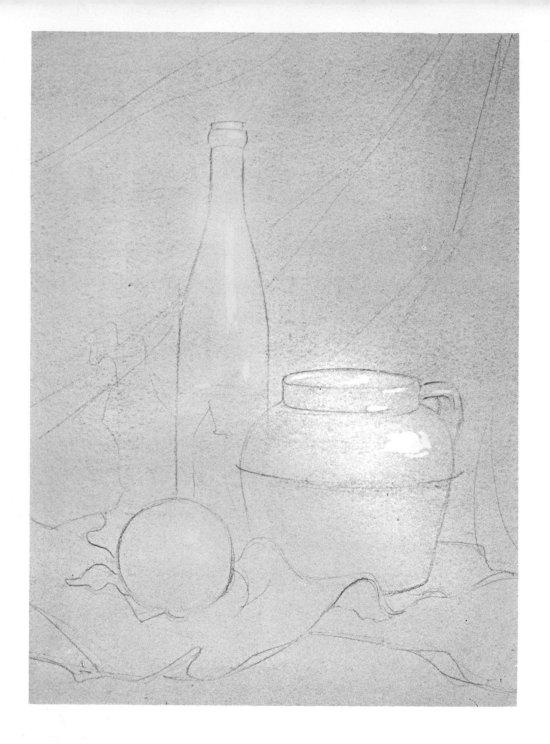

STAGE 2   Here I have a problem. The highlights on the bottle and glazed bean pot are much lighter (or higher) on the value scale than all the rest of the painting; so I have no choice but to take all other areas *down in value* to make these sparkling spots count. A neutral, *subduing* wash is put over everything but the highlights; these may be painted around or masked out as you choose.

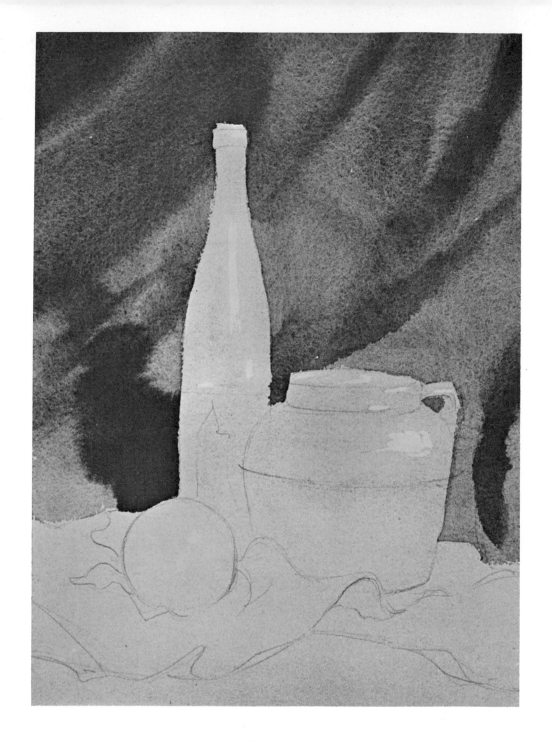

STAGE 3   From here on, I paint in the normal manner, keeping in mind, however, that every color and every wash will be influenced by the neutral wash underneath. It's like painting on gray paper. I silhouette the bottle and the bean pot with a fast drapery wash, adding soft, modeling darks while it's still wet. This exercise is much the same as the preceding white box study, giving you a chance to study the values and shapes. Let this stage dry before proceeding to the next step.

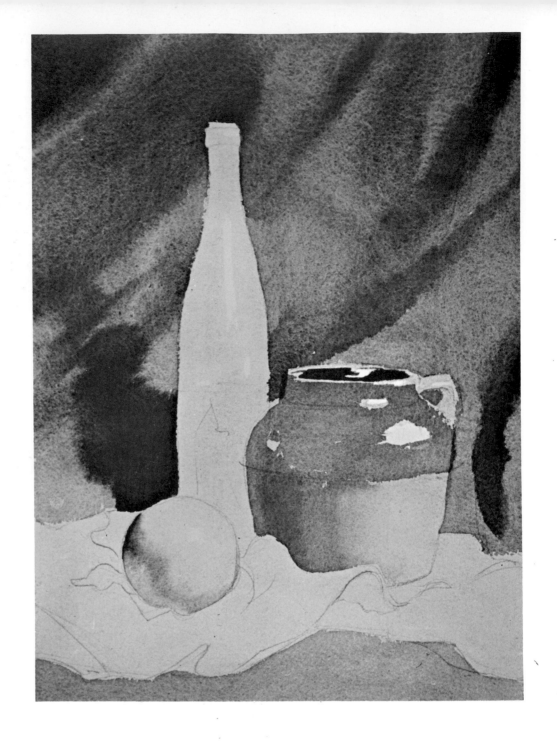

STAGE 4   In this step, I put in the first underpainting on the bean pot, on the orange,
and on the tablecloth in the foreground. On
the pot and on the orange, I soften the right
hand edges with clear water, remembering to
paint around the pure white highlights.

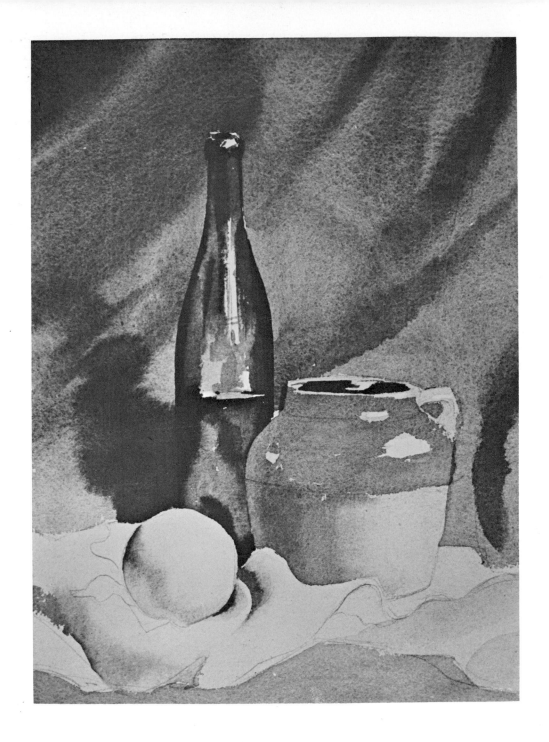

STAGE 5   On the bottle, I carefully study the highlights, reflections, and inner reflections —and what causes them—before proceeding. With a medium green wash, I paint around the highlights; I leave the secondary highlight and the surface of the liquid clear. While this is still wet, I come in with the very dark, soft green at the outer edge of the bottle, allowing the color to flow in with its own action. Additional modeling, below the surface line, is dropped in. Then I let it alone. Painting time: about forty-five seconds. Then come the light middle tones on the folds of the napkin to the left and right of the orange. Clear water is added to soften the edges toward the light source.

121

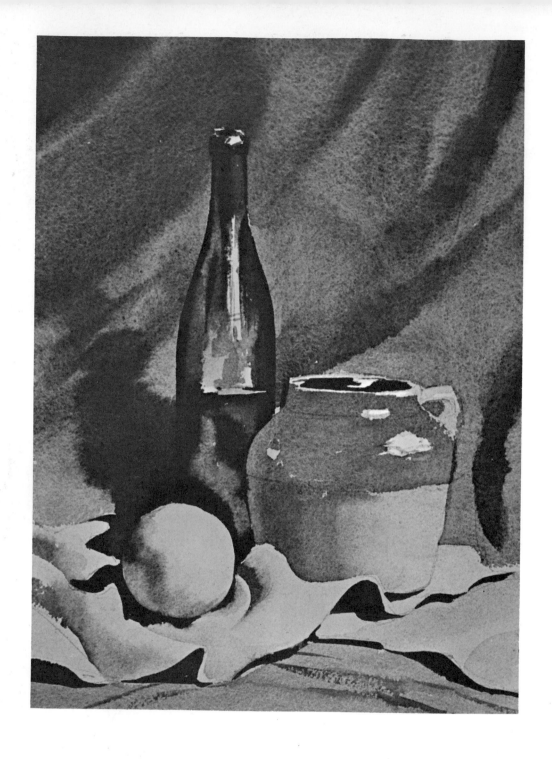

STAGE 6   Now come the dark shadows on the napkin, cast by the orange and bottle, and the darks under the edges. A couple of dry-brush strokes are added on the tablecoth for texture.

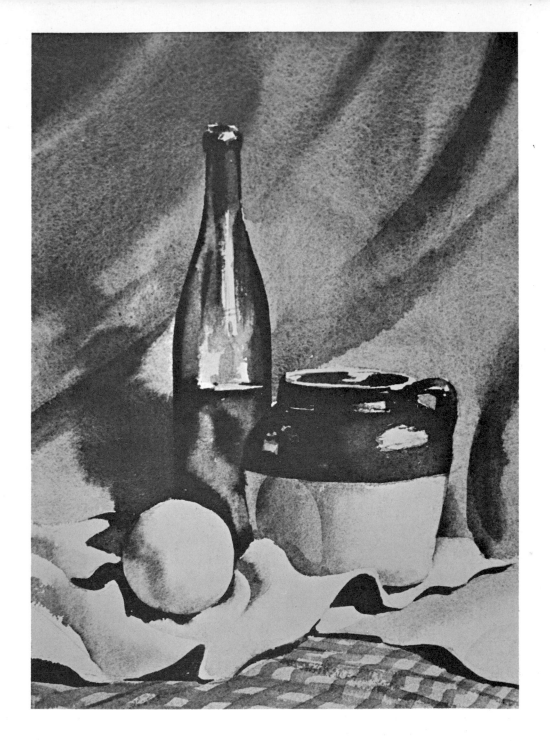

STAGE 7   I put in the rich, dark graded wash of the top portion of the bean pot, of course remembering to paint around the highlights. The plaid tablecloth is done with a ⅝″ flat brush, keeping in mind the contour of the wrinkles. Then I add the reflection of the orange on the shadow side of the bean pot. I model the dark side, add clear water to soften it, then do the right side with more clear water to blend around the curve of the pot.

10 Mountainous landscape: demonstration

My chief purpose in reconstructing "Chimborazo Volcano, Ecuador," is to demonstrate how to arrive at *hard* and *soft* edges in the same passage. Here, these edges are used mainly in the sky area; however, the same method can apply in countless ways. The idea isn't just to learn how to paint a sky, but how to control the medium so you can paint anything you wish.

First I brushed in clear water, down to the edge of the mountain and all across the sky area, with the exception of a little thin line of dry paper at the top of the cloud. I immediately dropped in the blues and the dark cloud underside, letting the wash take its own action.

In a situation like this, be sure to stay far enough back from your dry, thin line; if you add color too far up, the pigment will run up and form a hard edge where you want it soft. Do some practice exercises on scraps of watercolor paper. Find out what happens, how far the wash will flow before it takes hold. The entire answer to pulling off a good watercolor is in knowing the reasons *why*. That little dry line allowed me to have a hard or sharp top edge to my cloud, while at the same time, I kept a soft underside, and the color flowed into the areas both right and left.

The cloud shadow on the mountain is hard at the bottom, but soft as it enters the cloud. The underneath *must* be *dry*. Lay on clear water (your brush must be clean also or it will "rim") to the underside of the cloud and paint in the sharp shadows going *up* to the wet of the underside. From there, the wash will take its own form, which is one of the great charms of this medium. The same procedures are followed in "Hawaii, Shell Hunters" on page 105.

By the way, Ecuador is beautiful if you can stand the altitude. The two figures are walking by a pottery kiln, also used as an oven. The Indian lady is wearing a typical Andean bowler, or derby. If she were a chief's wife, she'd be wearing two—one on top of the other—as a symbol of rank. It's better than stripes.

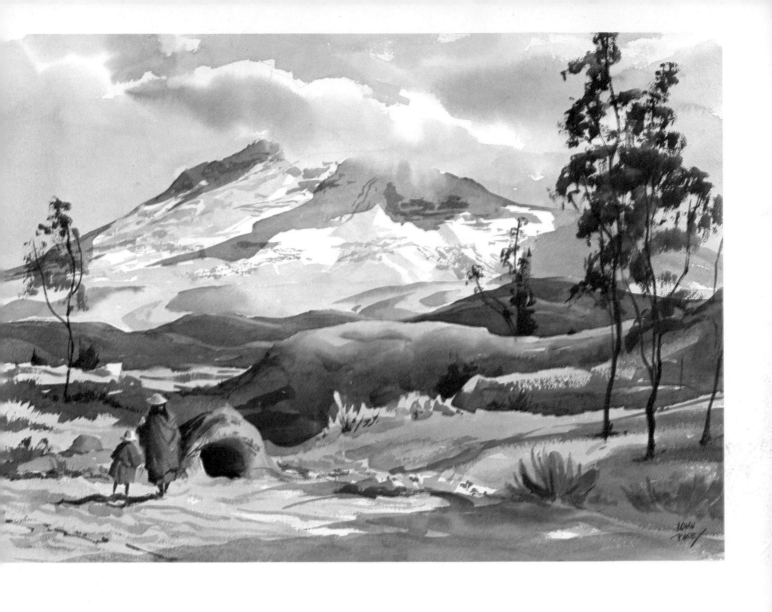

CHIMBORAZO VOLCANO, ECUADOR, 22" x 30"
Collection, General Tire International.

Pencil Sketch

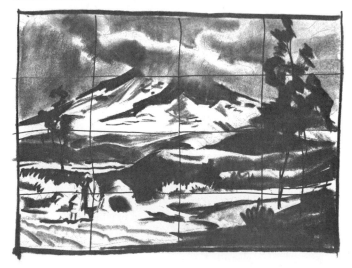

STAGE 1   After completing the sketch, I pencil in the outlines. My desire, here, is to paint the sky all in one pass and still retain a hard edge at the top of the cloud. This is accomplished by brushing clear water down to the edge of the mountain and all across the sky area, with the exception of a little, thin line of dry paper at the top of the cloud. While this is still very wet, I drop in the blue, letting it run to the edge of the dry paper line, then at once put in the dark underside of the cloud, letting the fluid color take its own action.

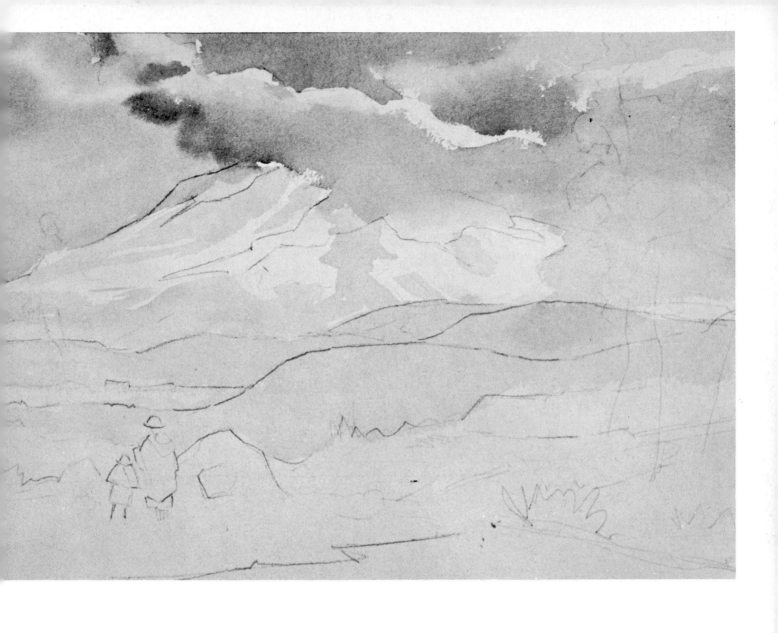

STAGE 2   A few of the basic color tints are added, to be textured and overpainted later.

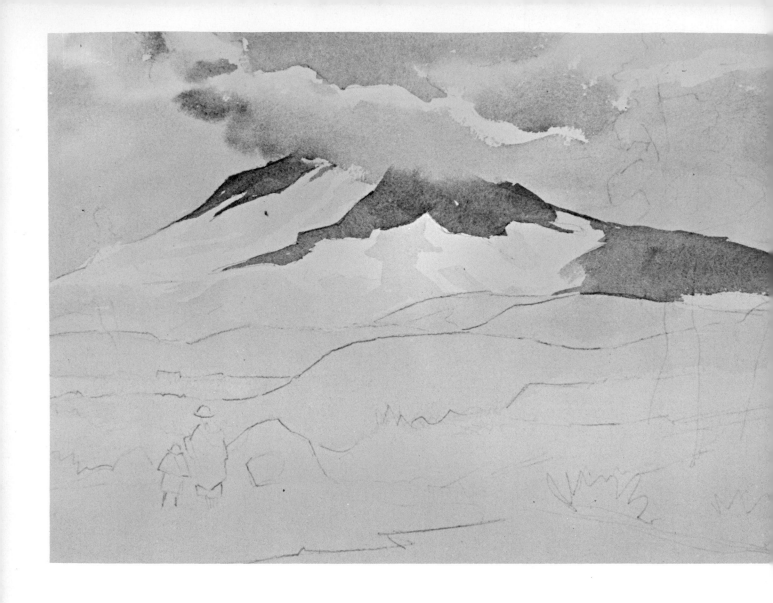

STAGE 3   This one is important. The cloud
shadow on the mountain is hard at the bottom,
but soft as it enters the cloud. The underpainting must be dry. I lay clear water over
the underside of the cloud. I then paint in the
sharp-edged shadows, bringing them *up* to the
wet underside. The color will take its own
shape at this point.

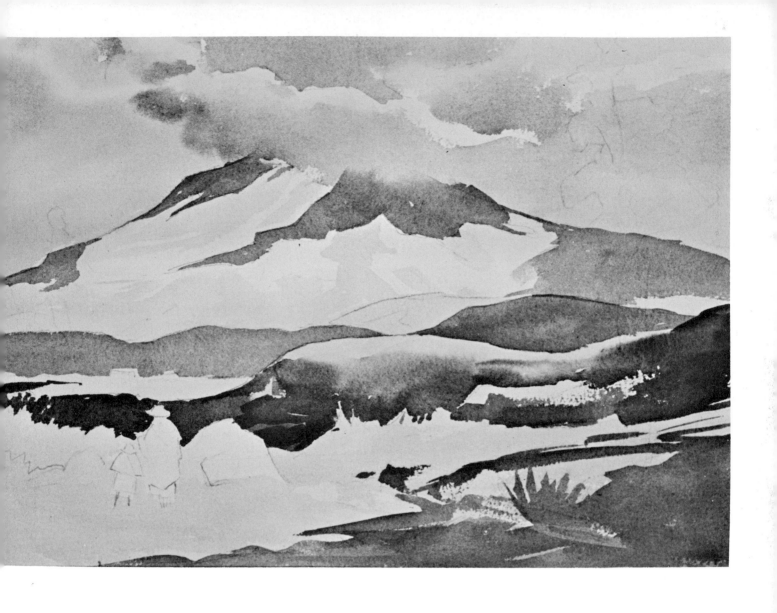

STAGE 4   The broad, dark areas of the middle and foreground are painted in, establishing my general value arrangement. On the rounded middle hill, I add clear water to soften the form. Note that I paint right through the trees. This can be done when the object to go on *top* is considerably darker than the wash underneath, if there's not too much color difference.

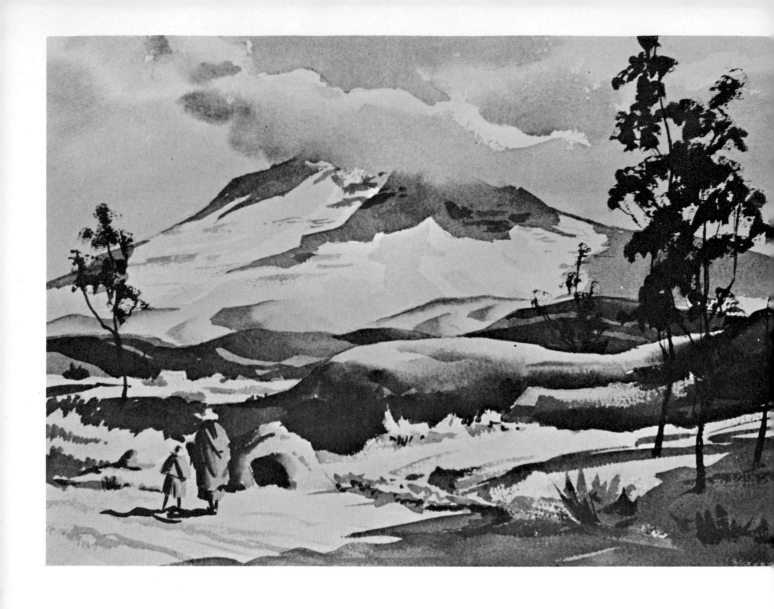

STAGE 5   In this final step, the trees are painted, using the brush as shown in the chapter on brushwork. I model the distant, rolling hills, remembering to soften the side toward the light source. There's a slight texture on the big mountain where the bare rock breaks through the snow. The two little figures and the oven come last.

11 Woods and snow: demonstration

I wandered through my woods for a good many years, looking for some way to make pictorial order out of chaos. In an opaque medium—like oil—it's not so difficult; we can always punch those sky holes on through with opaque color. But in transparent watercolor, how do we arrive at something fresh and clean, but still convey the feeling of all the "woods trash" that's there? There's the soft, springy bed of aromatic pine needles under our feet; the quiet; and the sharp tang of young fern and fungus on an old rotted stump. It's a charming sensation, but perhaps our eyes are too strongly influenced by our sense of smell. The question: is a subject like "Fox in Snow" paintable in watercolor?

It may seem mechanical, but about the only way I've found to paint a see-through woods picture in transparent watercolor is in the manner shown in this diagram. This isn't a formula—I don't believe in formulas—but simply an approach, a way to help you keep a crisp, clean painting. Vary the method to suit yourself. Use it as a starting point for your own thoughts.

Think of the subject as a theatrical stage with its cut-out pieces of scenery. The sky is your backdrop. The distant trees, back out in the far light, are cool in color, due to their distance. Even though you see very little of them in the finished painting, paint them in completely, in their silhouette form. Do the same as you come to the next, darker group, in under the shaded canopy or dome of the forest. All this time, you're painting around the shapes that are out in the light on the near side.

Put down the basic warm undertint on the big tree, and some of the broad shadows to help give the contour of the foreground. Continue with more shadows and a few accenting darks. You're coming into the home stretch: shaping, contouring, texturing; a sharp, dark cut here and there where

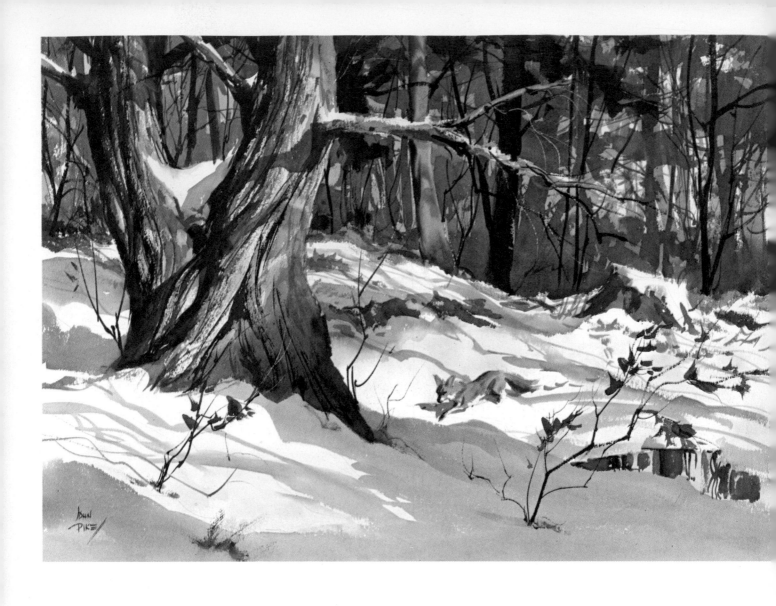

FOX IN SNOW, *22" x 30". Collection, General Tire International.*

needed; and down to the final little "fancies." Twigs, dry leaves, the pool of melting snow, darks to accent the fox, and there you have it.

This is *not* intended as a lesson in "how to paint the woods," but only an attempt to show how to analyze the procedure of painting *any* subject. In other words, what's the best way to go about transparent watercolor? Study it. Think it out most carefully. Then *hit it!*

If you want to have a wonderful experience on a painting trip in the woods, try this. Sit with your back against a tree. Get comfortable. If you're a gal, don't wear perfume; you lads, watch the shaving lotion. Don't smoke! Sit absolutely still; "twitchers" need not try. In about ten minutes, a wonder world of wild life will begin to appear. Chipmunks will run across your feet; red and gray squirrels will chase each other down the trees; birds of all kinds will come in for power landings; possibly a deer might graze by. If you're really rugged, try it on a moonlit night when the nocturnal club comes out. Skunks, raccoons, deer, porcupines, and owls are all members. Nothing will bother you if you don't startle it or (Heaven forbid) shoot at it. (Sadly, *man* is the only animal who kills for the love of killing.)

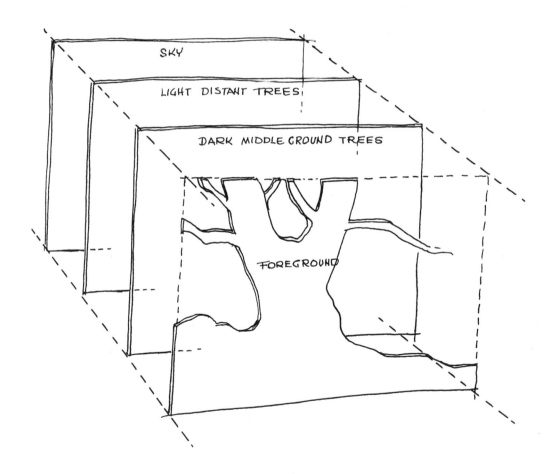

Diagram of Planes

Pencil Sketch

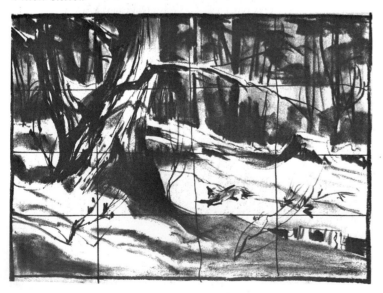

STAGE 1   After I've pencilled in my basic shapes, I lay in the cool sky wash over the entire dark woods area, as shown.

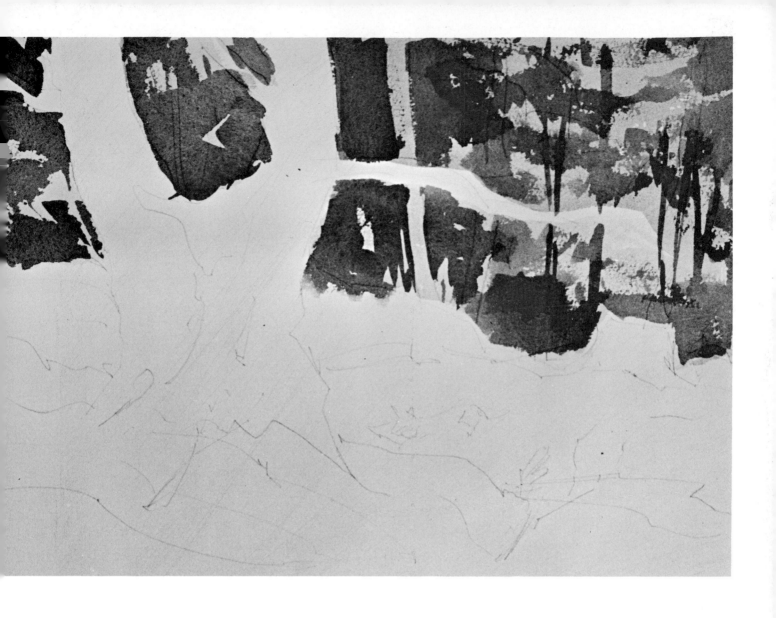

STAGE 2   Now I move away on through the distant trees and bushes, almost into the far light. Due to their distance and the atmosphere in between, they'll lean toward the cool side in color. This isn't always true, but for the sake of this demonstration, let's say they're cool. I paint in the entire silhouette. Little of this will show in the finished painting, but where it does, it will count properly.

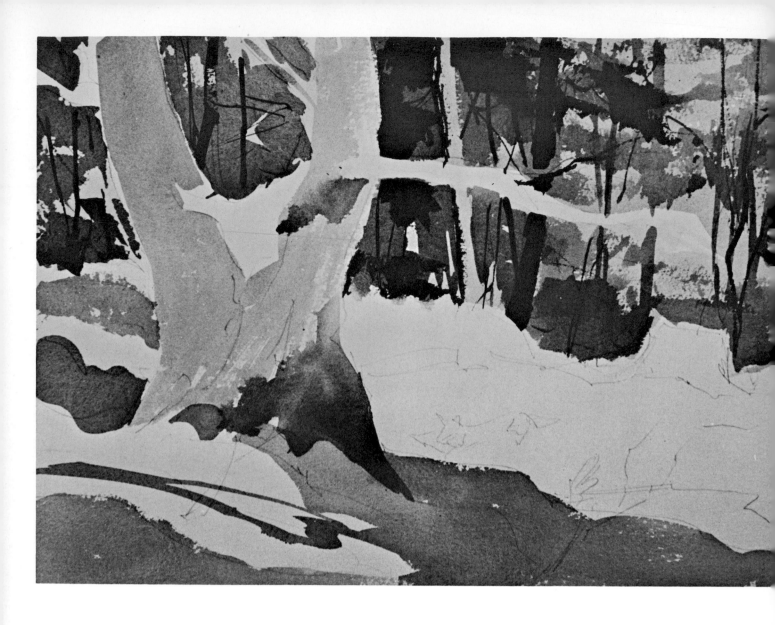

STAGE 3   Next, I put in the trees and trash
under the dark canopy of the big pines. Little
sunlight filters down, so they're much darker
in value. This also is painted quite completely
over the preceding color. All this time, I'm
painting around the tree and snowy foreground. At this stage, I put down a warm
undertint on the big tree, and some of the
broad, cool shadows to help create the contour of the foreground.

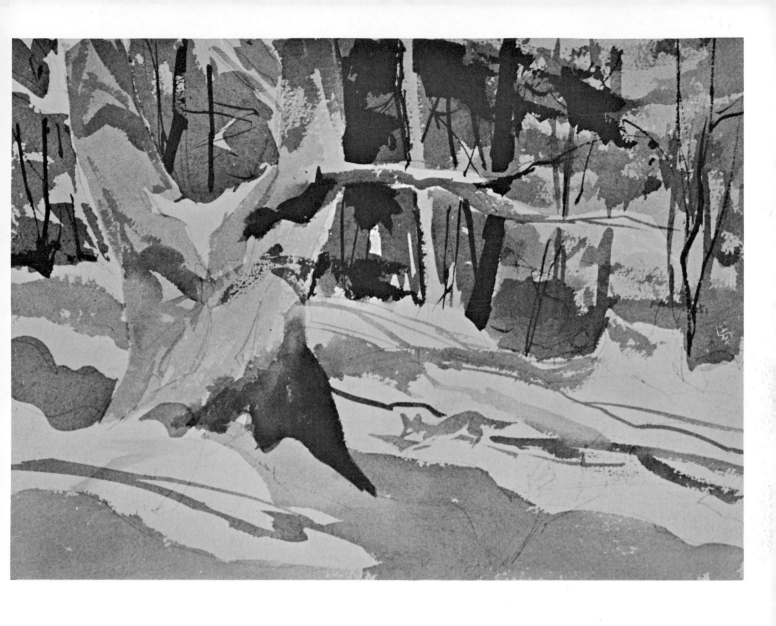

STAGE 4   Here I move forward to start shadowing and contouring the tree, as well as additional shadows across the middle ground. A touch of Burnt Sienna identifies the positioning of that beautiful pirate of the woodlands, Reynard Fox, Esq.

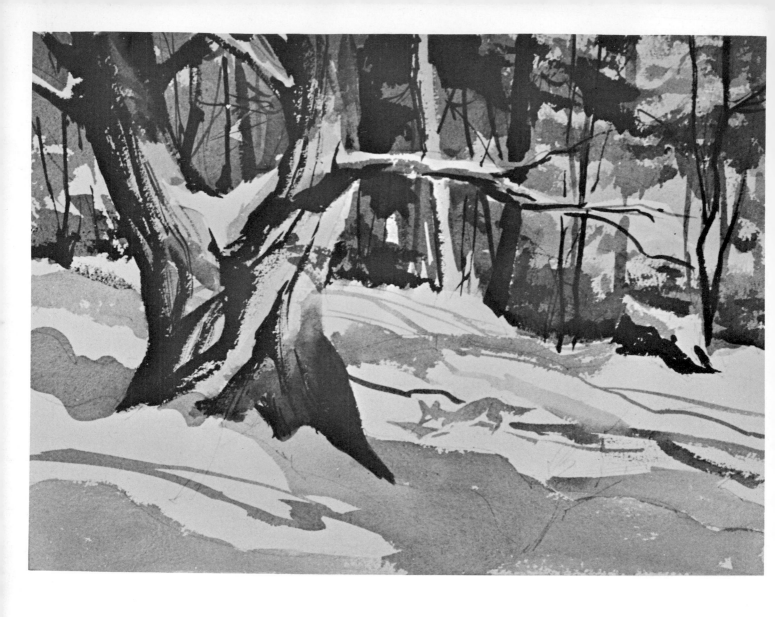

STAGE 5   In this step, I work in the dark
contouring textures of the big tree. This was
done in the manner shown in the section on
brushstrokes. The distant tree stump and a
few more ground bushes were added.

138

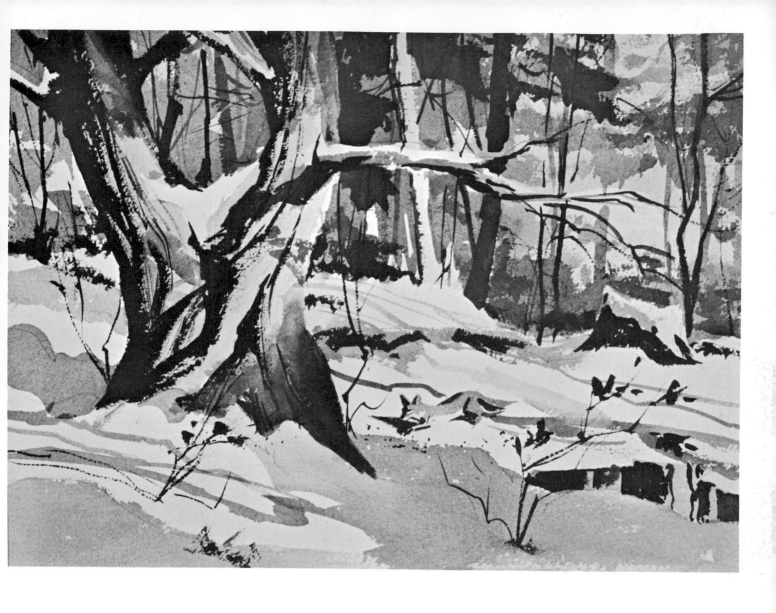

STAGE 6   Now is the time for my rigger. I play around with it and paint in all the small bushes and grass pushing through the snow. I add more little branches to the background. With a longer brush, I model and put in the shadows cast by the fox; the dark rocks breaking through the snow in the middle ground; the dried leaves on the bushes; and, last, the pool of melting snow, remembering what causes those reflections.

12 Woods, water, and figures: demonstration

"Breaking Camp" is a painting without a sky, yet you know that the sky is there by the sun, haloing the leaves of the foreground trees, and the blue sky reflections on the water.

The scene will look familiar to everyone who's ever done a day or two of camping and fishing. It could be an inlet of the great Mississippi, a Louisiana bayou, a small lake in New Hampshire or Maine, or a wide, still place in somebody's pet stream. Your clothes smell of wood smoke, fried fish, and Citronella, and you're tired; but what fun it's been!

I use "Breaking Camp" here to demonstrate large, simple patterns, and the need to study them well before the start of the painting. Also significant is the soft, wet value transition of the water.

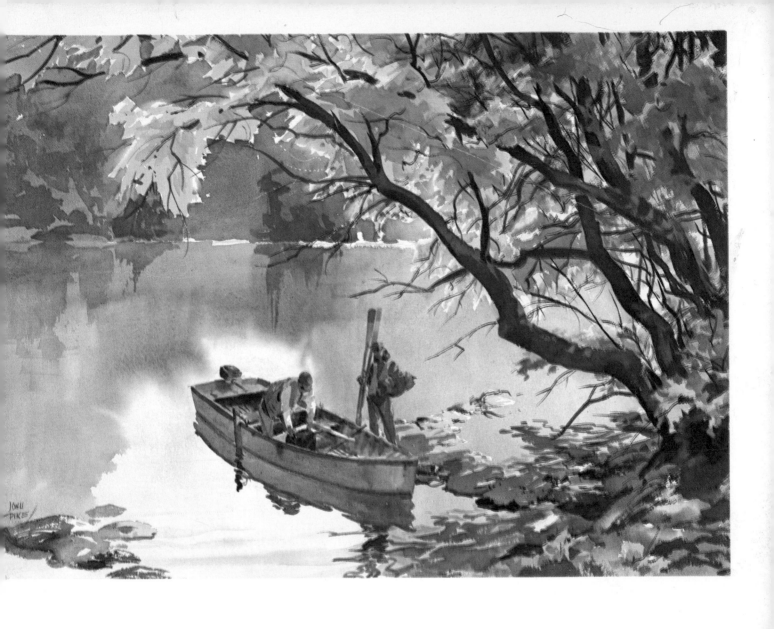

BREAKING CAMP, *22" x 30". Courtesy*
Osborne, Kemper, Thomas.

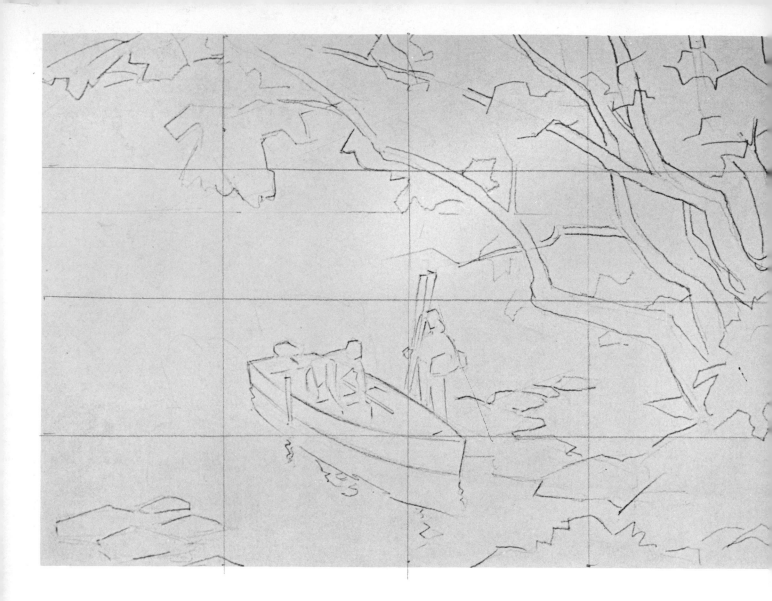

Pencil Sketch

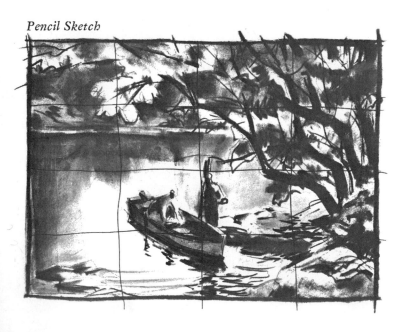

STAGE 1   "Breaking Camp" is a side and back lighted painting where the sunlight filters through the leaves of the trees. A pale yellow wash is put over all the leaf area to create warmth, as well as to create a foundation for the greens, which are rendered later in the process. This yellow doesn't show in the black and white photograph, but it's there. You really see only the drawing.

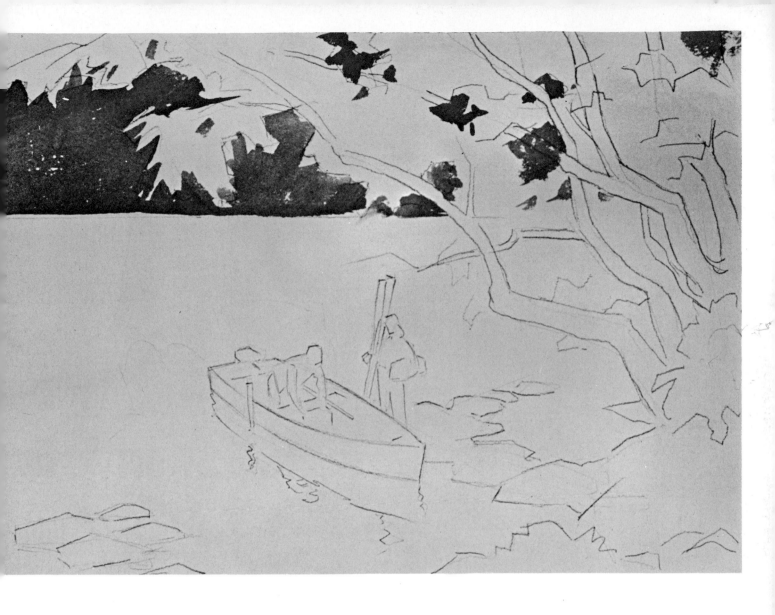

STAGE 2 The dark background of the far trees is cut in around the overhanging tree—to begin to give it shape and form—leaving the light yellow area. This is the time when design and patterning sense come into play. Such a direct statement, with the whole painting hanging on its success, must be thought out most carefully in advance. This picture again emphasizes the great value of the preliminary planning sketch. Make the pencil or crayon sketch your thinking and designing area, so you'll know exactly what you wish to say when you get to that big, white "moment of truth."

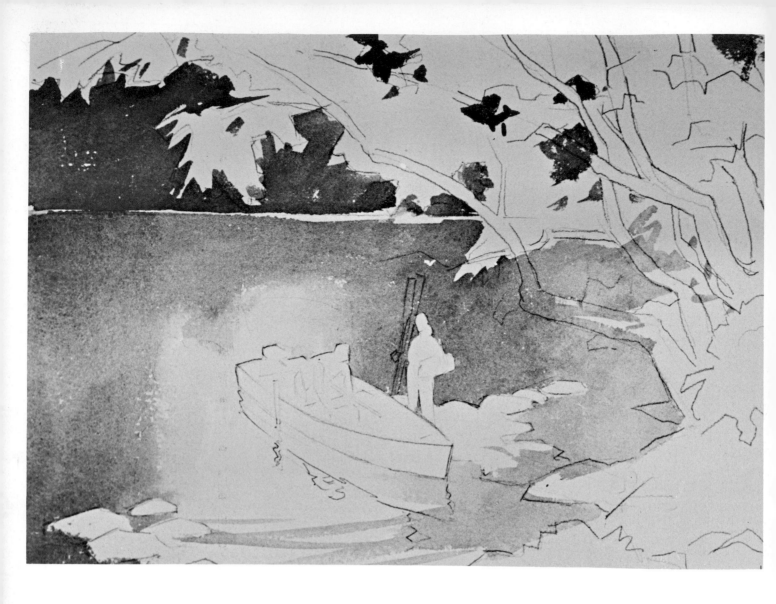

STAGE 3   I lay in a light blue wash over the water. (You can paint around or mask out the figures and rocks, as you wish.) I then come back in with darker pigment, very rapidly, to give the distant shore reflections down to the bottom of the picture. Don't waste any time at a moment like this, or you'll find a group of hard edges just where you want them soft.

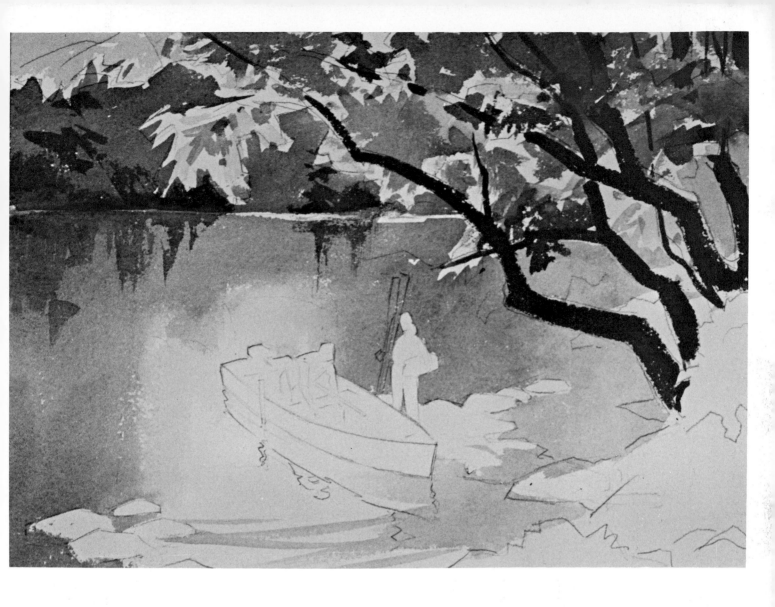

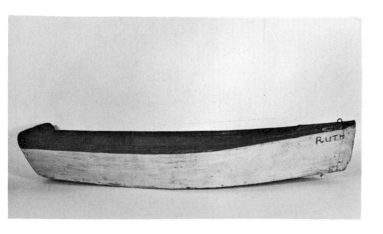

STAGE 4 Light and dark green rendering is added over the near foliage, remembering the effect of the yellow underpainting on the final color. The tree trunks are roughed in for form, as well as the underpainting of the figures, the rocks, boat, and foreground trash.

The little boat is a model of a Maumee River skiff, made for me in 1916 by Grandfather Pike. The proportions are perfect; in my many years of illustration, I've used it as a model many times. I used it in this painting as well. When the model isn't in service, it hangs, as a decoration, on my studio wall.

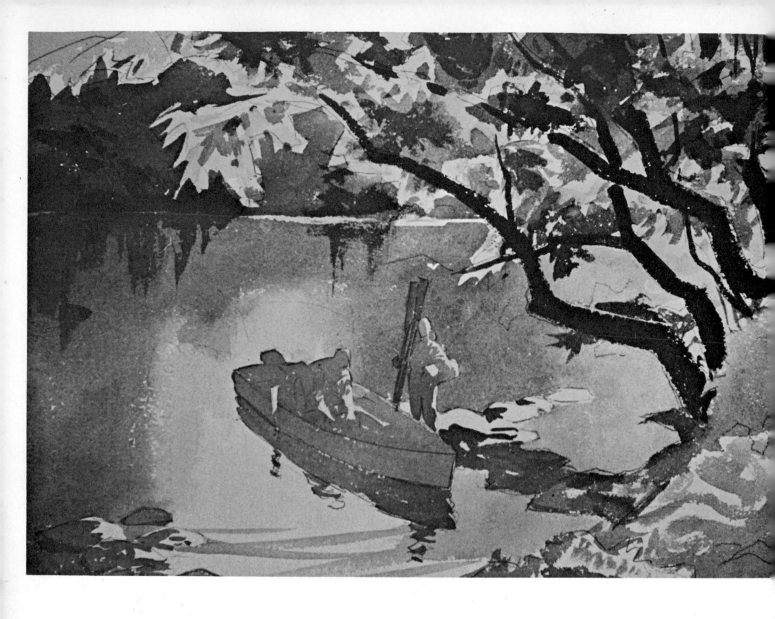

STAGE 5   I add the underpainting of the
figures, rocks, boat, and foreground trash.
Certain areas of the figures are untouched by
the dark wash to indicate the direction of the
light. Reflections are added beneath the boat.

146

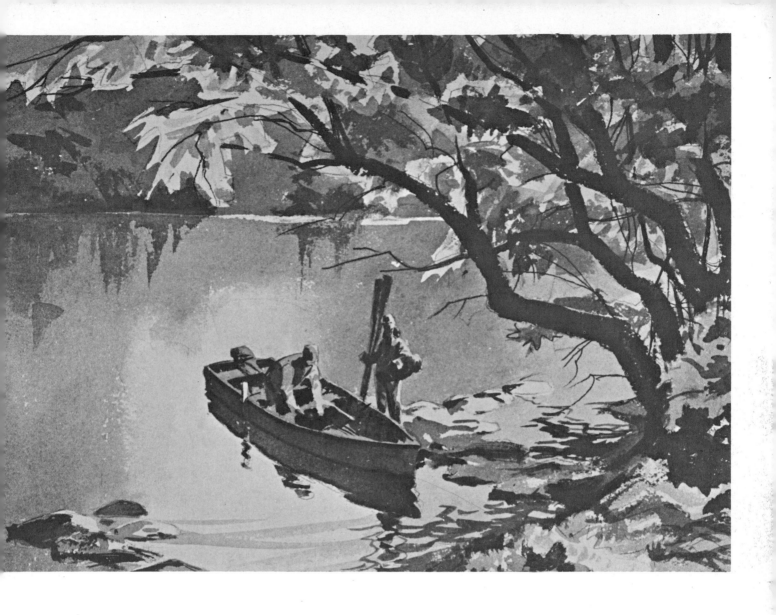

STAGE 6　The final step is the finishing: rendering the figures, the details on the boat, the texture of the rocks and foreground, as well as the little incidental branches. This is the time to review the whole effort, accenting here and there where needed, to achieve the proper over-all balance in the painting.

147

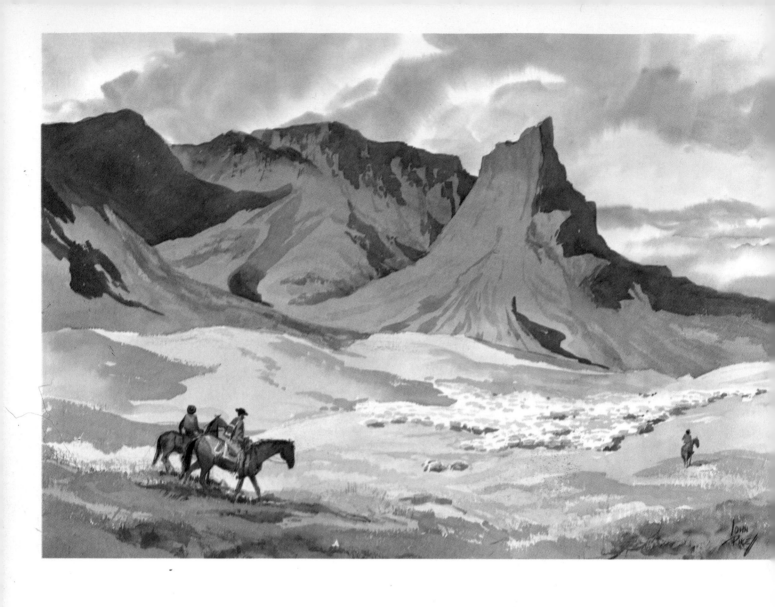

CHILEAN PATAGONIA, 22″ x 30″. Collection, General Tire International.

13 Mountains, sky, and figures: demonstration

"Chilean Patagonia" is really a painting with two main values; the sky and middle ground are the lighter value, and the dark sweep of the mountains and immediate foreground are the dark values.

The clouds in the sky and the texturing of the middle ground all contribute to a big, over-all light value, just as the texturing adds to the mountain darks.

Learn to see in the big, broad value terms.

Southern Chile is one of the largest sheep raising areas in the world, possibly the largest.

The gentleman who bought this watercolor inspected it in silence. Nothing had been said about what was represented by the white area in the right middle ground. He looked very closely at the spots of paint that make up the illusion of a flock. He stepped back, looked again, and said, "From those blobs, how do I know they're sheep?" Then, quietly: "But I guess I do."

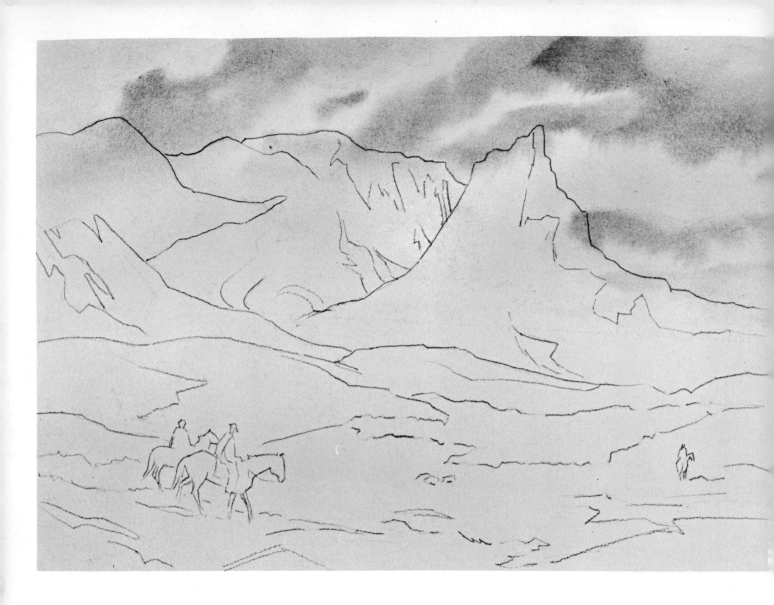

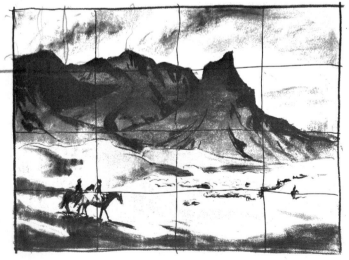

Pencil Sketch

STAGE 1   In the first stage of "Chilean Patagonia," I sketch in the drawing, taking care to outline my large shadow areas, which are so important to the depth and modeling of my far hills. I feel that I can, at the same time, put in my one and only pass at the clouded sky. Now, since the mountains are considerably darker than the sky, I allow the sky to get lost in the mountain tops (rather than paint around). This is done by putting clear, clean water over the entire upper half of my paper, then dropping in the pigment to create the cloud effect. In the mountain area, the wash simply fades off to nothing.

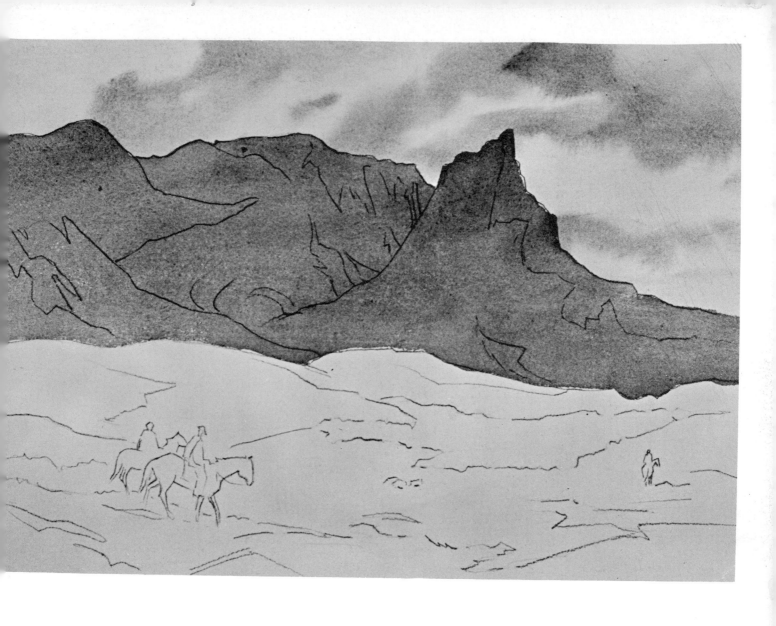

STAGE 2   Over the entire back mountains, I lay a flat, medium dark wash of the correct color and value, with no attempt to model at this time. Notice how it completely covers the bottom of clouds as they fade into the mountain area.

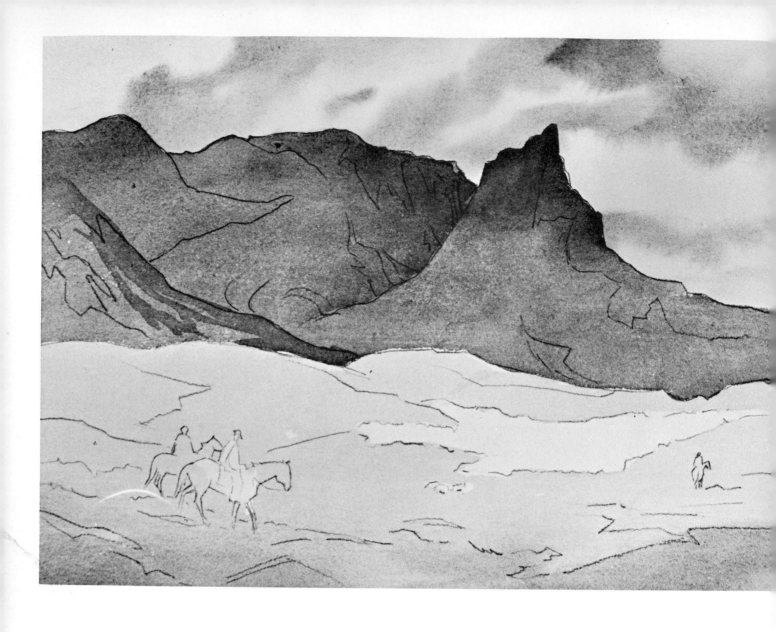

STAGE 3 Since the mountain wash has dried, I can go back in and start the modeling that will give the mountains shape and form. I also put in the broad underpainting (blue greens and yellow greens) of the distant fields and foreground, being careful to leave the white paper for my herd of sheep, as well as for the highlights on the mounted figures at the left.

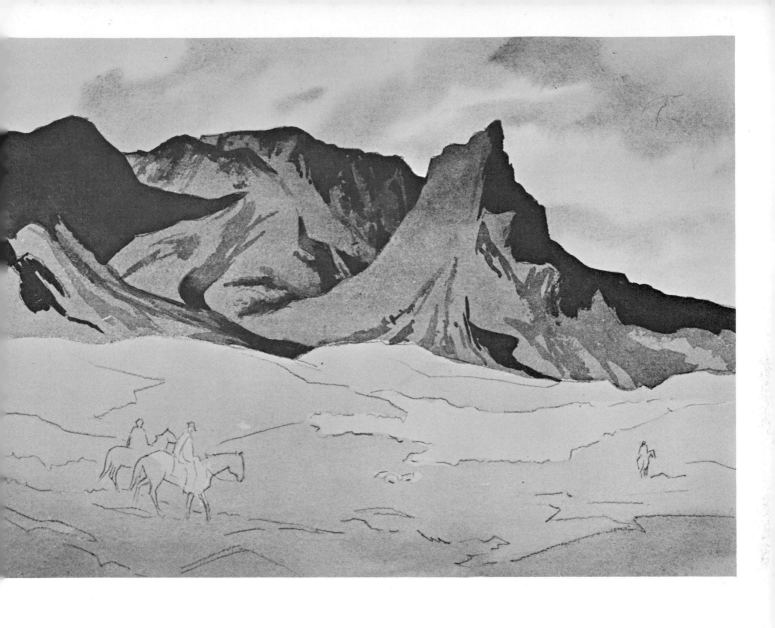

STAGE 4   In this step, I pretty much finish
up the modeling of the mountains, having
come in with the very dark areas. Some of the
areas are softened with clear water as they
round from the shadow sides to the sunny.

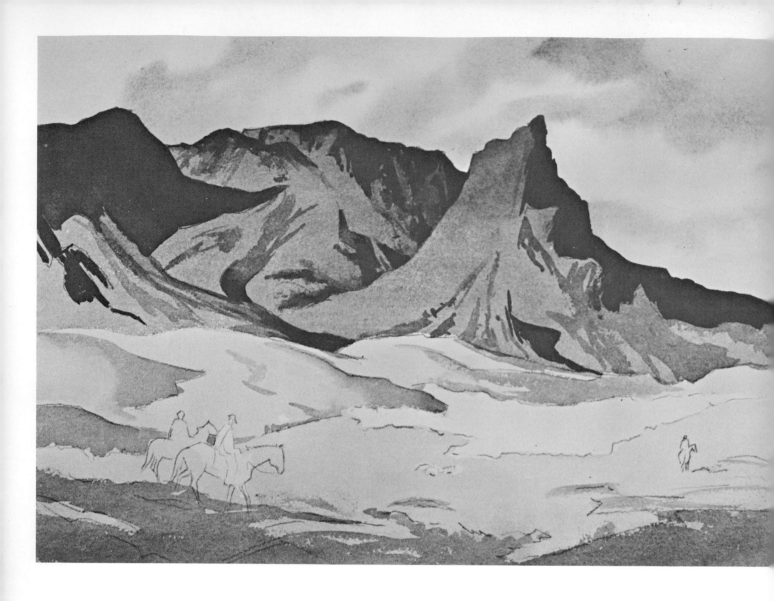

STAGE 5   I begin the shaping and contouring of the rolling plains, always softening the edge with clean water *toward* the light source, the sun. In go the dark foreground shadows that contribute so much to pushing back the middle areas, distant mountains, and sky. This effect creates the feeling of distance. The shadows are part of the fun of painting in mountain country. Where you have mountains, you have clouds; and where you have clouds, you have dramatic shadows. There's nary man nor boy who can argue with you about where you put the shadows. As the great Baron Munchausen said, "Vas *you* there, Charlie?"

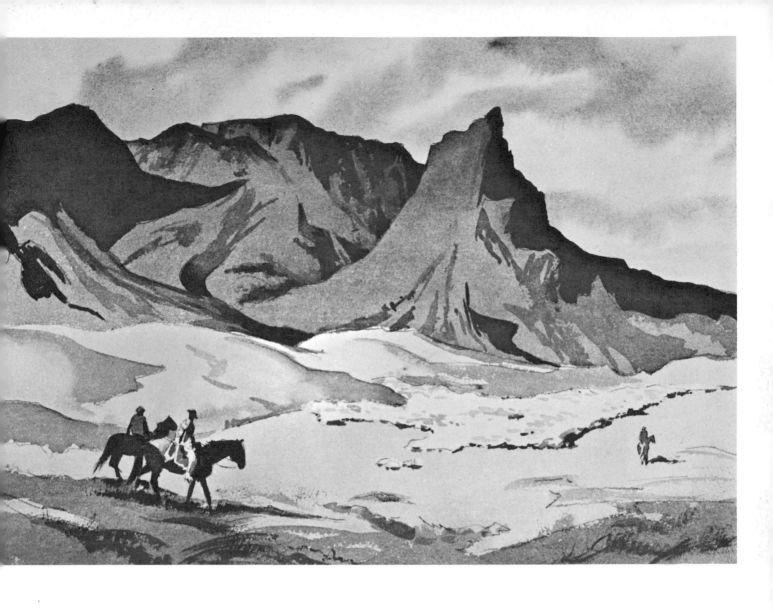

STAGE 6   Here I put in the finishes: the definition of the sheep by the darks and cast shadows underneath, and the slight graying blobs over their backs. I develop the three mounted shepherds and rough up the plains grass in the foreground to give identity to the simple handling of the middle ground plains.

14 Architecture in landscape setting: demonstration

"Torre de Belem on the Tagus, Portugal" was one of the historically famous spots from which men of great courage and dedication took off into the unknown. (In that day, I think it took more guts than brains, considering the quality of the ships they flung into the wild Atlantic!) The entire Portuguese court came to this spot to bid farewell to the great explorer, Vasco da Gama, a great and brave man.

In my mind's eye, I can see myself straining forward from the crow's nest, shouting in triumph, "Land ho! The New World!" But, in honesty, had I been a Portuguese at the time of Vasco, I would probably have found myself on the far side of the country, fixing a broken wagon wheel for a neighbor—or playing a guitar in the local bistro.

This demonstration combines a variety of elements, all of them challenging to the watercolorist: the intricate forms of historic architecture; distant landscape; water; trees; and moving figures. The rendering of light and texture is particularly tricky here.

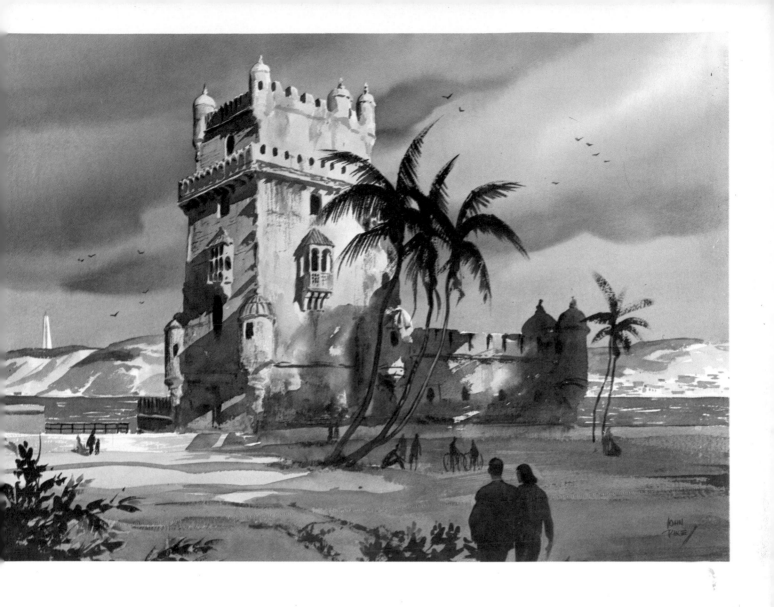

TORRE DE BELEM ON THE TAGUS, PORTUGAL,
*22" x 30". Collection, General Tire
International.*

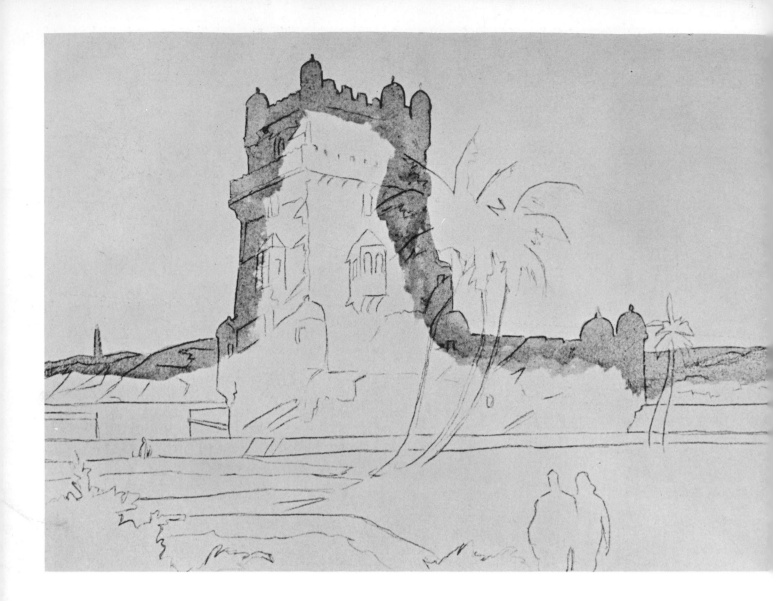

Pencil Sketch

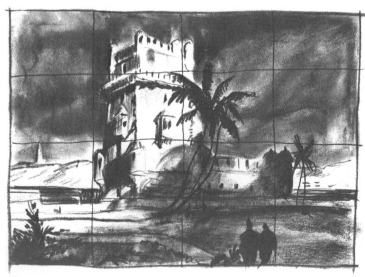

STAGE 1   Due to the rather intricate architectural features of this structure, I want to
keep a large, simple movement in the sky, so
the resultant whole wouldn't become too
busy. I want to make the sky in one big
sweep, so I decide to use a masking-out or
liquid frisket on the tower details. This frisket
is the dark you see in the photo.

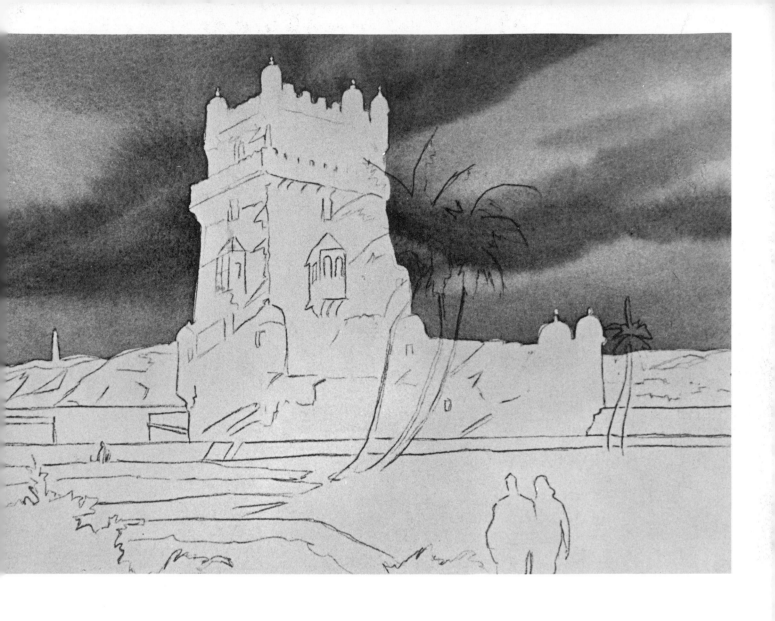

STAGE 2   I paint in the sky. After it's completely dry, I remove the rubber frisket, leaving my sketch and the pure white paper.

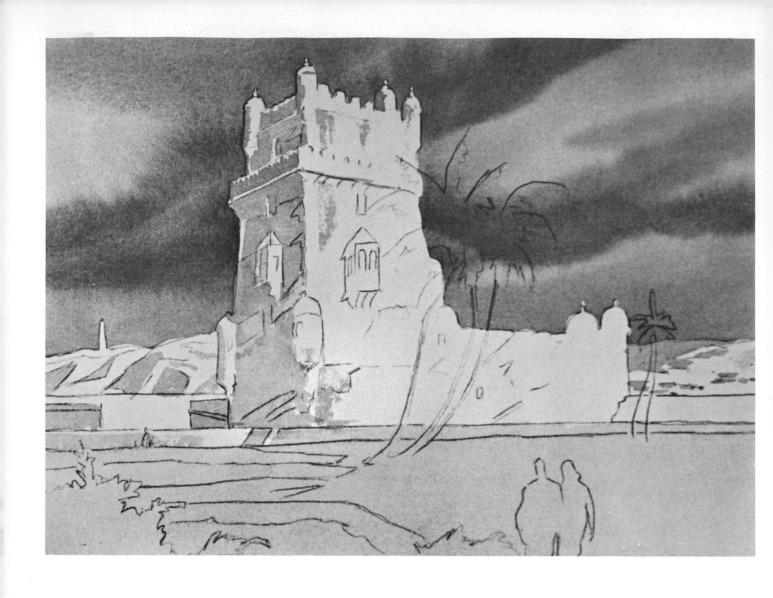

STAGE 3   I put in the warm underpainting of the building, the yellow-greens of the foreground, as well as the first modeling of the distant hills. These are all in pale tones, very transparent, so I can work and develop their textures a bit later.

160

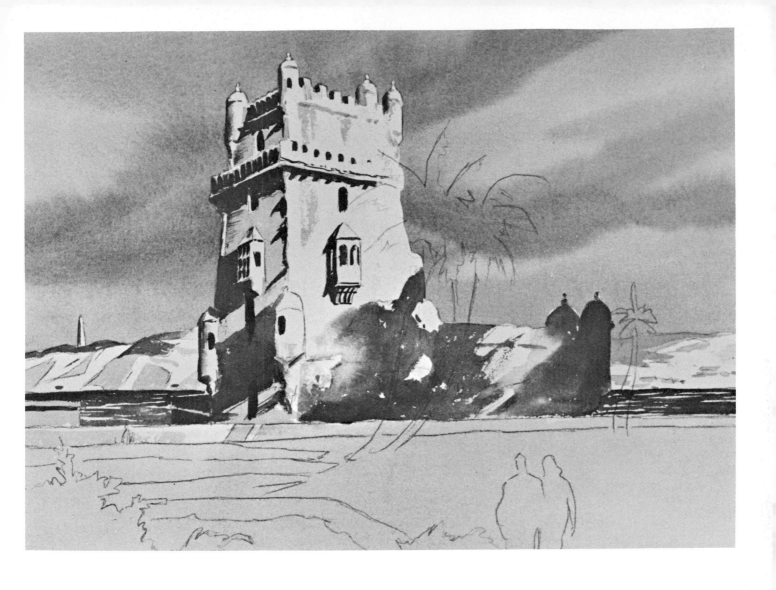

STAGE 4   Notice the half cast light on the left hand side of the building. It's still in sun-light, but isn't receiving the full rays of the sun, unlike the flat side nearest us. It's a sort of cross light, so I've taken it down in tone. On top of this, I add the elongated shadows. The distant hills need the darks of the top vegetation, and the deep blue-grays of the river all add to the result.

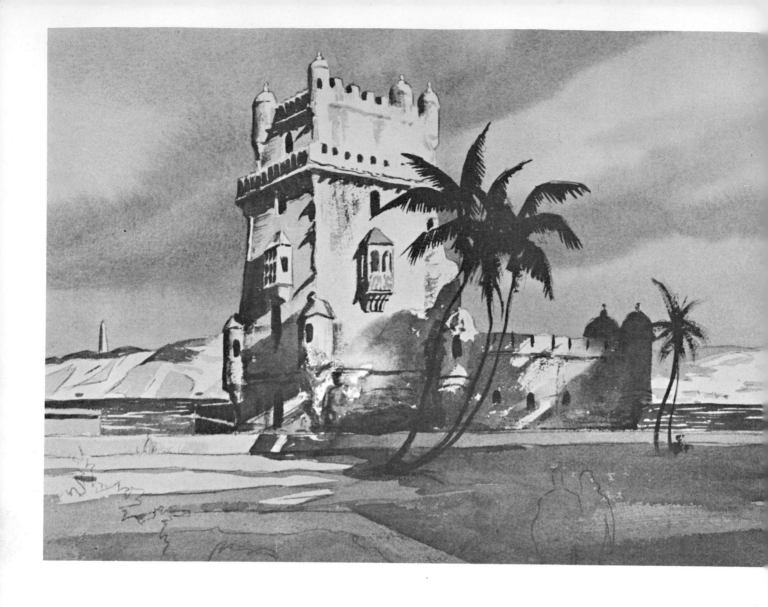

STAGE 5   The antique textures of our beautiful structure, the sweeping shadows across the foreground, plus the rendering of this strange type of palm tree are added.

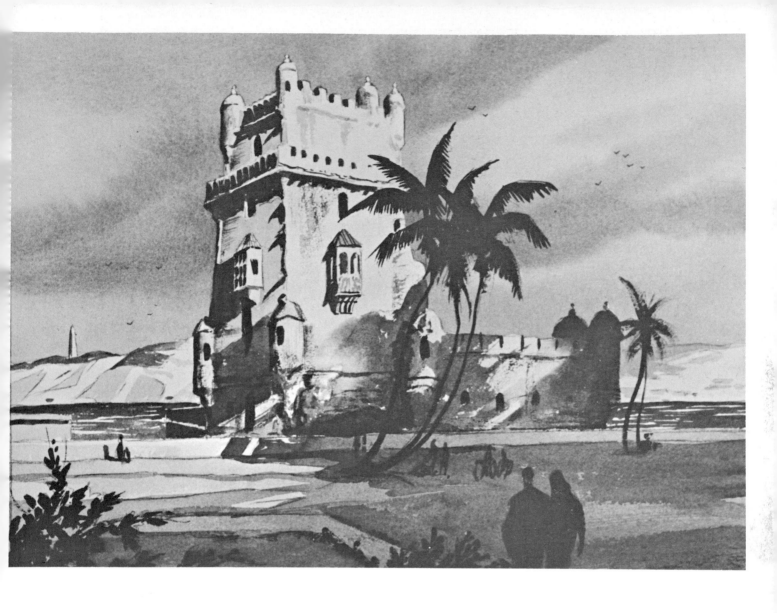

STAGE 6 At this point, I've pretty well established all of my values and the painting holds together. So now I add the kids under the trees with their bicycles, the lovers walking hand in hand in the right foreground, and a few little bushes and twigs to round out the composition.

15 *Low key landscape: demonstration*

This watercolor has a rather nostalgic quality for me. From my earliest memories, this time of day and year have always held both sad and delightful thoughts. Summer is over and from beyond the mountain comes the remote feel of frost. There is a stillness in the air that allows the smoke to go straight up. Tired from an afternoon's play and work (in my youth we all had our little jobs) we burst into the lighted house. A loving pat on the head, delicious warm smells from the kitchen—what luxury! And not a TV antenna in sight!

I reconstruct "Suppertime" here for two reasons: to show the handling of a *low key* or dark value painting; and to show how to mask out certain areas without making the effect look too contrived.

There's nothing as fresh as the white of your paper, even if it's retained by a lowly "trick" like masking. There are times when the need to keep an area clean would be defeated by the painting-around process. Going around these tiny lights might possibly make you slow up just enough to cause drying rings and mud. So I covered the vital spots with one of the many masking or frisket materials that are on the market. One simple method is to cut out a bit of masking tape or drafting tape, press it onto the watercolor paper, paint right over it, then peel it off, leaving the protected spot fresh and white. You can also brush on a dab of rubber cement, paint over the dry cement, then rub it off with a finger tip.

But please don't use a masking agent as a crutch. It's far better to paint around a white area if you possibly can do it, and much more satisfying too.

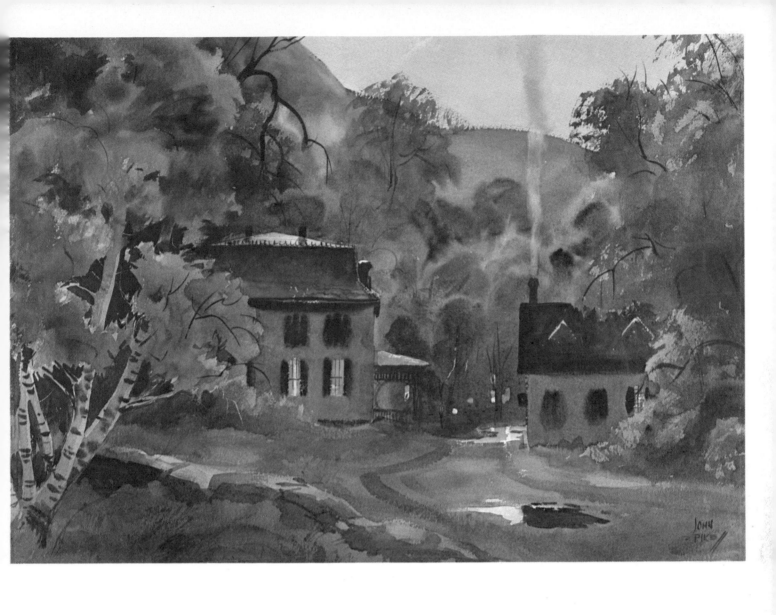

SUPPERTIME, *22" x 30". Collection,
General Tire International.*

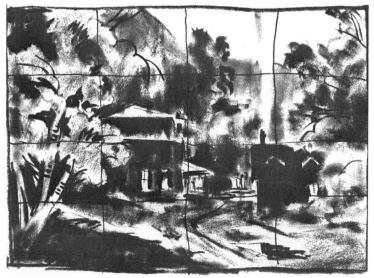

Pencil Sketch

STAGE 1 After composing carefully in my preliminary sketch—and being satisfied that it's the effect I'm looking for—I scale the sketch up to my watercolor paper. This illustration shows only the pencil outlines and the gray masking agent. The masking agent is colored gray so it will be visible on the white paper. This mask or *frisket* is liquid and is applied with a brush. Wash out the brush immediately after use. Some manufacturers suggest working a little soap into the wet brush *before* dipping into the liquid frisket. Masking or drafting tape may be cut to size and pressed into position; or a strip may be put on and cut around with a sharp knife, then the surplus peeled up. Tread lightly on this one. If you use tape, run the flat of your fingernail all around the edges to press it down so the paint won't bleed under.

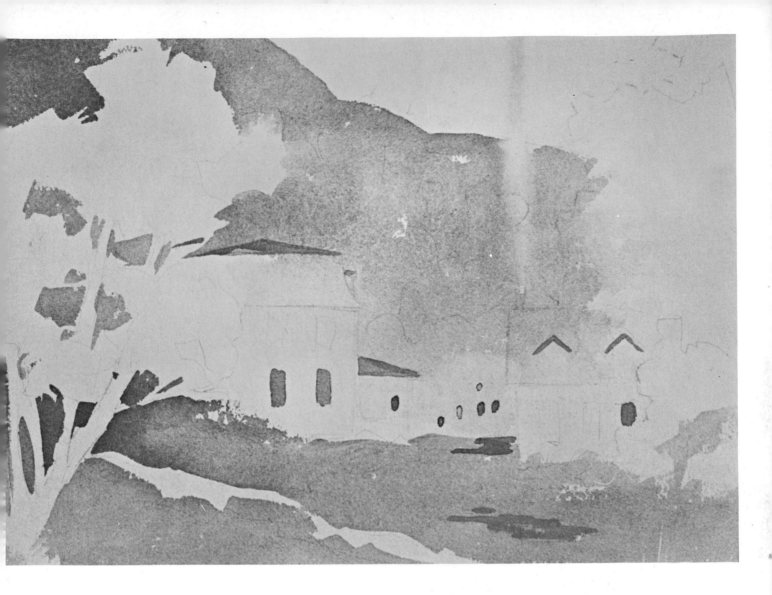

STAGE 2   The warm sky is put in and *lost* in the mountain area by the addition of clear water, faded off so as not to leave a hard edge. Where you have a dark value coming over a lighter one, always do this fade off. In this way, you avoid pigment buildup. For instance, if I bring the warm sky just to the edge of my blue mountain, then come in with the blue, I'd have a dark line (compound buildup) *every place* they overlap (no matter how hard I try to prevent it). This would completely defeat the feeling of distance, as I want *all my darks* in the middle and foreground areas. Now I put in the blue of the mountain, first touching the area of the smoke with a fairly broad band of clear water so it will be soft when I paint around it. At the same time, I come on down with a grayer color over most of the painting, beginning to establish its dark over-all value.

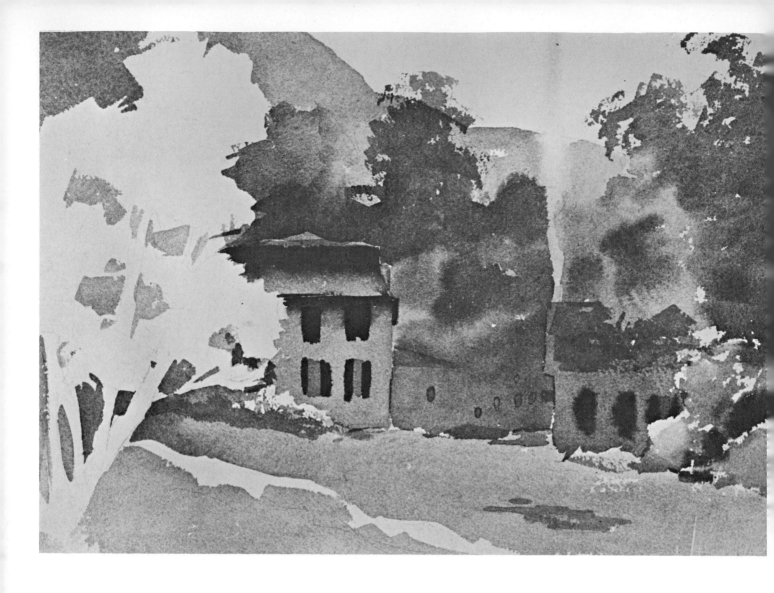

STAGE 3   I begin the detail of the buildings
and background, pretty much establishing their
final value relationship to the rest of the painting. I'm leaving the birches at this point so I
may think out how much darker I should
make them, relative to the rest of the painting.
Note that the masking is still on and I've been
painting over it. However, after the watercolor is absolutely dry, the mask is removed
before I go on to Stage 4.

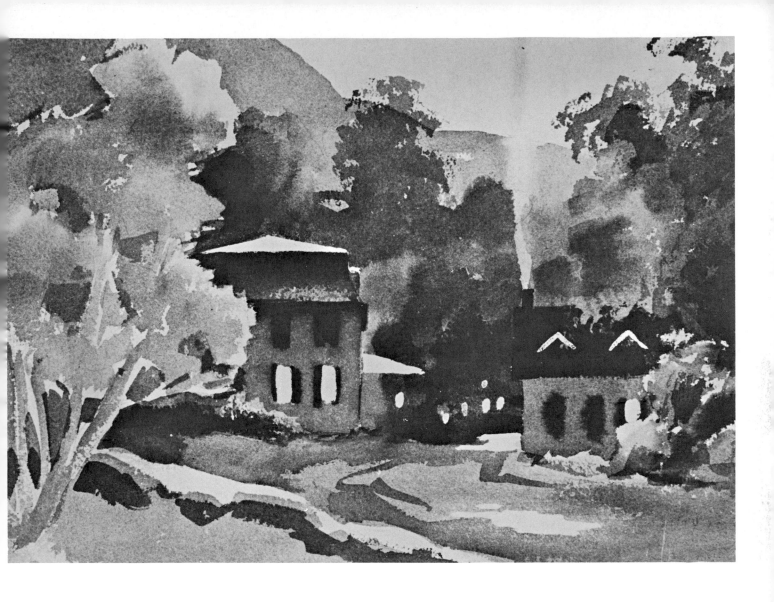

STAGE 4   Now that the mask has been removed, I can see value relationships more
clearly: the lightness of the sky, the rooftop,
and the lighted windows in relation to the
darks of the far and middle trees, and the
foreground. I put a tone over the clump of
birches at the left, and start to model them,
adding further darks in the distant trees above
the house and the porch. Then I add texture
to the large trees on the right. Clear water
is used in spots to soften a dark edge here and
there. I put in a dark wash over the roof of
the right hand house, painting around the
hanging leaves of the tree.

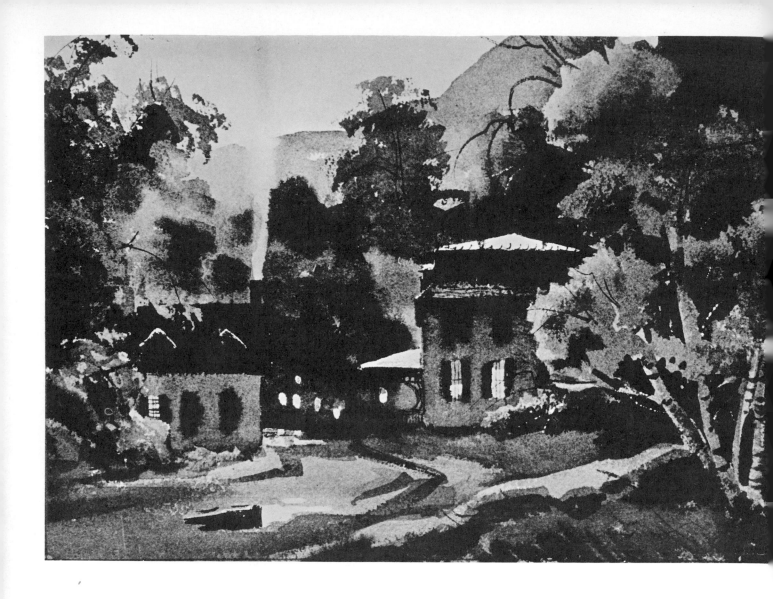

STAGE 5 All the large, basic values have been established, so now comes the fun of frosting the cake. First, a little more texture in the birch foliage and the stripes on the trunks. Now, general over-all texturing of the road and the left foreground grass. Then, the dark puddle reflections, the warm lights in the windows. Now, with one of my riggers, I put in the lacy scrollwork of the porch, the iron trim along the upper edge of the mansard roof, the crossbars in the windows and, finally, the twigs and small branches on the trees. All these little touches give character and interest, but it's the *big* value masses that make the painting.

16 *Winter landscape: demonstration*

Woodstock—the name of a little town away up the Hudson River in the heart of the Catskill Mountains, the town where I live. Unhappily, a name that has become famous the world over, synonymous with rock music, wild festivals, pot-smoking youth on a rampage, and "sin." (The last is pretty evenly spread around the globe.) Strange, because so little of it actually happened in Woodstock—they just borrowed our name.

Ah me, the swinging, raucous young have been with us generation after generation (I have an excellent memory), ever since we dropped from the trees and moved into the caves, and they will no doubt continue to be with us far into the distant future. But Woodstock, with its silent hills and snow-laden hemlocks and pines, will always stand high above any small unpleasantness far below. This is the Woodstock we love.

I used the word "silent." Did you ever observe a flock of crows resting quietly in the forest? Away, way up at the very top of the tallest pine sits the clown look-out who can't resist pushing the "panic button"—just for the hell of it!

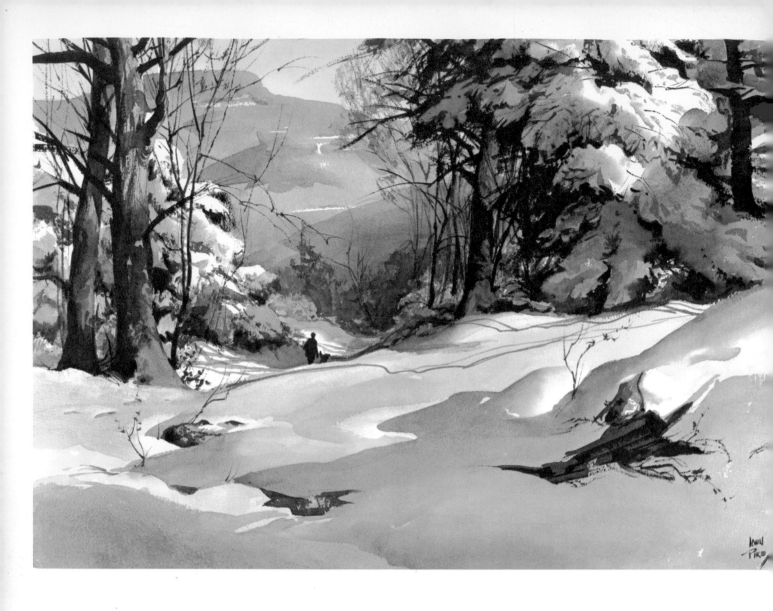

WOODSTOCK WINTER, 22" x 30".
Collection, General Tire International.

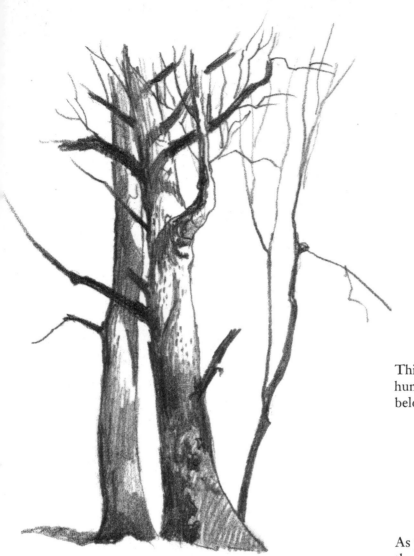

This thumbnail sketch of trees is one of many hundreds I've made. It was used in the sketch below.

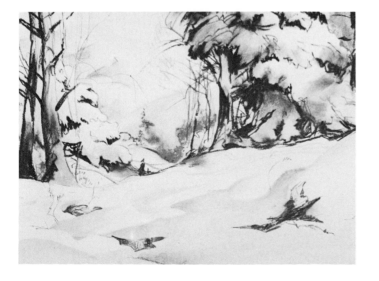

As you wade out into the fluffy snow to make the preliminary sketches for your painting, the first reaction to what you're seeing is dazzling white, blue, and spotty darks. If the landscape is flooded with sunlight, you're not far wrong. However, there are great subtleties in those blues. Study them carefully.

Learning to *see* is an art in itself. One can see the same subject in several ways. Example: you *drive* down a wooded country road and the lacy tree patterns are silhouetted against the sky. A rabbit runs across and disappears. You *walk* down that same road and the beautiful tree patterns are there, but in addition you see the bark textures of the big tree trunks with their moss and lichen, the soft undergrowth, the dead leaves and pine needles nestled among the rocks—*and* you have the fun of seeing where the rabbit went!

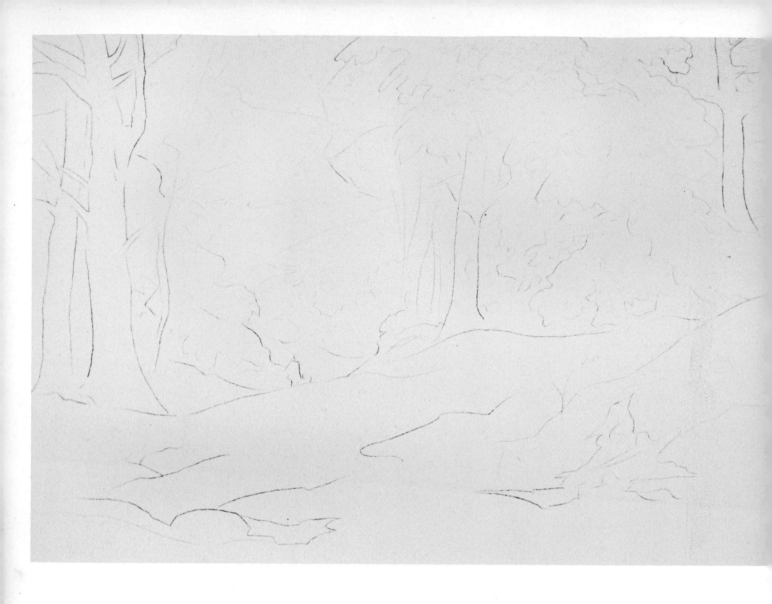

STAGE 1   Here is the simple pencil drawing
—for proper proportions and layout—scaled
up from the preliminary sketch. Speaking of
pencils, for drawing on watercolor paper I
find the average "advertising" pencils—you
know, the free ones from your insurance man,
the lumber company, etc.—are just about
right. They are usually No. 2 pencils, not too
hard and not too soft or smudgy.

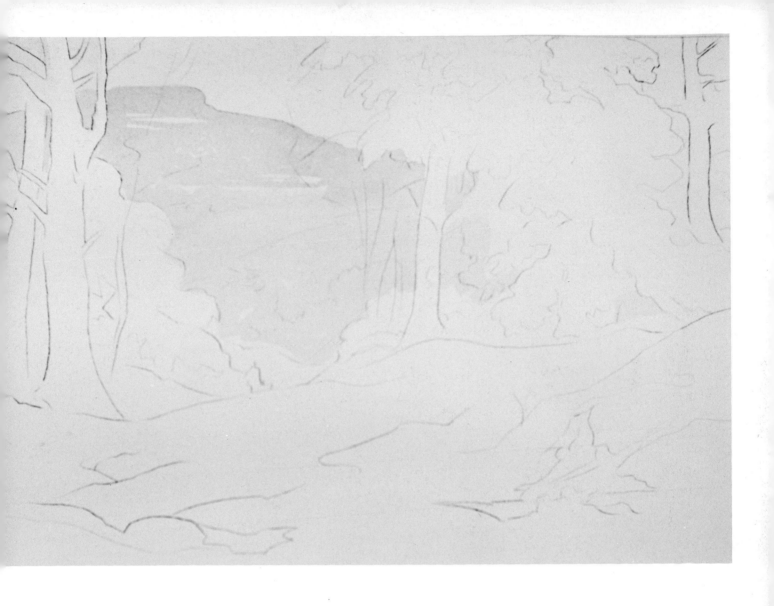

STAGE 2   No masking in this one. I put in
the blue-green sky and "lose" it in the upper
part of the mountain. By "lose," I mean that
I fade out the color by adding water, getting
rid of any hard edges and producing a "lost"
effect. When the sky area dries, I put in the
light brown-pink of the mountain.

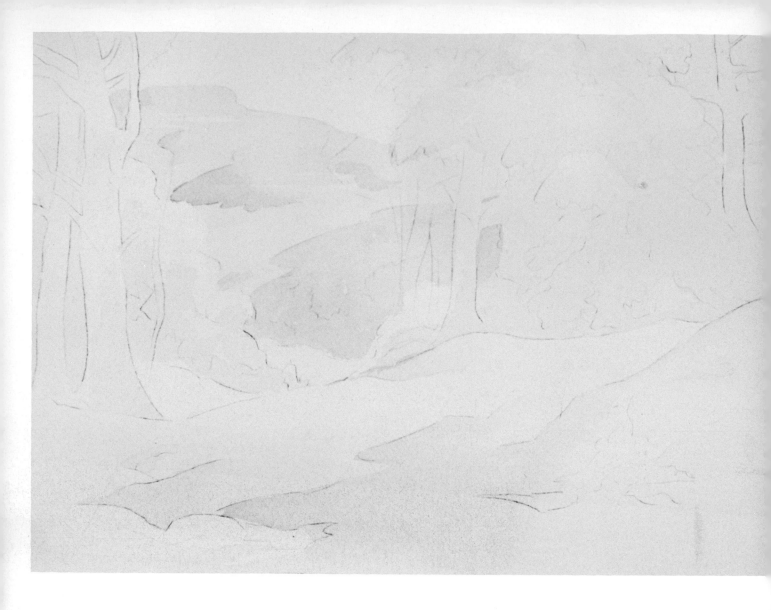

STAGE 3   I paint in the shadows on the mountains and model the snow on the trees with a blue-gray made with ultramarine blue and burnt sienna. Then I lay a pale, flat wash over entire middle and foreground, leaving the white paper in the spots you can see in the finished painting. When the wash is dry, I wash in the long foreground shadows, always keeping in mind where my light is coming from.

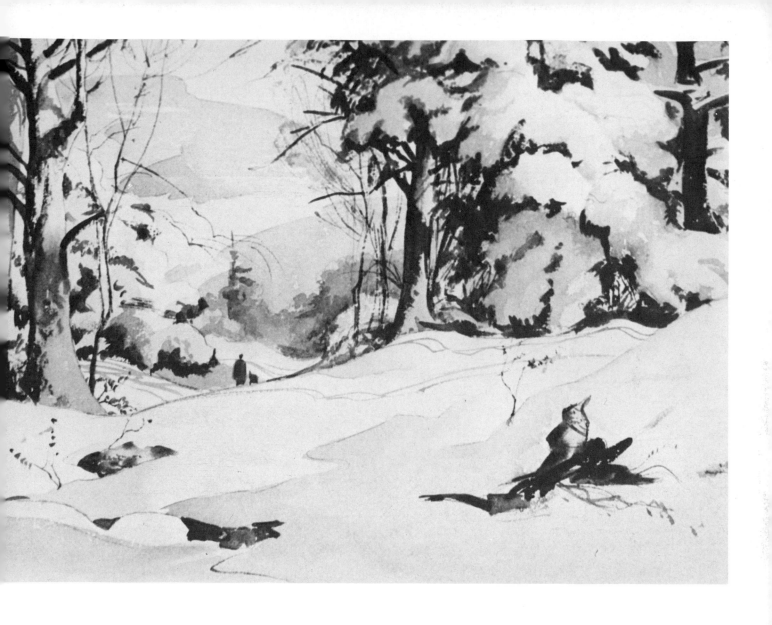

STAGE 4　This may seem like a big jump, but remember the sky, mountain, and snow are all in the light and middle tonal range. Now come the darks, with some solids and a lot of little scrawly bits. Don't get "rigger-happy." A rigger can be used just enough to create interesting detail, or it can lead the way to the cobweb factory. It's the *big* pattern that makes the painting. A little more modeling in the snow on the trees, and there you have the *real* Woodstock!

177

17   *Rocky coast: demonstration*

The aromas wafting about at low tide are sometimes offensive to landlubbers, but to the person who has grown up at the edge of the sea, the smell of decaying fish caught between the rocks, the dripping seaweed, and the tang of salt air combine to make the loveliest of all perfumes.

Near where I used to live, on the Massachusetts coast, the low tide exposed about a half-mile of juicy gray mud flats filled with delicious clams. As small kids, we fished, but "clamming" was our main sport. The mud would ooze up between our toes, and as we walked along, the clams would shoot streams of water into the air, stupidly showing us where to dig.

My maternal grandfather, John Weatherly Callard, had been a newspaper writer. He had a wild imagination and sense of humor. One summer day, as a group of us was setting off with our buckets and clam hooks, he called to us with a warning to keep our eyes peeled for rabid quohogs! (A quohog is a species of giant clam and is great in chowders.) He noted that it was the time of the moon when they (the quohogs) occasionally went completely berserk and were known to have chased clam-diggers, at terrific speeds, for miles across the flats. He quietly went back to his gardening and several round-eyed youngsters approached the mud flats with new-found respect, not really believing, but just suppose . . . ?

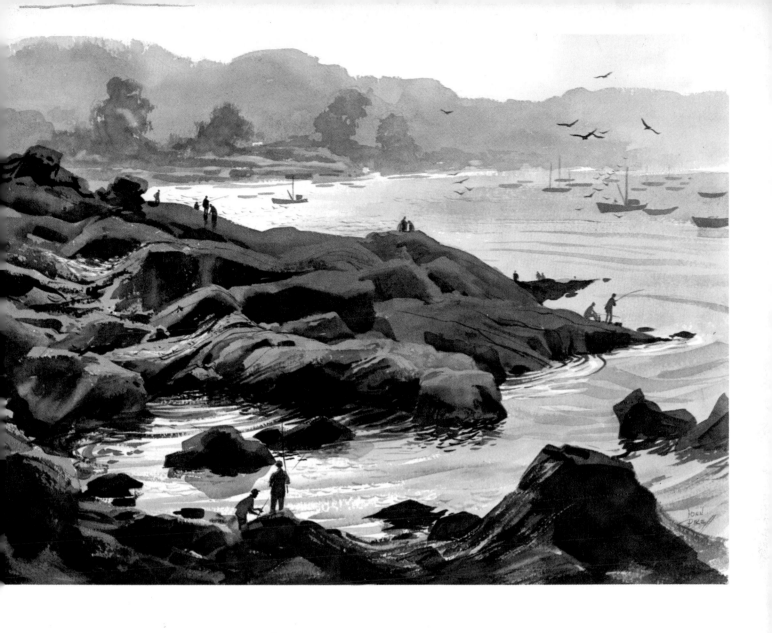

CAPE ANN ROCKS, 22" x 30".
Collection, General Tire International.

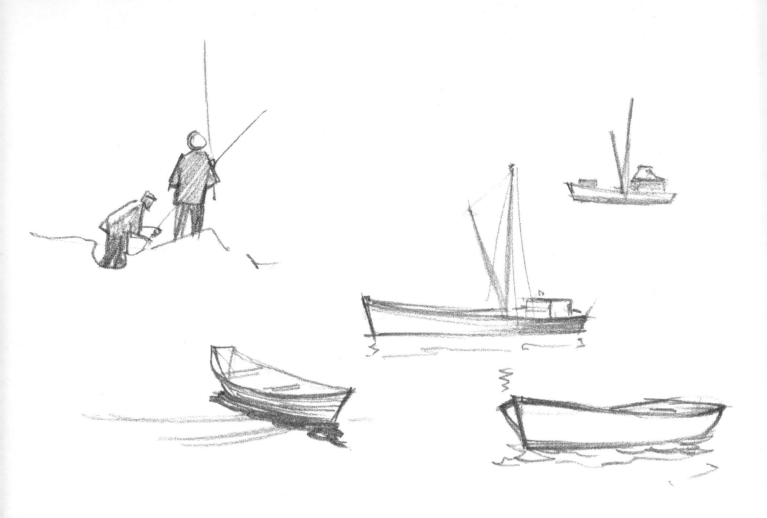

(Above) Here are some small figure and boat sketches.

Pencil Sketch

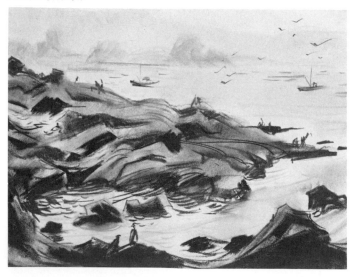

(Left) In this sketch we have two large values, light and dark, with secondary darks in the big low-value (dark) rocks. Play them with care.

To do a sketch with square-on back-lighting almost demands dark glasses. I use neutral gray glasses that simply take everything down in value—even when I work with color. I must admit I lift and check once in a while, but squirrely as it sounds, it works! In the tropics dark glasses are indispensable.

Every once in a while, in every man's existence, it's refreshing—and necessary—to step far back from fixed thoughts and take a *good long look*. This goes not only for people in the arts, but for those in every endeavor. You, with your education as a painter, must of necessity have a greater awareness of the big wide world around you than most people—because you're an interpreter. Learn to see around and far and away, beyond the simple structure and color of that "charming red barn."

STAGE 1   The penciling is put in quite simply, and in this same stage I put in the pale sky and allow it to dry before I wash in the distant hills. No liquid frisket or tape was used.

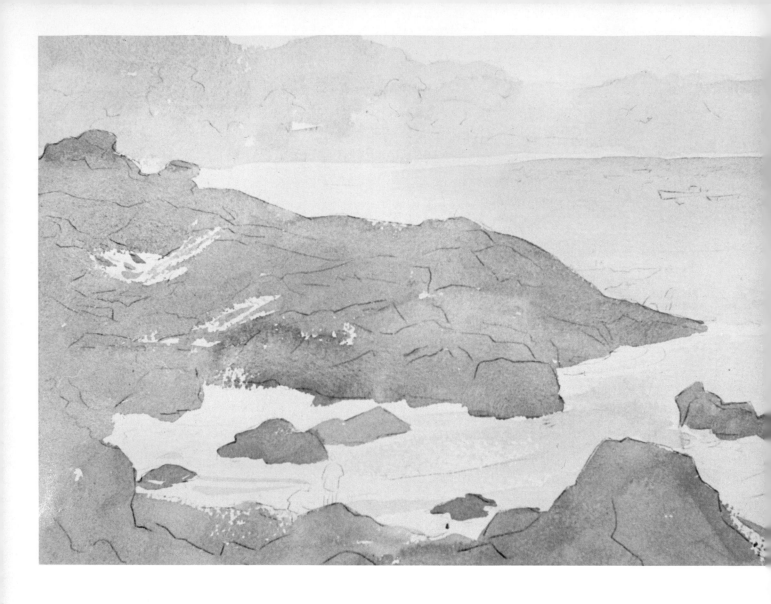

STAGE 2 The light blue of the water is washed on, leaving, by means of a little tricky brushwork, the sparkles and highlights. No effort is made to hold to the exact outline of the large rock area, the value of which is so much darker than the sea that any slippage of the lighter value into the darker will not be noticed. When this is dry, the middle and foreground rock mass is put down.

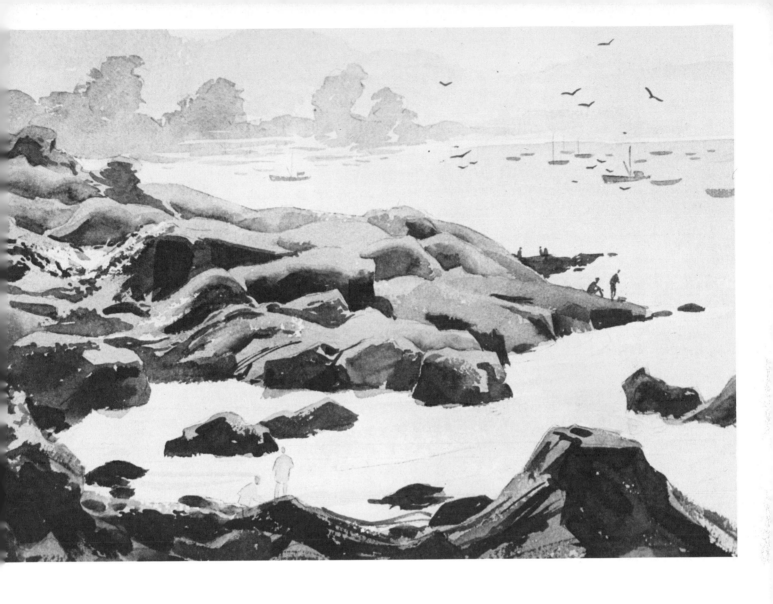

STAGE 3   Next comes the pale silhouette of the large trees against the distant hills, and then the modeling of the rocks, always keeping in mind the light source. Couldn't resist putting in a few gulls and boats at this point.

183

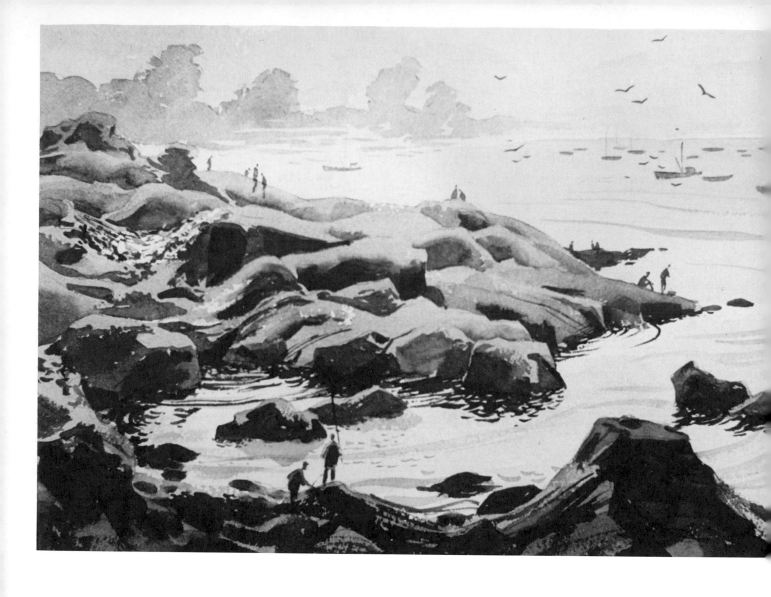

STAGE 4 Now, down the home stretch to
the finish—the reflections in the water, the
little fishing figures, and the general pulling-
together of the whole painting. A touch of
deeper dark here, a little scrape there—and
voila! Cape Ann Rocks! A perfect example of
a painting done in pure high-back lighting.

18 *Breakers, rocks, beach, and figures: demonstration*

Many claim that Oregon has the most beautiful coastline in the country. Warm winds from off the Pacific Ocean give it an unusually mild climate for its high 40's, north latitude location. The warm air also contributes to creating highly dramatic, theatrical effects. I attempted to capture some of the drama here. To produce the value-graded step-back silhouette effect, think out your procedure carefully. If the distance and the mist is to be convincing, those large rock washes must be put down right the first time!

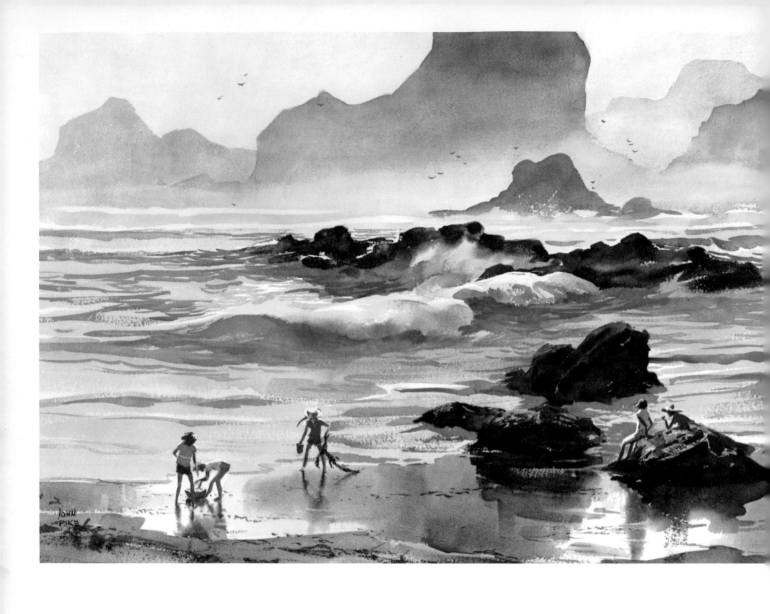

YOUNG BEACHCOMBERS ON THE
RUGGED OREGON COAST, *22" x 30".*
Collection, General Tire International.

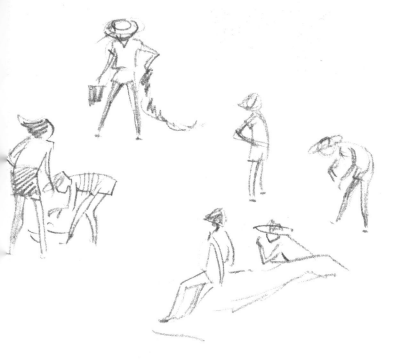

The little figure doodles are fun to do and they tend to loosen up your drawing.

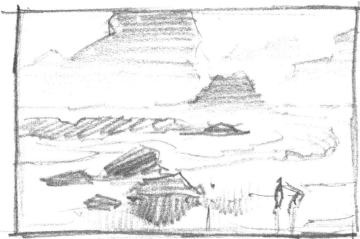

Here's one of many thumbnail sketches I did before arriving at the final sketch below. As you can see, it's not the same as the final version.

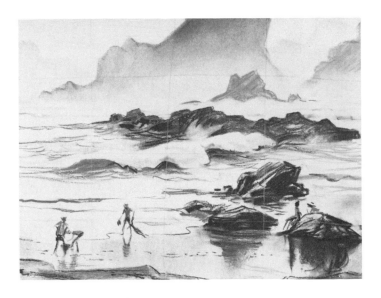

Pencil Sketch

The great value of your preliminary sketch is that it removes most of the guesswork when you come to the final painting. You've arrived at the composition you like, the drawing, and —most important of all—you've established the values. I like to take the salient ingredients —in this case, large and small rocks, the sea and the little figures—and juggle them around until I get something that pleases me. This is possible in a landscape as it's not offensive to move a tree here or a rock there to gain your desired objective. However, in doing historical sites and such it's best to stick to the actual layout of the buildings and the land, but the lighting and atmosphere can still be your own.

187

STAGE 1   First the drawing—mainly just an
outline of areas. No masking is used in this
watercolor.

STAGE 2   After putting in the pale sky over the whole upper area, and allowing it to dry, the most distant (left and right), and lightest, rock formations are painted in right over the dry sky. These are faded at the bottom by adding clear water. Also, the edges are "lost" into the center area where the big rock will be.

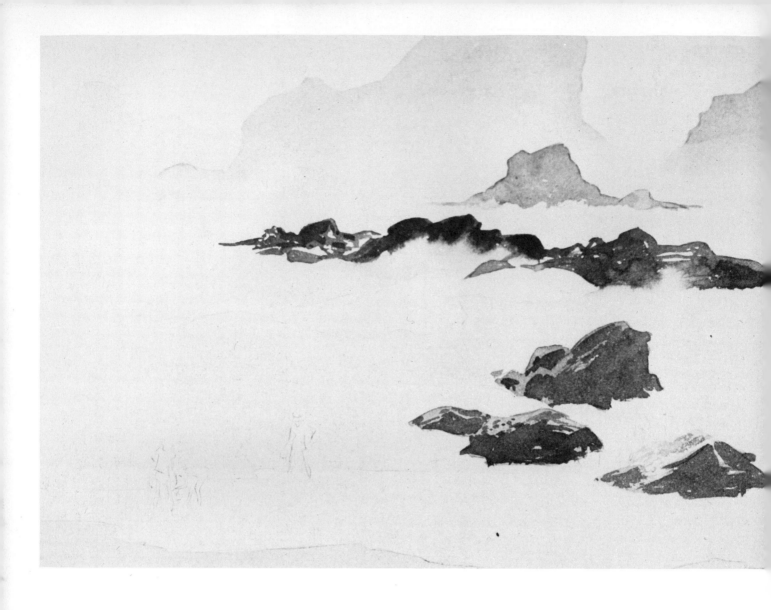

STAGE 3   The large rocks in the center and to the right are graded, or faded down, by adding clear water as I go along. Remember, we want a sharp edge, so the washes underneath must be dry. A light blue-green wash is put over the entire sea with the exception of a few sparkles and the white foam. Then the dark rock shapes in the middle and foreground are painted in. The paint is allowed to dry between each step.

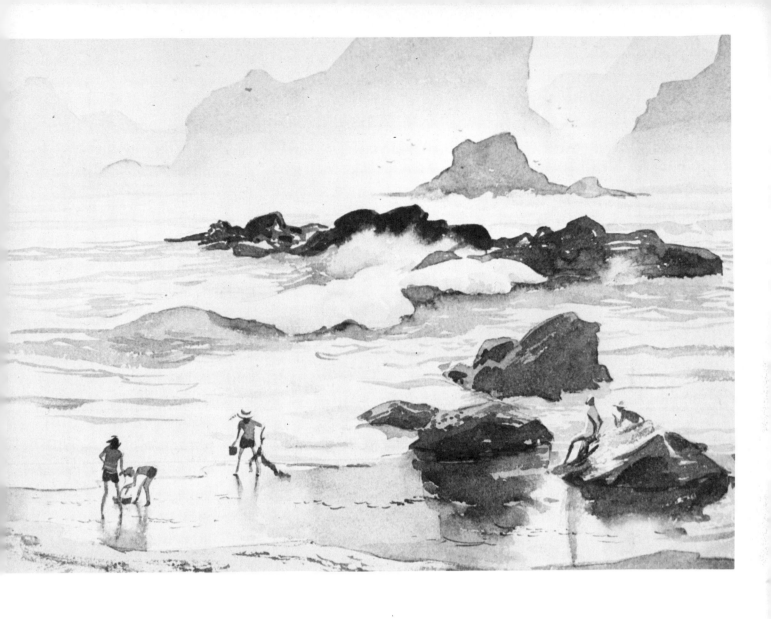

STAGE 4   Now the simple texturing of the water and the rocks, the sand, the little figures, and the all-important reflections in the wet sand. Keep in mind the objects causing those reflections. Bet those kids are having fun!

19 *Forest waterfall: demonstration*

A beautiful spot—the damp coolness, the sounds, and the sheer beauty of rushing water. But when I start to paint a watercolor problem like this, I think of the possible wisdom of my Great Aunt Laura's question to my Mother, "Why doesn't John get a position in a bank like all decent people?"

Water is a moving thing, always on the go, seeking a lower level or another shore. There can be great confusion in watching it move; it goes here, there, everywhere. How do you stop it enough in your mind's eye to paint it? Of course there is always the camera, which can serve as a wonderful back-up. But that back-up is only meaningful as an aid to your own close scrutiny of what is actually happening to the water.

Sit on the shore where waves are breaking. Painting-wise it's most confusing. But every marine painter knows that those big-water, roll-over shapes will *repeat* themselves, at least for a while. So rather than try to see the entire thing at one time, sketch a small area when the action happens, then wait for the next time the same action happens again until you have that area down. Then sketch another section, and so on until you have all the information you need for your painting. The foregoing also applies to waterfalls—which happily don't have tides.

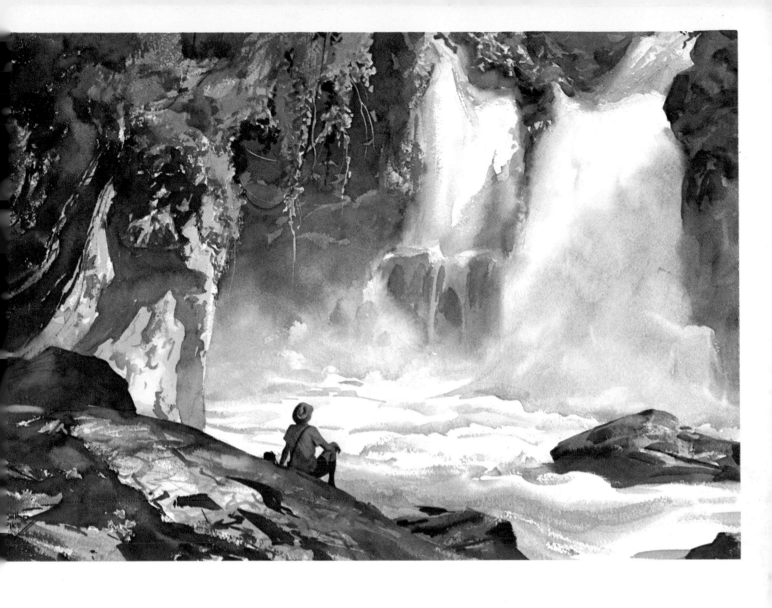

GRANADA CASCADE, MEXICO, 22″ x 30″.
Collection, General Tire International.

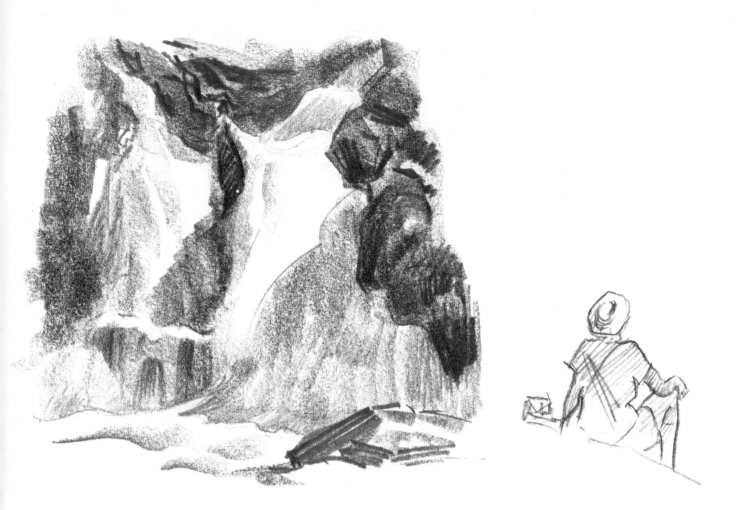

This little sketch was a preliminary to the one below.

This roughly sketched figure also appears in the more finished sketch below.

Pencil Sketch

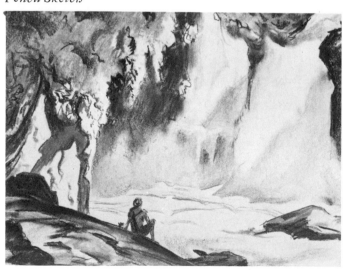

When I started this sketch, I'd already established the rock formations underneath and the sunlit patterns on the foamy water flowing over the rocks in my preliminary sketch, above left. Study and try to *see* beneath the surface. What makes the water act that way? *Seeing* not only concerns looking, but also knowing what you are looking at. Try to learn all you can about your subject. The more you know, the less insecure (the middle name of transparent watercolor!) you'll feel about the beautiful painting you visualize.

STAGE 1   First the drawing. Then the frisket, or rubber cement (the same thing, in a sense. It keeps the paint you put over it from reaching the surface of your paper, and may be removed later by rubbing or "pick-up"). The frisket is used just on the trailing vines hanging from the big rock on the left.

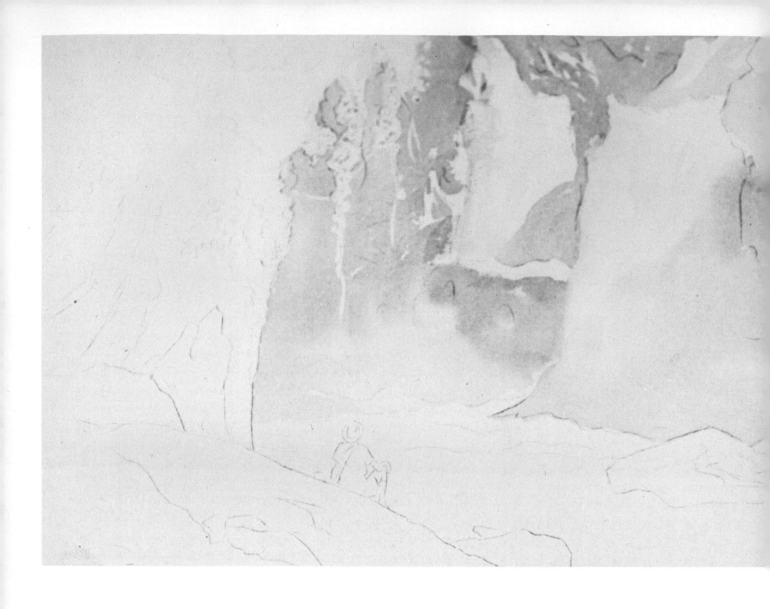

STAGE 2   The water is the most difficult area to play with—also the lightest, or highest, in value. The action and modeling is done first and when it dries, the lighter darks around it are put in to make the falls come forward.

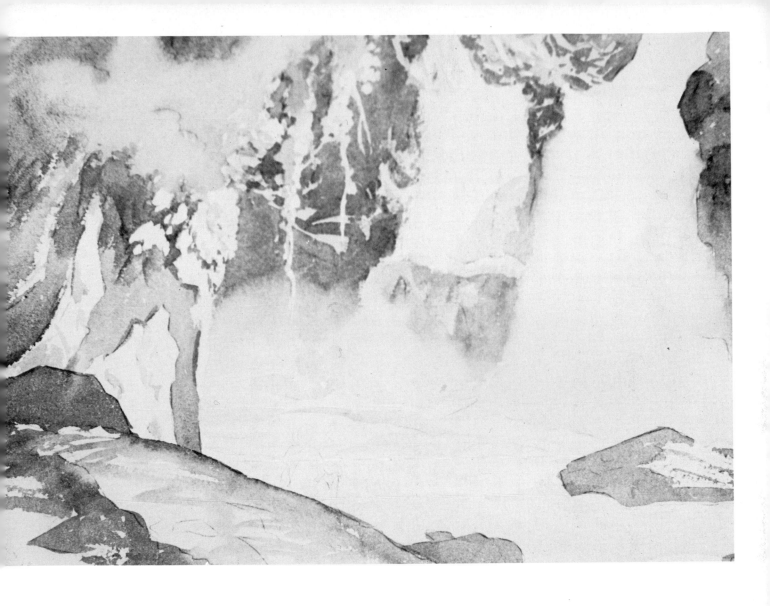

STAGE 3   More darks are added around the falls where needed, then the broad surface colors on the big rock at the left, as well as foreground, are painted in. The frisket is removed so the bright yellows and greens may be dropped in to make the falls take one more step backward—or you, forward, however you want to look at it.

197

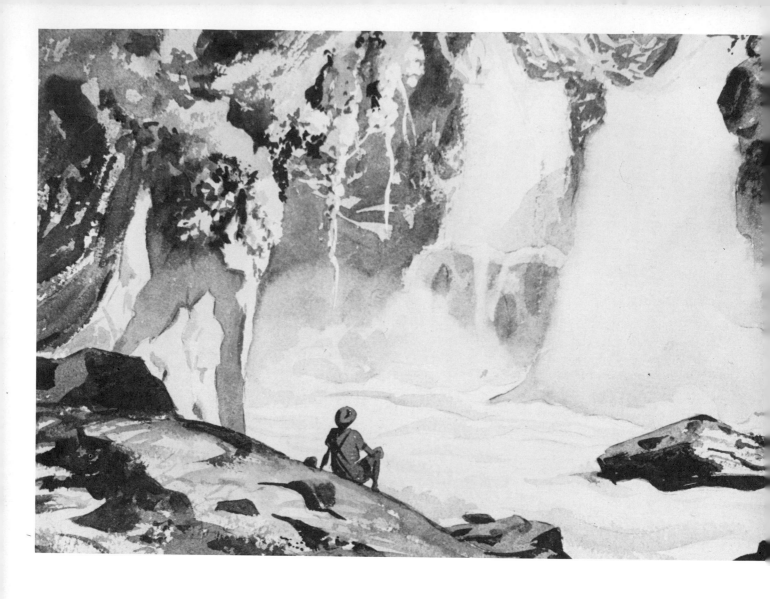

STAGE 4   Details of the figure and overall texturing make the last stage for the wind-up. Please remember that it's the pre-planning—in sketch and procedures—that makes everything fall easily into place for the success of your great watercolor painting.

20 Architecture and figures: demonstration

A couple of things bothered me in Ecuador and some of the other Central and South American countries. Perhaps the least important is the altitude, which doles out an intolerable amount of oxygen to us stupid smokers. Another is the history of the place, the realization of what the barbarians from Europe, starting three centuries ago, did to these proud people, under the guise of bringing Culture and God to their lives.

I have been one of the fortunate people who have traveled to many lands, East and West, over a long period of time. Many otherwise closed doors are opened to people in the arts—music, painting, theater, etc.—so communication is never a barrier. Artists seem all to speak a Universal Language. Over the years, my feeling has grown that *all* men of the earth are searching for exactly the same thing—a great Universal Power or God to give help, comfort, and encouragement to lighten the load of each of us in his time on this mad planet.

There, you've had your sermon. My Mohawk blood is cooling down and we can get on with the watercolor.

This painting was chosen for the high right, but basically down, lighting. The great church is in shadow on this side, but has reflected illumination from the sunlit courtyard of flowers below. Altitude is about 10,000 feet.

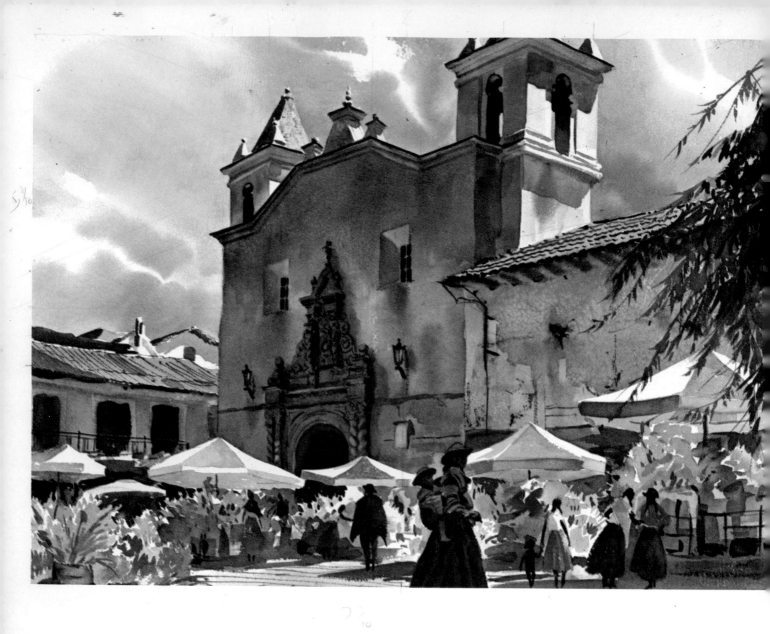

FLOWER MARKET AT EL CARMEN CHURCH,
CUENCA, ECUADOR, *22″ x 30″*.
Collection, General Tire International.

200

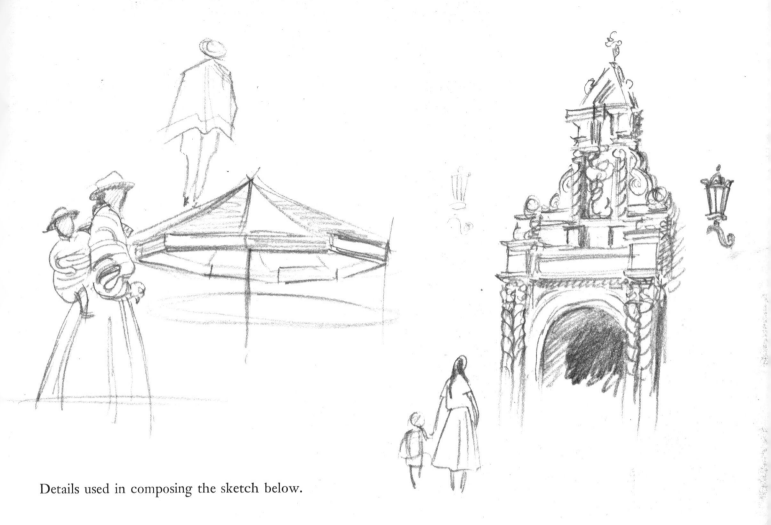

Details used in composing the sketch below.

Pencil Sketch

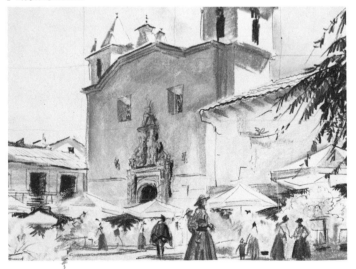

I've heard many young students state that they didn't want to bother with sketching—they just wanted to paint. That's fine if they don't give a damn about where they are going and happily possess lots of loot for endless supplies of very expensive paper.

Sketching is an art in itself—it develops dexterity in both hand and mind. Get it all down in your sketch book or pad for future reference. You think you'll remember, but you won't. Draw all kinds of things—create your own drawing "shorthand" so you can make quick records. Doing this will also help develop your "pictorial memory," just as writing down a person's name will help you remember it—at least in theory!

STAGE 1   Two types of masking are used
for this stage, tape and liquid, because I will
not be able to paint around the details in the
drawing and still gain the big, juicy sky effect
I want. After the drawing is completed, masking tape, cut to shape, is placed over the
canopy areas. Liquid frisket is used on the
little details at the top of the building (which
doesn't show in the photo).

STAGE 2   The clouds and the blue sky are painted in, using ultramarine blue and burnt sienna for the warm grays, and Thalo blue with a touch of Thalo green in the sky itself. This combination gives you a pleasing color play—warm and cool in the same passage. When dry, the liquid masking at the top of the building is removed; the tape on the canopies is left on.

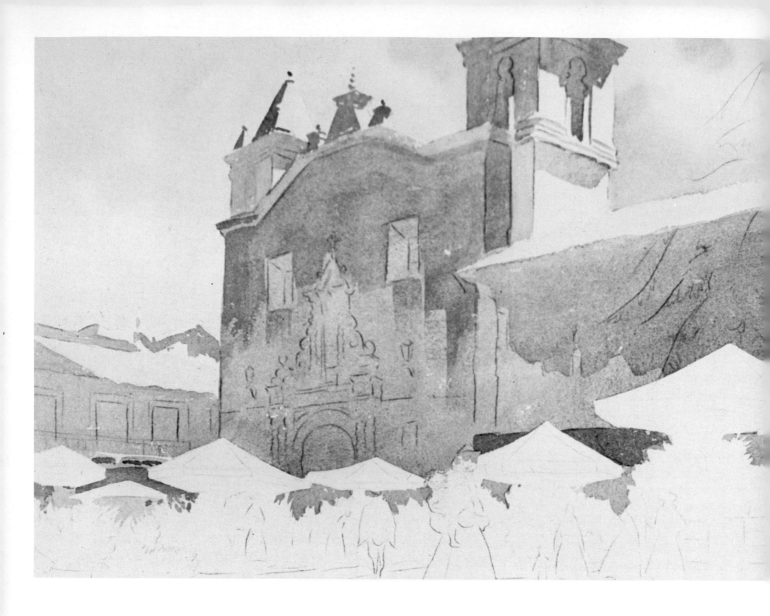

STAGE 3   A pale yellowish tint is put on the sunlit side of the building and the plaza floor. This is allowed to dry. Then I wash in the large shadow sides of the church and adjoining structures, working from fairly cool blue-grays at the top, on down to the warmer darks caused by the light reflections from the courtyard. While this is still wet, I sprinkle in a little table salt for texture. Try it, it's fun. I peel up the masking tape on the canopies.

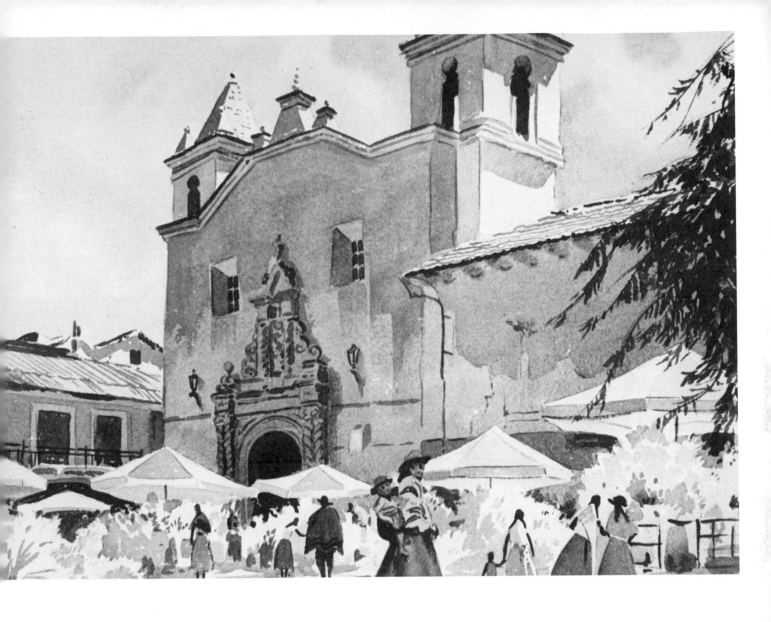

STAGE 4 The finish comes with a lot of little darks and textures, the colors on the canopies and flowers, the deep green of the tree at the right, the figures, and, as always, the general pulling-together to make all areas *simpatico* to each other. A pox on "conquistadors," then and now!

21 Sailing boats: demonstration

The beauty of the "Lateen" sail has to be seen to be really appreciated. Its design dates back thousands of years and was, I believe, a product of the great early engineer-seafarers of the eastern Mediterranean. The boats and sails come in all sizes—working boats such as these, boats for heavy cargo, and a few just for pleasure. When I was stationed in Cairo for a time during WW II, one of the great treats was to charter a pleasure "Felucca" for a moonlight sail, all night, up and down that section of the Nile. The larder would be well-stocked with goodies, the boat paved with colorful Egyptian cushions—and I had a guitar. That was a real tough part of the war for me! I can still see that long slim boom angling some fifty or sixty feet toward the stars, and the handsome captain walking in barefoot silence along the gunwhale to make an adjustment here and there. Ah, but that's another story for another book.

I chose this painting to demonstrate because it is pretty close to a two-value picture. Also, it demonstrates a rather liberal use of masking tape as an aid. Splash on!

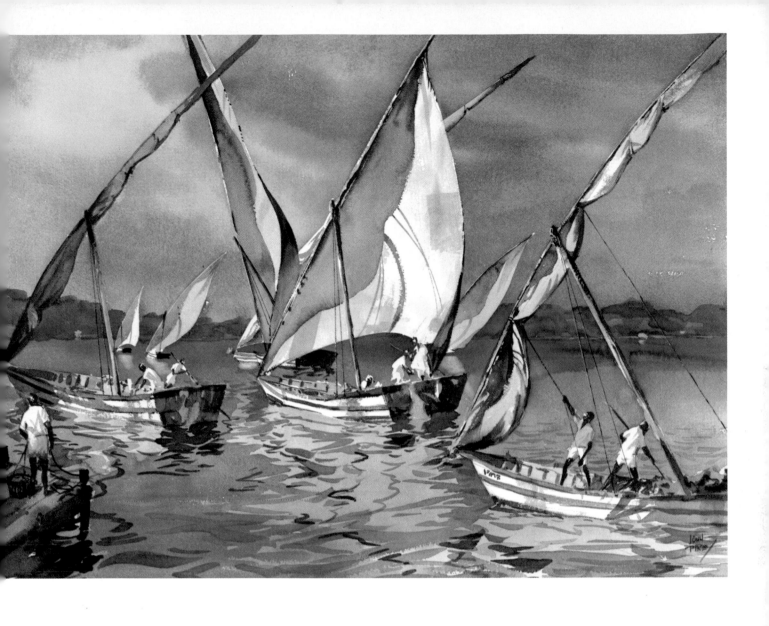

LAKE VICTORIA FISHERMEN, *22" x 30".*
Collection, General Tire International.

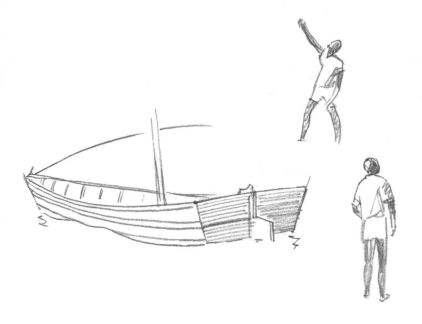

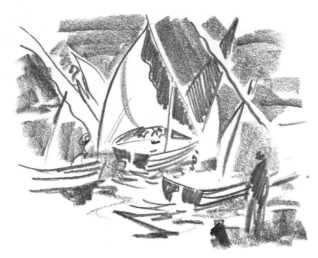

The line drawing of the "Felucca" was done for detail, and the little figures are just two of many action sketches.

Here we have another small preliminary sketch with a different composition than the final sketch below.

Pencil Sketch

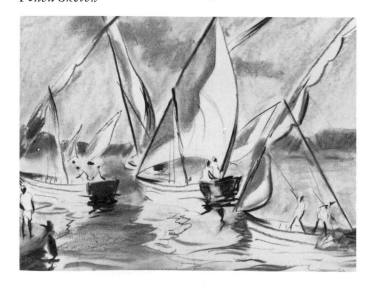

Most anything can be sketched, but that doesn't necessarily mean that all your information has to go into any one painting. However, find out all you can about your subject —learn all "the reasons why." A tree leans, a roof sags, a ground mist rises. Knowing the cause will help you to understand the effect. A thorough knowledge of these will help in making a convincing and believable painting. Your thorough understanding of the construction—the way and why it happens—will allow you to take the liberties with nature and man-made structures that will make you a truly creative painter. The photographer, after all, is stuck with exactly what's in front of his lens.

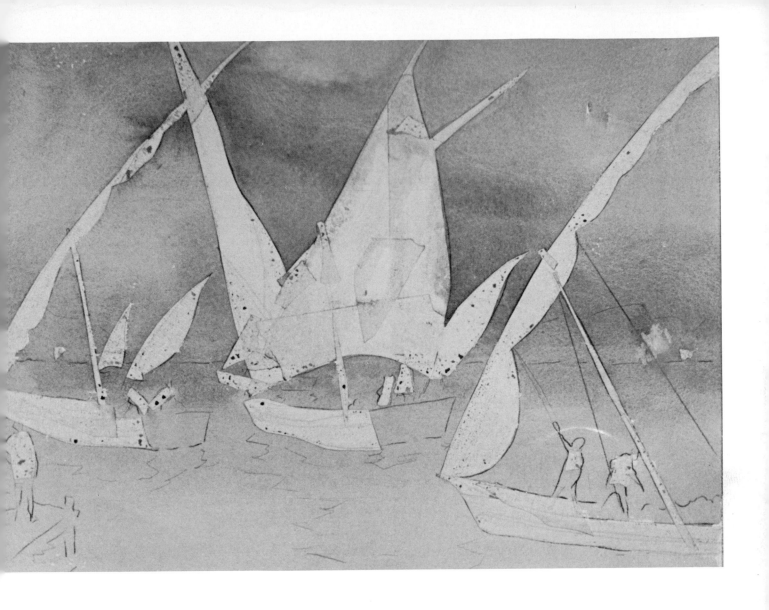

STAGE 1　Before we begin, a word about using masking tape as a block-out agent. First, lay it over the parts of your drawing you want to keep white. The pencil lines will show through just enough so you can cut your various shapes and contours. For cutting, use a very sharp mat or frisket knife. Cut through *just* the tape and not your watercolor paper. (Do a test hop on another paper.) If you are using a very heavy paper, such as 300 lb., it's not so important, but if you are using a very lightweight paper, tread lightly or forget it and go back to the liquids. In this stage, I put on the tape, cut it, then put in the sky wash and carry it down, changing color, to the lightest color in the water.

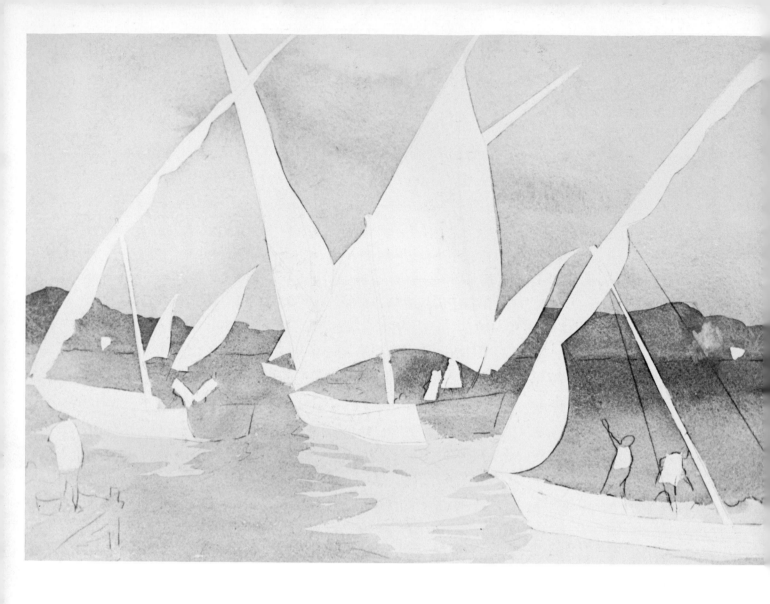

STAGE 2   I paint in the distant hills. Then
I go down to the foreground with the water
surface color, painting around the lighter reflections of the sails and boats. When this is
dry, I remove the tape—and wow! How
white that paper is!

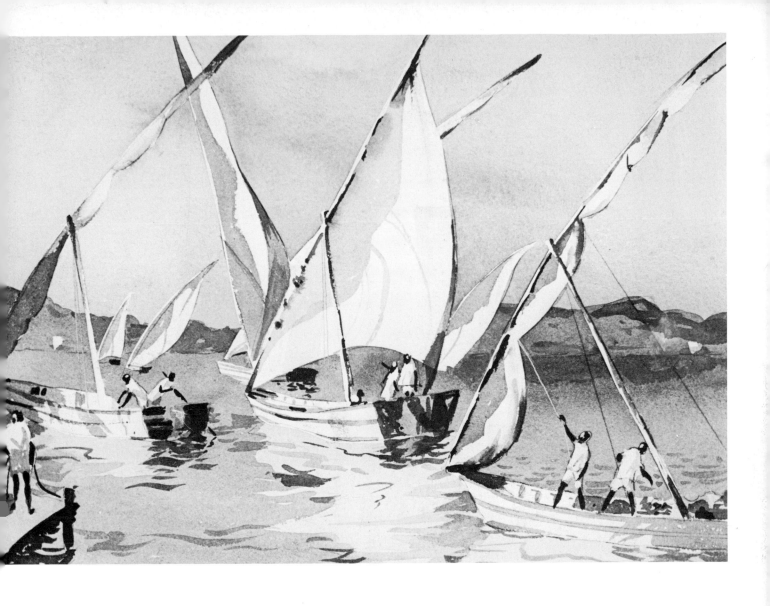

STAGE 3 On those white areas left when the masking tape is removed, I work the subtleties and textures, the translucent shadows on the sails, the darks of the figures, the stern sections and the many little details—pulling the values down and balancing them against the background darks until the areas are compatible with each other. Sail on, O Victoria! I might add a touch of phonetic Arabic: "*Bookra fra mish mish,*" which very roughly translates into, "I'll see you tomorrow when the apricots bloom."

22 Windmills against the sky: demonstration

Ah, dear Don Q. and Sancho, in this mad, fascinating and unpredictable world, methinks you are not the only ones who have jousted with giants! Or a windmill—just a little, teeny windmill?

Man's efforts to harness the winds to give him power and energy go back into prerecorded history, and in many cases he was most successful. On the water, from the small, reed, basket-like boat with a palmetto leaf held high to ease the poling or rowing before the wind, on, in time, to the beautiful but clumsy tub-like round ships, on to the sleek, racy, and highly maneuverable clipper ships, the developments advanced. Most intriguing! Man took to the skies, and since the wind was not constant, he built himself an engine to push him through the still air. It seems now, in "Monday morning quarterbacking," that the great aircraft inventor-designers would have been far wiser to have turned to the ancient windmills for their source of design, rather than to the bird—because in the windmill, however crude, was the essence of a true airfoil!

Enough of history. Here we are jousting with windmills in watercolor. This painting is a good example of the use of two types of masking agents, tape and liquid. Bear with Don Q. and me through the various steps, perhaps at the finish we can all shout, "Olé!"

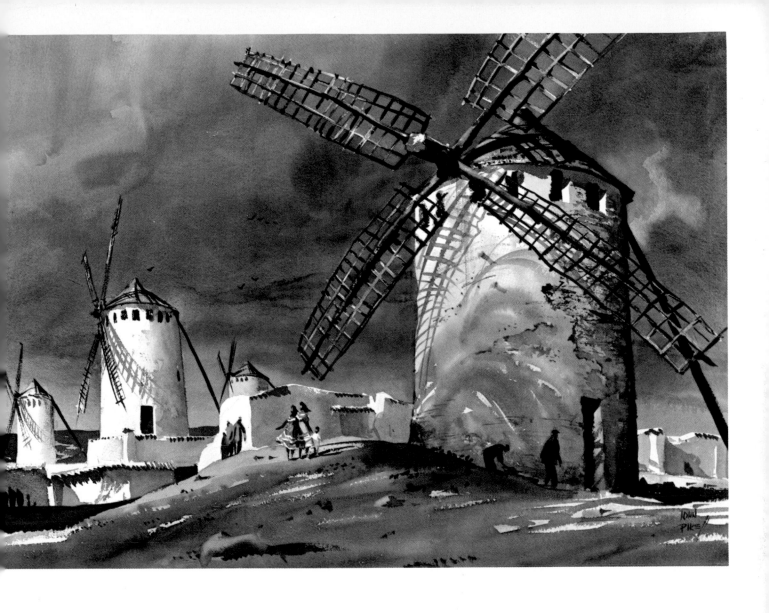

WINDMILLS IN SPAIN, *22" x 30".*
Collection, General Tire International.

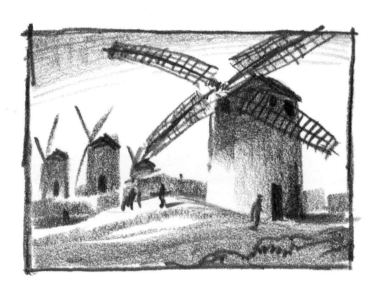

Windmills offer a great opportunity for dramatic effects. The small sketch shown here, dark against a light background, had real possibilities in that department. But it had a bit too much of the Daumier–Rembrandt sort of feeling. (Nothing like putting myself in good company!) Also, in the many times I've been to Spain, bright sunlight seemed to cover everything—at least most of the time. So I reversed the value order to sunlit windmills against a dark sky. The sketch below and the painting are my final conclusion.

Pencil Sketch

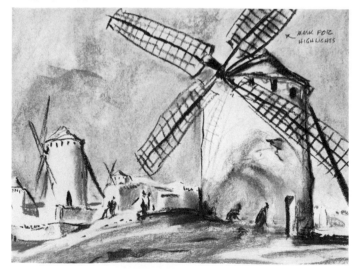

To all you jousters with transparent watercolor, a poem:

> Fancy people—a fancy life
> Of paint and song—a lovely bash!
> Comes Shakespeare's "shove off the mortal
>   coil"
> To Angel's wings—or Southern Broil,
> There's bound to be a fancy splash!

If you don't like that one, how about:

> Into each life some rain must fall;
> Why not take up watercolor?

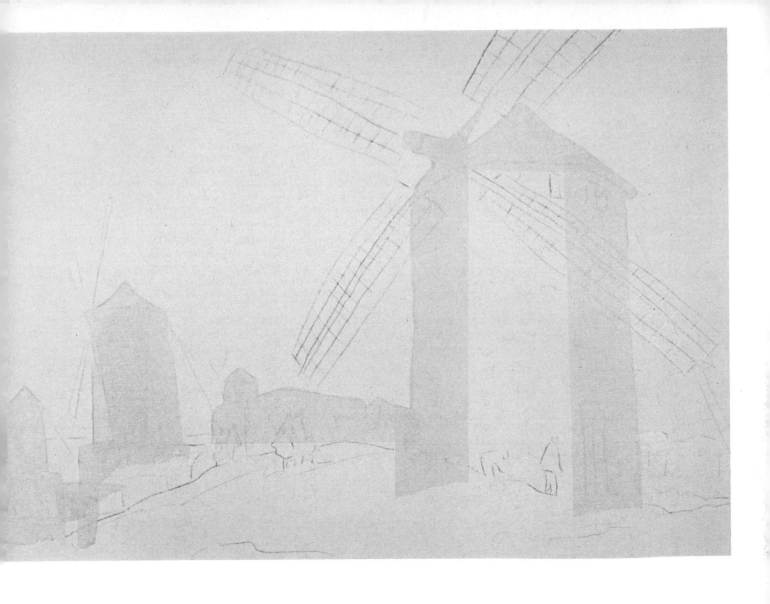

STAGE 1   Ordinary masking tape of most any brand is great for blocking out large areas. We can use this device to good advantage here, where the windmills are lighter than the dark, glowering sky behind them. Using liquid masking, I touch in some of the possible highlighted spots of the huge sweep-wings, denuded of their canvas. As I mentioned earlier, with most masking tapes you can see through to your pencil line, which gives you the opportunity to cut and waver the edge to suit your purpose. Use a *very* sharp knife, cutting through *only* the tape.

215

STAGE 2   Here, I wash in the big dark sky, at the same time loosely working in some modeling to create the cloud feeling. I use sienna and umber along with my old pal, ultramarine blue. The cold blues are Thalo. When this is thoroughly dry, all masking is removed. The real reason for masking in a subject such as this is to give you the freedom to say what you want to say in that sky.

STAGE 3   At this stage I model the roundness of the windmills, cast the soft shadow wash over the one at the right, and paint the shadow areas of the various walls in the middle and background. Now to the pale green of the grass. When the grass is partially dry, I add the large dark shadow mass of the foreground.

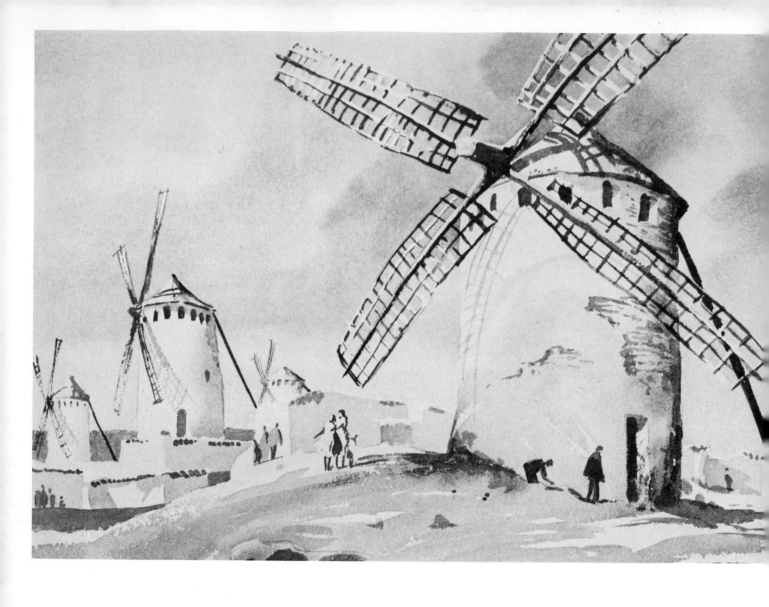

STAGE 4 Now for the darks that make those middle values count and bring the painting to life. All the little details—texture of the massive stones and the darks on the great wings—are done at this stage. I doodle around until I feel the painting holds together, each area and value in proper relationship to all other areas. Olé?

23   *Some general thoughts*

In a lifetime of painting and teaching, I've picked up a few tricks and tips that may be worth bearing in mind. . . .

THAT BLANK
WHITE PAPER

Dead white paper has always had, at least for me, a rather lackluster quality. I'm thinking particularly of the large white areas in snow paintings, as well as the whiteness of skies and water in misty or foggy pictures.

I've found that by covering the entire paper with clear water and then dropping in little spots of the three primaries—*very pale* Alizarin Crimson, Thalo or Winsor Blue, and yellow—I could overcome the white curse. While still very wet, I criss-cross this with more clear water, more or less blending the colors together. It looks pretty horrible at first, but when it dries, you'll find that you have quite a beautiful luminous, or iridescent, quality. Then, when you paint directly over it (after it's dry), all of your whites come up smiling. Just another watercolor trick that helps.

My theory is that the ice crystals in snow and the water droplets in fog actually have a tendency to break the light into its natural spectrum—however pale and remote. So I think this trick of mine makes some scientific sense. In any case, I think you'll like the results. But if you're working for reproduction, watch the yellows; they sometimes come through stronger than intended.

PAINTING MANNERS

Some thoughts on painting in the field, both at home and abroad.

Always remember that no matter *where* you are, you're on *somebody's* property.

Painting, like music and the dance, is a language that needs no translation. Art is one of the greatest jumpers of geographical and cultural boundaries.

During the war years, I often found myself being group "interpreter" in a half dozen or more languages. I speak none of them, but I took the pains to learn how to say "hello" and "thank you" in each. All the rest of my translating was done with my little blank sketchbook and a pencil. The results were most pleasant.

You, as an artist, are something a little bit special in the eyes of the layman. He may be a primitive savage in the darkest jungle, or a Parisian sophisticate. For the primitive soul, you're a lover of beauty; therefore you mean him no harm. The sophisticate is a lover of the Arts, so there's a common ground (he may think what you do stinks, but, as a person of culture, he'll admire you for giving it a try).

Probably the prime requisites for working at home or abroad are an open mind and heart, a healthy curiosity, and the ability to *accept* the new and the strange, without making an inward comparison with what you've got back home. Respect and try to understand what you see and the people you're with. Know the taboos, and there are *many*. If you're abroad, check with your consulate or embassy. After all, even at home, there are many religious groups who also have restrictions. Don't step on toes; find out.

As I said above, no matter where you are, you're on someone's property, so here are a few little rules:

In the country, always ask permission to set up and paint. You don't have to know the language; your equipment (brushes, paper, and paints) are your passport. A farmer may think you're a bit of a nut for wanting to paint what *you* consider his "romantic" broken-down barns, when he's a bit ashamed that he hasn't kept up repairs too well for the last thirty years.

Always have a spare paper bag or plastic bag with you. (In other countries, these aren't as plentiful as in the U.S.). This is for your clean-up, and this means *everything*, from used tissue, paper towels, and cigarette packs down to the cigarette butts, themselves, and empty tubes of paint. In other words, leave the place just as you found it. Your simple courtesy will bring you many a glass of cool well water, or a sparkling touch of wine just when you need it most.

I remember a story of a summer art school that let its young hopefuls roam the countryside in search of subject matter. A local dairy farmer generously gave them full use of his meadows. Unhappily, the students weren't very tidy people and five or six of the farmer's prize milk producers died from eating oil paint rags. I still can't decide which were more stupid, the students or the cows.

In the city, ask the policeman on the corner (or the *gendarme*, or the *carabiniere*). He has the job of keeping hundreds of thousands of humans flowing past a given point. If you're going to be a slower-upper, then don't do it. Make a quick sketch. Then finish and develop it back at your studio.

Always be aware of local and religious do's and don'ts, the taboos I mentioned earlier. It's extremely easy to say to oneself, "No one thinks like *that* in this day and age!" But they do, and it's up to you to respect their thinking, agree or not.

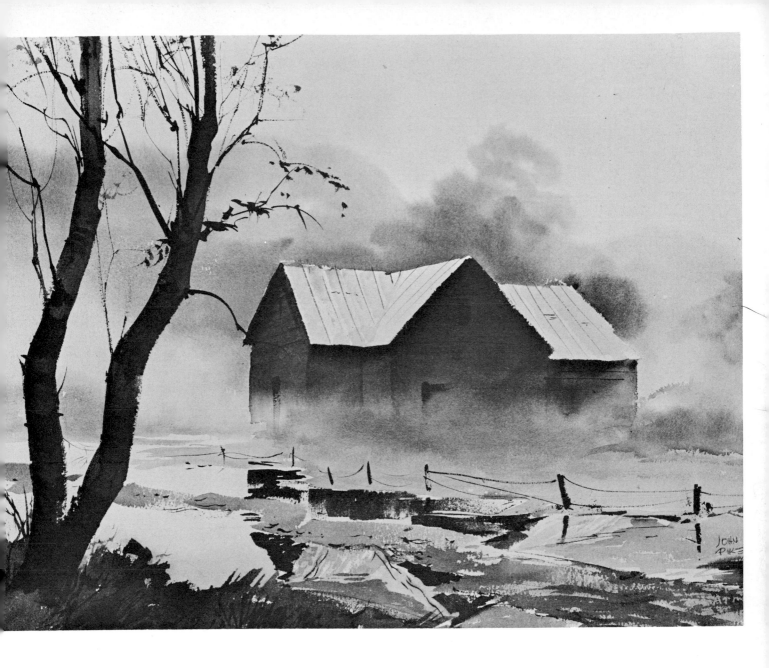

GROUND FOG, *22" x 30". Private collection.*

The sky and the misty trees were painted in one pass, bringing the surplus water (with slight pigment) all the way down to the fence area. When this was dry, the dark barn was put in and handled just as you would a graded wash from dark to light, achieved by adding more and more clear water as you move down. Last, I added the dark birches and foreground to the left, the fence posts, and the reflections in the water.

221

For example, in the Islamic or Mohammedan world, the portrayal of the human figure in a drawing or painting will have many reactions, running all the way from delight in a portrait sketch, down to complete hostility. I happen to have experienced the full gamut. But this is only one of many areas where one must *know*. When we swing out from Squaresville, we must respect all our fellow world citizens and understand which foot follows the other.

HOW NOT TO PRAISE AN ARTIST

In collecting the photographs of watercolors for this book—several of which I hadn't seen in twenty or twenty-five years—somehow I was reminded of a family story. First let me set the stage . . .

Father was Victorian, having been born in the early 1870s.

Father was opinionated. (Anybody see "Life With Father?" My father's name was also Clarence.) He loved the arts, but, good God, you don't have one in the family!

Father had been a great athlete.

He seemed to me a remote, but wonderful, man. His humor was delightful, and, at times, caustic.

A great many years ago, some distant relative, a concert pianist, came through Boston on a tour. She was considered by the critics quite a capable young lady of eighteen years. Mother and Father went to the recital and enjoyed it too.

Some twenty years later, as they were leaving Symphony Hall after her next concert in that city, Mother asked, "What did you think of her performance tonight?"

"Excellent!" said my father. "She plays just as well now as she did at eighteen!"

Index

Edited by Donald Holden
Designed by James Craig
Composed in eleven point Janson by Atlantic Linotype Co., Inc.
Offset by The Haddon Craftsmen, Inc.
Bound by The Haddon Craftsmen, Inc.